Young Black bear cubs weigh up to one pound when they are born. They weigh 15—pounds by their first autumn, although they can weigh much more.

YOUNG Females most often give birth to two cubs. Cubs remain with their mother until they are about 17 months of age.

SPRINGTIME DIET After black bears emerge from their dens in spring, they eat mostly newly sprouting plants, leaves, and flowers.

CHARACTERISTICS Black bears in Georgia have black coats. In other parts of the U.S. and North America, their coats can be brown, cinnamon, blond, or blue-grey.

HSP Science Georgia

Harcourt
SCHOOL PUBLISHERS

Visit *The Learning Site!*
www.harcourtschool.com

HSP Georgia
Science

Black bear

SCHOOL PUBLISHERS

Science and Technology features provided by

Printed in the United States of America

ISBN-13: 978-0-15-358541-8
ISBN-10: 0-15-358541-2

4 5 6 7 8 9 10 032 16 15 14 13 12 11 10 9 8

Series Consulting Authors

Michael J. Bell, Ph.D.
Associate Professor of Early
  Childhood Education
College of Education, West
  Chester University of
  Pennsylvania
West Chester, Pennsylvania

Michael A. DiSpezio
Curriculum Architect
JASON Academy
Cape Cod, Massachusetts

Marjorie Frank
Former Adjunct Professor,
  Science Education
Hunter College
New York, New York

Gerald H. Krockover, Ph.D.
Professor of Earth and
  Atmospheric Science Education
Purdue University
West Lafayette, Indiana

Joyce C. McLeod
Adjunct Professor
Rollins College
Winter Park, Florida

Barbara ten Brink, Ph.D.
Austin Independent School
  District
Austin, Texas

Carol J. Valenta
Senior Vice President
St. Louis Science Center
St. Louis, Missouri

Barry A. Van Deman
President and CEO
Museum of Life and Science
Durham, North Carolina

Georgia Curriculum and Classroom Reviewers

Amy Benson
Tritt Elementary
Marietta, Georgia

Joyce Brooks
Alpharetta Elementary
Alpharetta, Georgia

Julie Barnhart Burns
Blandford Elementary
Runcon, Georgia

Shelley Crittenden
Grantville Elementary
Grantville, Georgia

Calandra Eineker
Alpharetta Elementary
Alpharetta, Georgia

Jennie Haynes
A. B. Merry School
Augusta, Georgia

Gail Hines
A. B. Merry School
Augusta, Georgia

Dawn M. Hudson
Paulding County Schools
Dallas, Georgia

Valerie E. King
Big Shanty Intermediate
Kennesaw, Georgia

Sondra M. Lee
Grantville Elementary
Grantville, Georgia

Stacey N. Mabray
Richmond County Board of
  Education
Augusta, Georgia

Heather L. Nix
Berrien Primary School
Nashville, Georgia

Lisa E. Reynolds
Holsenbeck Elementary
Winder, Georgia

Vicki Roark
Little River Elementary
Woodstock, Georgia

Karol H. Stephens
Northeast High School/
Bibb County Board of Education
Macon, Georgia

Karen W. Sumner
G.O. Bailey Primary School
Tifton, Georgia

Beth Thompson
Alpharetta Elementary
Alpharetta, Georgia

Gina A. Turner
Troup County Schools
LaGrange, Georgia

Nan Ward
Lake Park Elementary
Albany, Georgia

Dianne Wood
Woody Gap School
Suches, Georgia

Georgia HSP Science and the Georgia Performance Standards for Science

Dear Students and Parents,

The Georgia Performance Standards for Science (GPS), shown here for your reference, were designed to provide students with the knowledge and skills necessary for science proficiency at the fourth grade. Therefore, the GPS will drive science instruction. Since science is a way of thinking and investigating, as well as a body of knowledge, students need an understanding of both the Characteristics of Science and its Content. The GPS require that instruction treat these together, so they are shown here as co-requisites.

Georgia HSP Science was developed to provide complete coverage of the GPS. Throughout the book you will find exciting investigations, engaging text, and ties to Georgia people and places. These help ensure mastery of the GPS, while providing a rewarding science experience for all students.

Harcourt School Publishers

Co-Requisite—Characteristics of Science

Habits of Mind

S4CS1 **Students will be aware of the importance of curiosity, honesty, openness, and skepticism in science and will exhibit these traits in their own efforts to understand how the world works.**

a. Keep records of investigations and observations and do not alter the records later.

b. Carefully distinguish observations from ideas and speculation about those observations.

c. Offer reasons for findings and consider reasons suggested by others.

d. Take responsibility for understanding the importance of being safety conscious.

S4CS2 **Students will have the computation and estimation skills necessary for analyzing data and following scientific explanations.**

a. Add, subtract, multiply, and divide whole numbers mentally, on paper, and with a calculator.

b. Use fractions and decimals, and translate between decimals and commonly encountered fractions—halves, thirds, fourths, fifths, tenths, and hundredths (but not sixths, sevenths, and so on)—in scientific calculations.

c. Judge whether measurements and computations of quantities, such as length, area, volume, weight, or time, are reasonable answers to scientific problems by comparing them to typical values.

S4CS3 Students will use tools and instruments for observing, measuring, and manipulating objects in scientific activities utilizing safe laboratory procedures.

a. Choose appropriate common materials for making simple mechanical constructions and repairing things.

b. Measure and mix dry and liquid materials in prescribed amounts, exercising reasonable safety.

c. Use computers, cameras, and recording devices for capturing information.

d. Identify and practice accepted safety procedures in manipulating science materials and equipment.

S4CS4 Students will use ideas of system, model, change, and scale in exploring scientific and technological matters.

a. Observe and describe how parts influence one another in things with many parts.

b. Use geometric figures, number sequences, graphs, diagrams, sketches, number lines, maps, and stories to represent corresponding features of objects, events, and processes in the real world. Identify ways in which the representations do not match their original counterparts.

c. Identify patterns of change in things—such as steady, repetitive, or irregular change—using records, tables, or graphs of measurements where appropriate.

S4CS5 Students will communicate scientific ideas and activities clearly.

a. Write instructions that others can follow in carrying out a scientific procedure.

b. Make sketches to aid in explaining scientific procedures or ideas.

c. Use numerical data in describing and comparing objects and events.

d. Locate scientific information in reference books, back issues of newspapers and magazines, CD-ROMs, and computer databases.

S4CS6 Students will question scientific claims and arguments effectively.

a. Support statements with facts found in books, articles, and databases, and identify the sources used.

b. Identify when comparisons might not be fair because some conditions are different.

The Nature of Science

S4CS7 Students will be familiar with the character of scientific knowledge and how it is achieved.

Students will recognize that:

a. Similar scientific investigations seldom produce exactly the same results, which may differ due to unexpected differences in whatever is being investigated, unrecognized differences in the methods or circumstances of the investigation, or observational uncertainties.

b. Some scientific knowledge is very old and yet is still applicable today.

S4CS8 Students will understand important features of the process of scientific inquiry.

Students will apply the following to inquiry learning practices:

a. Scientific investigations may take many different forms, including observing what things are like or what is happening somewhere, collecting specimens for analysis, and doing experiments.

b. Clear and active communication is an essential part of science. It enables scientists to inform others about their work, expose their ideas to criticism by other scientists, and stay informed about scientific discoveries around the world.

c. Scientists use technology to increase their power to observe things and to measure and compare things accurately.

d. Science involves many different kinds of work and engages men and women of all ages an backgrounds.

Co-Requisite—Content

EARTH SCIENCE

S4E1 **Students will compare and contrast the physical attributes of stars, star patterns, and planets.**

a. Recognize the physical attributes of stars in the night sky such as number, size, color, and patterns.

b. Compare the similarities and differences of planets to the stars in appearance, position, and number in the night sky.

c. Explain why the pattern of stars in a constellation stays the same, but a planet can be seen in different locations at different times.

d. Identify how technology is used to observe distant objects in the sky.

S4E2 **Students will model the position and motion of the earth in the solar system and will explain the role of relative position and motion in determining sequence of the phases of the moon.**

a. Explain the day/night cycle of the earth using a model.

b. Explain the sequence of the phases of the moon.

c. Demonstrate the revolution of the earth around the sun and the earth's tilt to explain the seasonal changes.

d. Demonstrate the relative size and order from the sun of the planets in the solar system.

S4E3 **Students will differentiate between the states of water and how they relate to the water cycle and weather.**

a. Demonstrate how water changes states from solid (ice) to liquid (water) to gas (water vapor/steam) and changes from gas to liquid to solid.

b. Identify the temperatures at which water becomes a solid and at which water becomes a gas.

c. Investigate how clouds are formed.

d. Explain the water cycle (evaporation, condensation, and precipitation).

e. Investigate different forms of precipitation and sky conditions (rain, snow, sleet, hail, clouds, and fog).

S4E4 **Students will analyze weather charts/maps and collect weather data to predict weather events and infer patterns and seasonal changes.**

a. Identify weather instruments and explain how each is used in gathering weather data and making forecasts (thermometer, rain gauge, barometer, wind vane, anemometer).

b. Using a weather map, identify the fronts, temperature, and precipitation and use the information to interpret the weather conditions.

c. Use observations and records of weather conditions to predict weather patterns throughout the year.

d. Differentiate between weather and climate.

PHYSICAL SCIENCE

S4P1 **Students will investigate the nature of light using tools such as mirrors, lenses, and prisms.**

a. Identify materials that are transparent, opaque, and translucent.

b. Investigate the reflection of light using a mirror and a light source.

c. Identify the physical attributes of a convex lens, a concave lens, and a prism and where each is used.

S4P2 **Students will demonstrate how sound is produced by vibrating objects and how sound can be varied by changing the rate of vibration.**

a. Investigate how sound is produced.

b. Recognize the conditions that cause pitch to vary.

S4P3 **Students will demonstrate the relationship between the application of a force and the resulting change in position and motion on an object.**

a. Identify simple machines and explain their uses (lever, pulley, wedge, inclined plane, screw, wheel and axle).

b. Using different size objects, observe how force affects speed and motion.

c. Explain what happens to the speed or direction of an object when a greater force than the initial one is applied.

d. Demonstrate the effect of gravitational force on the motion of an object.

LIFE SCIENCE

S4L1 **Students will describe the roles of organisms and the flow of energy within an ecosystem.**

a. Identify the roles of producers, consumers, and decomposers in a community.

b. Demonstrate the flow of energy through a food web/food chain beginning with sunlight and including producers, consumers, and decomposers.

c. Predict how changes in the environment would affect a community (ecosystem) of organisms.

d. Predict effects on a population if some of the plants or animals in the community are scarce or if there are too many.

S4L2 **Students will identify factors that affect the survival or extinction of organisms such as adaptation, variation of behaviors (hibernation), and external features (camouflage and protection).**

a. Identify external features of organisms that allow them to survive or reproduce better than organisms that do not have these features (for example: camouflage, use of hibernation, protection, etc.).

b. Identify factors that may have led to the extinction of some organisms.

Contents

Big Idea
You can answer your science questions by carrying out careful investigations.

UNIT A — EARTH SCIENCE   52

Big Idea
We can predict where the sun, the moon, the planets, and the stars will be in the sky.

Big Idea
The sun's energy causes water and air to move in ways that result in predictable weather patterns.

UNIT B PHYSICAL SCIENCE 152

Big Idea
Sound and light are forms of energy that interact with matter in ways that enable us to see and hear the things around us.

Big Idea
Forces act on and change the motion of objects in measurable ways.

Big Idea
The six main kinds of simple machines make work easier by changing the force needed to move objects.

Big Idea
All living things need energy and matter to live and grow.

Big Idea
Certain body parts and behaviors can help living things survive, grow, and reproduce.

References

North Atlantic right whale off the coast of Georgia

Getting Ready for Science

Georgia Performance Standards in This Chapter

Characteristics of Science

S4CS1 Students will be aware of the importance of curiosity, honesty, openness, and skepticism in science and will exhibit these traits. . . .

S4CS2 Students will have the computation and estimation skills necessary for analyzing data and following scientific explanations.

S4CS3 Students will use tools and instruments . . . in scientific activities utilizing safe laboratory procedures.

S4CS4 Students will use ideas of system, model, change, and scale in exploring scientific . . . matters.

S4CS5 Students will communicate scientific ideas and activities clearly.

S4CS6 Students will question scientific claims . . . effectively.

S4CS7 Students will be familiar with the character of scientific knowledge and how it is achieved.

S4CS8 Students will understand important features of the process of scientific inquiry.

What's the Big Idea?

You can answer your science questions by carrying out careful investigations.

Essential Questions

Go online for student eBook
www.hspscience.com

Science in Georgia

Dear Angel,

We're having a great time in the mountains. Today, we walked along the Appalachian Trail.

My dad taught me how to measure how far we walked by counting our steps. For me, every 35 steps is about 100 feet. I lost count after 2,000 feet, but it seemed that we walked for miles!

I'll see you on Sunday!

Your friend,
Kyle

USA

How far do you walk every day? What tools could you use to measure the distance? How does this relate to the **Big Idea?**

Characteristics of Science

S4CS3 Students will use tools and instruments for observing, measuring, and manipulating objects in scientific activities utilizing safe laboratory procedures.

S4CS5c Use numerical data in describing and comparing objects and events.

S4CS7a Similar scientific investigations seldom produce exactly the same results, which may differ due to unexpected differences in whatever is being investigated, unrecognized differences in the methods or circumstances of the investigation, or observational uncertainties.

Essential Question

What Are Inquiry Tools?

Georgia Fast Fact

Eyes on the Planet

The Aura satellite was developed by the National Aeronautics and Space Administration (NASA). Launched in July 2004, Aura monitors the protective layer of ozone in Earth's atmosphere. Scientists from Georgia Tech have helped analyze data collected by Aura.

standard measure
[STAN•derd MEZH•er]
An accepted unit of
measurement (p. 6)

microscope
[MY•kruh•skohp] A tool that
makes an object look many
times bigger than it actually
is (p. 8)

spring scale [SPRING SKAYL]
A tool that measures forces,
such as weight (p. 11)

Aura spacecraft in orbit around Earth

Measuring with Straws

Guided Inquiry

Start with Questions

When you visit the doctor, he or she measures how tall you are. You might also use a height chart at home to keep track of how much you've grown.

- What exactly is measuring?

- What are some different ways to measure objects?

- Are there standard ways to measure the same objects?

Investigate to find out. Then read to find out more.

Prepare to Investigate

Inquiry Skill Tip

When you measure, you make observations by using numbers. Look for ways in which a straw can be used to measure things. Then think about other ways you might measure the same things.

Materials

- plastic straws
- classroom objects
- 2 cups
- water
- marker

Make a Data Table

Object	Measurement(s)

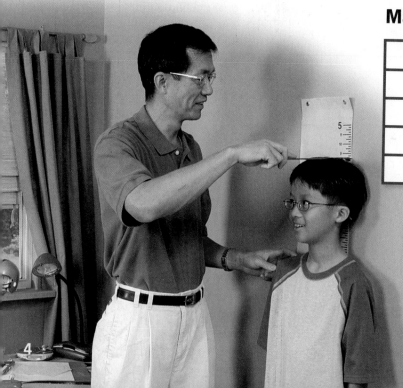

Follow This Procedure

1 Use straws to **measure** the length and width (distance along and distance across) of several objects. For example, you might begin with this textbook. **Record** your measurements.

2 Now use straws to **measure** the circumference of a round object (the distance around it). (Hint: Flatten the straws before you start.) **Record** your measurements.

3 Next, work with a partner to find a way to use straws to **measure** the volume (amount) of water in one of the cups. **Record** your measurements.

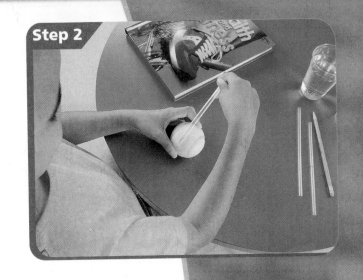

Step 2

Step 3

Draw Conclusions

1. Compare your measurements with those of other students. What can you conclude?

2. **Standards Link** Which of the objects you measured was the longest? Which cup held the greater volume of water? How can you tell? **S4CS5c**

3. **Inquiry Skill** Scientists **measure** carefully and record numbers accurately. Why do all scientists need to use the same unit of measurement when working on the same problem? **S4CS5c**

Independent Inquiry

How could you use straws to measure weight? What other tools would you need? Plan and carry out a simple investigation to find out. **S4CS7a**

VOCABULARY
standard measure p. 6
microscope p. 8
spring scale p. 11

SCIENCE CONCEPTS
▶ how scientists use tools to measure, observe, and manipulate
▶ how to use tools properly and safely

Focus Skill MAIN IDEA AND DETAILS

Look for tools that scientists use.

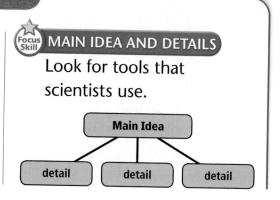

Tools for Measuring Distance

Long ago, people sometimes used body parts to measure distance. For example, in the early 1100s, King Henry I of England had several identical iron bars made. The bars supposedly equalled the distance from his nose to his fingertips. They became a standard length—one yard. A **standard measure** is an accepted amount that is used to measure other things.

When it was introduced, the meter, another unit of length, was not based on a body part. It was defined as $\frac{1}{10,000,000}$ of the distance from the North Pole to the equator. Imagine measuring that distance!

These units of measurement may seem strange. Yet they helped people agree on the lengths of objects and the distances between places.

Focus Skill MAIN IDEA AND DETAILS

Why do we use standard measures?

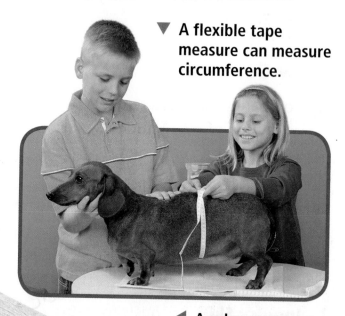

▼ A flexible tape measure can measure circumference.

◀ A ruler measures length. Place the first line of the ruler at one end of the object. The line closest to the other end of the object shows its length.

Geologists and surveyors use this tool to measure large distances.

Tools for Measuring Volume

Cooks measure ingredients for recipes with cups and spoons. Scientists also measure volume with tools. To find the volume of a liquid, you can pour it into a measuring cup or beaker. You can also use a graduated cylinder, or graduate. The numbers on the side of each container show the volume of the liquid. Never use tools from your science lab for measuring food or medicine!

To measure the volume of a solid, multiply its length by its width by its height. For example, a box has a length of 4 centimeters and a width of 2 centimeters. Its height is 2 centimeters. The volume is 4 centimeters × 2 centimeters × 2 centimeters = 16 cubic centimeters.

This is sometimes abbreviated 16 cm³. All volumes are given in cubic units. So you may see cubic meters (m³), as well.

Focus Skill — **MAIN IDEA AND DETAILS**

How do you measure the volume of a solid? Of a liquid?

Droppers are used to measure small amounts of liquid.

To measure a liquid, place a graduated cylinder on a flat surface. Your eyes should be even with the flat top of the liquid. The volume is the marking that is closest to the top of the liquid.

Tools for Observing and Handling

Sometimes scientists need to observe objects closely. Certain tools can help them observe details that they might not be able to see with just their eyes.

A hand lens makes things look larger than they are. It magnifies them. Hold the lens a few centimeters in front of your eye. Then move the object closer to the lens until you can see it clearly. Never let the lens touch your eye. Never use it to look at the sun!

Forceps let you pick up sharp or prickly objects without getting hurt. You can also use them to hold delicate objects without handling those objects too much. However, you must squeeze the forceps gently.

A magnifying box is sometimes called a bug box. Students often use it to observe live insects. An insect can move around in the box while you watch.

A **microscope** makes objects look several times bigger than they are. The microscope shown on the next page has one big lens. Two knobs enable the user to adjust the image until he or she can see it clearly.

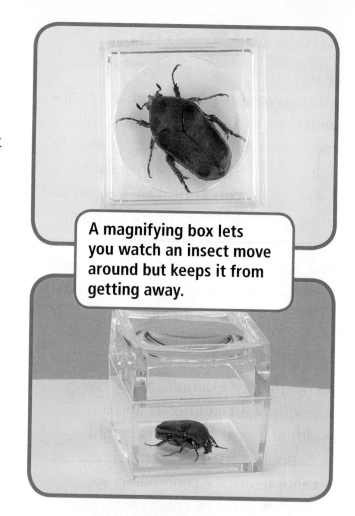

A magnifying box lets you watch an insect move around but keeps it from getting away.

Focus Skill MAIN IDEA AND DETAILS

How do the tools on these pages help scientists?

A hand lens helps you see many details. When you use forceps to hold an object, you can observe the object without having your fingers in the way. ▶

8

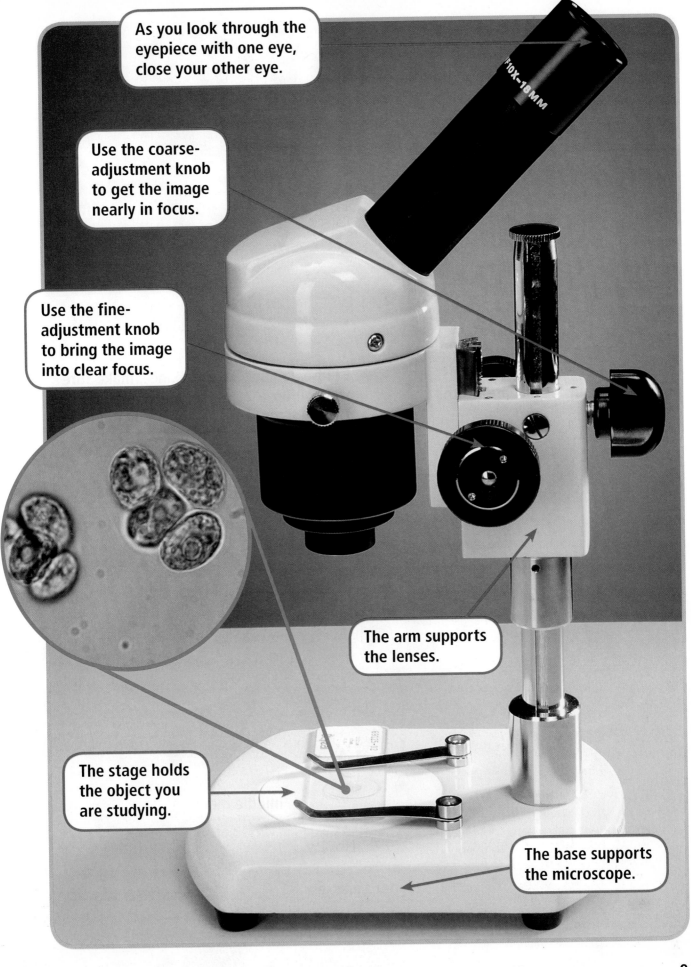

As you look through the eyepiece with one eye, close your other eye.

Use the coarse-adjustment knob to get the image nearly in focus.

Use the fine-adjustment knob to bring the image into clear focus.

The arm supports the lenses.

The stage holds the object you are studying.

The base supports the microscope.

Other Tools

Many other tools can help you measure. For example, a thermometer measures the temperature of the air or of a liquid. A thermometer is a hollow glass tube that has a bulb at one end. The bulb contains a liquid. The air or liquid around the bulb warms or cools the liquid inside the bulb. As the liquid inside the thermometer gets warmer, it expands and rises up the tube. Numbers on the thermometer tell how warm the air or liquid being measured is.

When you are using a thermometer, be sure to touch the bulb as little as possible. If your fingers are on the bulb, you will just measure the warmth of your fingers! Also, be careful—glass thermometers break easily. If one breaks, tell your teacher or another adult.

The number closest to the top of the liquid in the thermometer is the temperature.

▼ Before you use a pan balance, make sure the pointer is at the middle mark. Place the object in one pan, and add standard masses to the other pan. When the pointer is at the middle mark again, add the numbers on the standard masses. The total is the mass of the object.

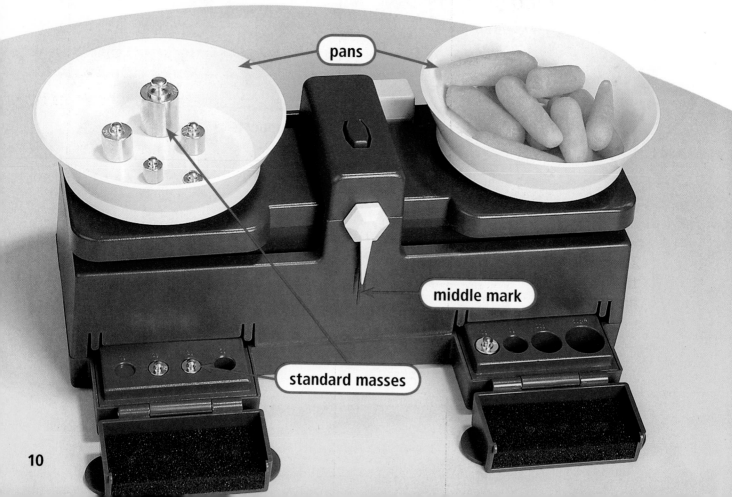

pans

middle mark

standard masses

This girl is using a spring scale to measure the rabbit's weight. ▶

A rock hammer can chip away smaller samples from a large rock. How might you observe these samples?

A pan balance measures mass. Mass is the amount of matter in an object. It is measured in grams (g). A **spring scale** measures forces, such as weight. Force is measured in newtons (N).

Other tools help scientists as well. The rock hammer shown on this page can help scientists gather samples from larger rocks. The scientists then identify the rocks by using other tools, such as hand lenses, to observe the patterns of crystals and other properties.

Focus Skill) MAIN IDEA AND DETAILS

What properties do a pan balance and a spring scale measure?

11

Essential Question

What are inquiry tools?

In this lesson, you measured length and volume and learned about the tools used to measure weight, length, and volume.

1. (Focus Skill) **MAIN IDEA AND DETAILS** Draw and complete a graphic organizer to give details that support this main idea: *Scientists use many different tools to measure, observe, and handle.* **S4CS3**

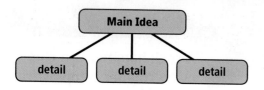

2. **SUMMARIZE** Write two sentences that tell what this lesson is mostly about. **S4CS3**

3. **DRAW CONCLUSIONS** How would scientific experiments be different if scientists had no tools to use? **S4CS3**

4. **VOCABULARY** Write a fill-in-the-blank sentence for each vocabulary word. Trade sentences with a partner. **S4CS3**

5. **Critical Thinking** How do mass and weight differ? **S4CS3**

CRCT Practice

6. Which tool measures length?
   A beaker
   B thermometer
   C pan balance
   D tape measure **S4CS3**

7. Which tool measures volume?
   A meterstick
   B pan balance
   C spring scale
   D graduated cylinder **S4CS3**

8. How can you decide which tool to use in a certain experiment?

The **Big** Idea

S4CS3

Writing
ELA4W2

Persuasive Writing
You are a scientist, but you can afford only two of the tools described in this lesson. Choose two tools, and write a persuasive paragraph explaining why they are the most important.

Math
M4N5e

Solve a Problem
You are using a measuring wheel to determine the width of a street. A rotation of the wheel is 1 meter (3.3 ft). The wheel rotates $9\frac{1}{2}$ times. About how wide is the street?

bee stinger and sewing needle

Art

Up Close and Closer
Draw an object as you would see it with your eyes. Then draw the same object as you think it would look under a hand lens. Now draw it as though it were under the highest-power microscope lens.

For more links and activities, go to **www.hspscience.com**

Characteristics of Science

S4CS1 Students will be aware of the importance of curiosity, honesty, openness, and skepticism in science and will exhibit these traits in their own efforts to understand how the world works.

S4CS2c Judge whether measurements and computations of quantities, such as length, area, volume, weight, or time, are reasonable answers to scientific problems by comparing them to typical values.

S4CS3a Choose appropriate common materials for making simple mechanical constructions and repairing things.

S4CS4 Students will use ideas of system, model, change, and scale in exploring scientific and technological matters.

S4CS6b Identify when comparisons might not be fair because some conditions are different.

Georgia Fast Fact

A New Building
1180 Peachtree has 41 floors and rises to a height of 198 meters (650 ft). Before structures of this size are built, architects plan and build models. They work hard to make designs that are interesting and safe.

Essential Question

What Are Inquiry Skills?

1180 Peachtree in midtown Atlanta

observation [ahb•zuhr•VAY•shuhn] Information that you gather with your senses (p. 18)

inference [IN•fuhr•uhns] An untested interpretation of observations (p. 18)

prediction [pree•DIK•shuhn] A statement of what will happen, justified by observations and knowledge of cause-and-effect relationships (p. 19)

estimate [ES•tuh•mit] An educated guess about a measurement (p. 22)

hypothesis [hy•PAHTH•uh•sis] A scientific explanation that can be tested (p. 23)

experiment [ek•SPER•uh•muhnt] A controlled test of a hypothesis (p. 23)

15

Build a Straw Model

Guided Inquiry

Start with Questions

Engineers use models to help them design buildings and bridges. People who build amusement park rides, such as roller coasters, also build and test models to make certain the rides are fun and safe.

- What is a model?
- How can using models help you answer questions about science?

Investigate to find out. Then read to learn more.

Prepare to Investigate

Inquiry Skill Tip

A model is an object that looks or acts like the thing you are studying. Every model has limits. It can never be exactly the same as the thing you are studying.

Materials

- 16 plastic straws
- 30 paper clips
- 30-cm piece of masking tape

Make an Observation Chart

Building Method	Ideas and Observations

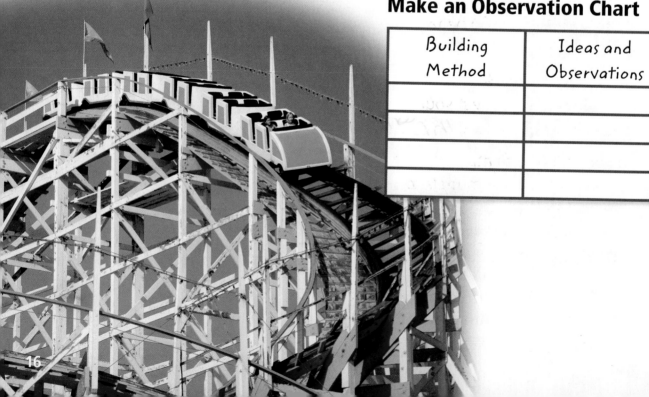

Follow This Procedure

1 Work with a group to construct a model of a building. First, discuss questions such as these: What should the building look like? What are some ways to use the paper clips and the tape with the straws? What will keep the building from falling down?

2 Have one group member record all the ideas. Be sure to respect each other's suggestions.

3 **Predict** which building methods will work best, and try them. **Observe** what works, **draw conclusions**, and **record** them.

4 Plan how to use your building methods to **construct a model** building. Then carry out the plan.

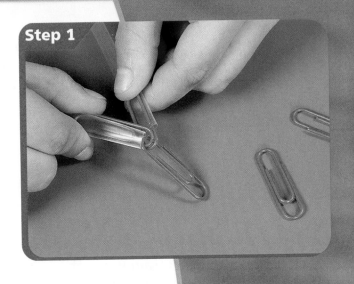
Step 1

Step 3

Draw Conclusions

1. Why was it important to share ideas before you began construction?

2. **Standards Link** How did your observations affect your conclusions? **S4CS1b, c**

3. **Inquiry Skill** Scientists and engineers often **use models** to see how parts work together. What did you learn about building by making the model? **S4CS4a, b**

Independent Inquiry

Choose one additional material or building method to use in making your **model**. **Predict** how it will improve your model. Justify your prediction. Then test it. **S4CS3a**

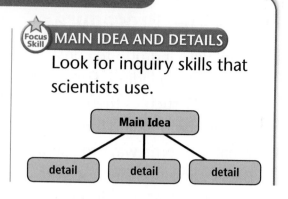

VOCABULARY
observation p. 18
inference p. 18
prediction p. 19
estimate p. 22
hypothesis p. 23
experiment p. 23

SCIENCE CONCEPTS
▶ how scientists think
▶ how asking questions helps scientists learn and understand

Focus Skill **MAIN IDEA AND DETAILS**
Look for inquiry skills that scientists use.

```
Main Idea
   |
detail  detail  detail
```

Observe and Infer

Scientists practice certain ways of thinking, or *inquiry skills*. You can use these skills, too. Learning them will help you think like a scientist.

Did you notice the clouds when you woke up today? If so, you made an observation. An **observation** is information from your senses. You can *observe* how tall a tree is and the color of its leaves.

An observation is information from your senses. You can record your observations with notes or drawings. ▼

Did you ever try to explain why a tree's leaves are green or why its bark is rough? You were not observing. You were inferring. An **inference** is an untested interpretation based on your observations and what you know. Scientists might observe that one star looks brighter than others. They could *infer* that the brightest star is bigger, hotter, or closer to Earth.

Focus Skill **MAIN IDEA AND DETAILS**
Why do scientists use inquiry skills?

18

Predict

You often use your knowledge to guess what will happen next. When you do this, you are predicting. A **prediction** is a statement of what is likely to happen, justified by what you know about cause-and-effect relationships.

A scientific prediction isn't just a wild guess. It is an educated guess. Scientists justify their predictions by their observations, their experience, and what they already know.

When you *predict*, you figure out patterns of events. Then you suggest what is likely to happen next. For example, scientists might observe a series of small earthquakes. They might use that information to predict a volcanic eruption.

MAIN IDEA AND DETAILS

How are predictions different from guesses?

You use inquiry skills to predict that a flower's buds will open. You might even predict what color they will be. ▼

▲ How are these plants the same and different? What words and numbers can be used to describe them?

Compare, Classify, and Use Numbers

How would you describe the plants in the picture above? Scientists—and you—often compare objects and ideas. When you compare, you identify how two or more things are alike and different. You can learn about plants, for example, by comparing their leaves and flowers.

Suppose you want to find a book in the library. Books in libraries are organized based on an observation. For example, fiction is sorted alphabetically by the author's name.

Scientists also classify, or sort, objects. For example, they group plants by the types of flowers they have. Classifying helps you see patterns.

Using numbers helps scientists—and you—experiment and learn. Scientists use exact numbers to measure the mass of a seed. How might you use numbers to learn about the plants in the picture?

Focus Skill **MAIN IDEA AND DETAILS**

Name a way in which you use each inquiry skill on this page in your daily life.

20

Time/Space Relationships and Models

How do the orbits of the planets relate to one another? How does a pulley work? How does a seed grow into a plant? To answer these questions, you need to understand *time/space relationships*.

Space relationships tell where things belong in relation to each other. Time relationships tell the order of events.

Look at the pictures of the plant at the right. How has the plant changed? If you know the order of the events in its life cycle, you can infer that the plant has grown over time.

Have you ever used a little ball and a big ball to show Earth orbiting the sun? You were *using a model*. Models help you understand how things work. Scientists often use models to understand things that are too big, small, fast, slow, or dangerous to observe in person.

Focus Skill MAIN IDEA AND DETAILS

How would you use time/space relationships when building a model of an ecosystem?

Knowing the order in which events happen over time can help you understand the life cycle of this plant. You could find out more by recording how long it takes the plant to grow and change. ▶

Measure and Estimate

When you investigate, you usually need to *measure* your results. Measuring allows you to compare your results to those of others. Scientists use the measurements of the International System of Units (SI), also called the *metric system.*

Measuring is one way of using numbers. Sometimes, scientists make exact measurements. They use tools such as metersticks to measure distance, and they use thermometers to measure temperature. They use graduated cylinders to measure volumes of liquids, pan balances to measure masses, and spring scales to measure forces such as weight. Each tool gives a measurement as an exact number.

Sometimes, it's not possible to measure exactly. If something is too big, small, fast, slow, or dangerous to investigate up close, scientists may use their observations to make an estimate. An **estimate** is an educated guess about a measurement.

(Focus Skill) **MAIN IDEA AND DETAILS** How is measuring related to using numbers?

▲ This girl is estimating a length of about 75 cm.

▼ Careful measurements help these boys collect accurate data about distance and time.

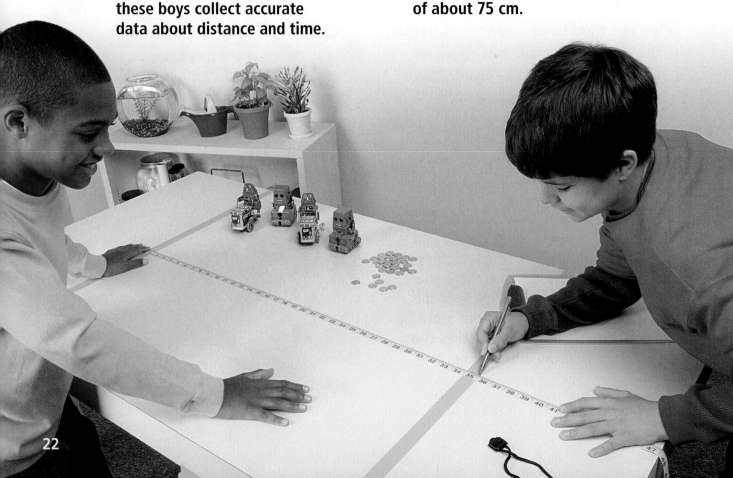

◀ **What is a possible hypothesis for an investigation that uses these materials?**

Plan and Conduct an Investigation

Your CD player will not work. You think of several possible causes, such as dead batteries. Then you plan and conduct a simple investigation. You find and fix the problem. Scientists also solve problems in this way.

Suppose you have a more complex problem. For the school fair, your class is designing a large board with holes cut in it for a beanbag toss. You already have the beanbags. They measure 6 centimeters ($2\frac{1}{3}$ in.) around. You must decide how large to make the holes in the board.

You decide that the holes in the board should also measure 6 centimeters in diameter. This idea becomes your **hypothesis**, or scientific explanation that you can test. Next, you test your hypothesis.

You plan an **experiment** to test your hypothesis. Your teacher cuts different-size holes in a board, and you toss the beanbags through them. You find that the beanbags go through an 8-centimeter hole more easily. But is it really the larger hole that makes the difference? Could the difference be your distance from the board? Could it be how high or low the hole is? How can you find out?

Focus Skill **MAIN IDEA AND DETAILS** What is a hypothesis?

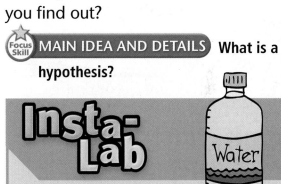

Insta-Lab

Full Measure
Choose an object in the classroom. Measure it in as many ways as you can. Record the measurements. Give them to your teacher. You will be given another list. Try to find the object that the new list describes.

These students are measuring how fast loaded and unloaded toys move. What variables are they controlling? What variable changes? What variable are they observing?

Identify Variables and Gather/Display Data

In an experiment, you must identify the variables—things that can change. In the beanbag experiment, the variables are the size of the holes, the distance of the player from the board, and the height from the ground to the holes.

To make a test fair, keep all of the variables the same except the one you are testing. In the first trial of the experiment, you change only the size of the holes. In the next trial, you change only the height from the ground to the holes. By controlling variables, you can make sure your results are due only to the thing you changed.

As you do your experiment, you write down your results. Then you display them in a graph or table.

 **MAIN IDEA AND DETAILS** Why is it important to control variables?

24

Draw Conclusions and Communicate

During your beanbag experiment, you recorded your results for each size hole. Next, you need to interpret your data, or draw a conclusion about it.

After you study your data, you find that the results do not support your hypothesis. But that's OK! Remember, a hypothesis is just one possible explanation. The purpose of an experiment is to test a hypothesis. You still got the information you needed!

You can share the results of your experiment by discussing with your classmates how to build the game for the school fair. If the experiment were for a science fair, you would use other tools—writing, pictures, and graphs—to communicate the information. You might even display the beanbag board that you used to test your hypothesis.

Focus Skill **MAIN IDEA AND DETAILS**

Why is communication an important skill?

▼ These students are using words, objects, and pictures to communicate. They are sharing how they conducted their experiment and what conclusions they drew.

Essential Question

What are inquiry skills?

In this lesson, you learned about important skills scientists use to explain the world around them. These skills include observing, inferring, predicting, measuring, and estimating. Scientists use these skills and others when they experiment to test a hypothesis.

1. (Focus Skill) **MAIN IDEA AND DETAILS** Draw and complete a graphic organizer in which you list three different inquiry skills. **S4CS1, 2**

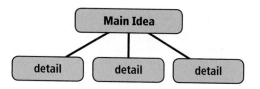

2. SUMMARIZE Write several sentences that tell the most important information in this lesson. **S4CS1, 2**

3. DRAW CONCLUSIONS You cannot understand a classmate's science project. What inquiry skill or skills does your classmate probably need to improve? **S4CS8b**

4. VOCABULARY Make a crossword puzzle with the vocabulary terms. **S4CS1**

5. Critical Thinking How is an estimate like a prediction? **S4CS2c**

CRCT Practice

6. Which inquiry skill helps you notice a change in something?
  A hypothesize
  B communicate
  C observe
  D predict **S4CS1**

7. In an experiment, how can you make sure your results are due only to what you've tested?
  A by forming a hypothesis
  B by controlling variables
  C by drawing conclusions
  D by making a prediction **S4CS6b**

8. Which skills could you use to help you find out what kind of muscle tissue is shown on a microscope slide? **S4CS1**

The **Big Idea**

Writing

ELA4W2

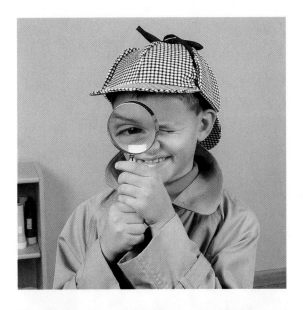

Narrative Writing

Write a story about how you or an imaginary person your age uses several inquiry skills to solve a problem. At the end of the story, name the skills that were used.

9÷3 Math

M4M1a

SI Units

Find out more about the International System of Units (SI). What SI unit is used in place of each of the following customary units: inch, yard, mile, gallon, ounce, pound, and ton?

Health

Get Moving

What do you think is the main reason some people do not like to exercise? Think of a way to find out whether this reason—your hypothesis—is supported. Write the steps you would take to test your hypothesis.

For more links and activities, go to **www.hspscience.com**

LESSON 3

Characteristics of Science

S4CS4b Use geometric figures, number sequences, graphs, diagrams, sketches, number lines, maps, and stories to represent corresponding features of objects, events, and processes in the real world. Identify ways in which the representations do not match their original counterparts.

S4CS4c Identify patterns of change in things—such as steady, repetitive, or irregular change—using records, tables, or graphs of measurements where appropriate.

S4CS5c Use numerical data in describing and comparing objects and events.

Essential Question

How Do Scientists Use Graphs?

Georgia Fast Fact

Shake and Quake

A seismograph measures earthquakes and records the data on graphs. The strength, or magnitude, of an earthquake is measured by using the Richter scale. Earthquakes with a Richter magnitude of less than 3.5 are mild. Quakes with a magnitude of 7.0 can cause serious damage. In this lesson, you'll learn how scientists—and you—can use graphs to display data like this.

Modern seismogram

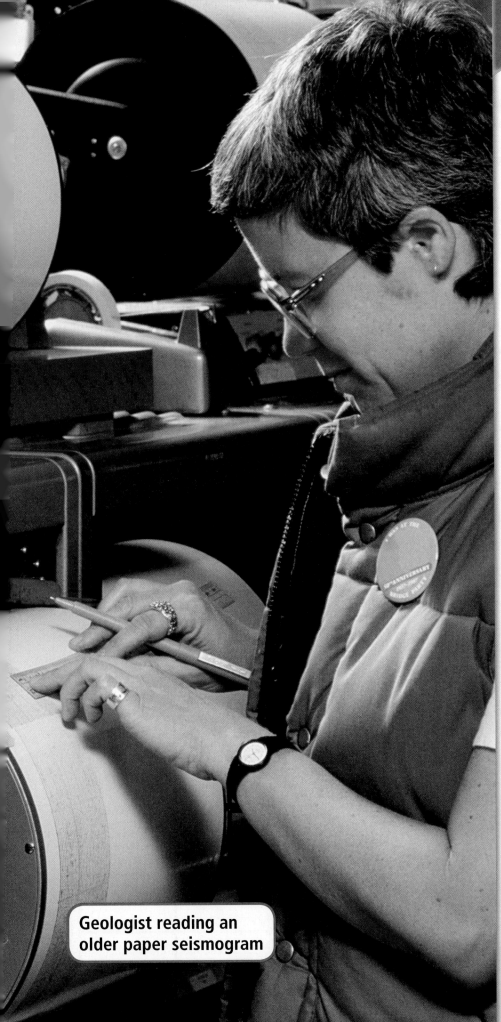

Geologist reading an older paper seismogram

interpret [in•TER•pruht]
To analyze data to draw
conclusions (p. 32)

scale [SKAYL] One of the lines
on a graph, used to show
the sizes of the units on the
graph (p. 33)

Testing Beam Strength

Guided Inquiry

Start with Questions

The steel beams in this equipment can hold a lot of weight. You will investigate the strength of model "beams"—drinking straws.

- What force can you apply to the straws to test their strength?

- How will you display your data?

Investigate to learn about using data. Then read to find out more.

Prepare to Investigate

Inquiry Skill Tip

Graphing is one way to display data from an investigation. Graphing makes it easier for you to see patterns and draw conclusions.

Materials

- 10 plastic drinking straws
- masking tape
- large paper clip
- paper cup
- pennies

Make a Data Table

Predictions and Results		
Number of Straws	Predicted Number of Pennies That Will Be Supported	Actual Number of Pennies That Were Supported
1		
2		
3		
4		

Follow This Procedure

1 Work with a partner. Use tape to make straw bundles. Make one bundle of 2 straws, one of 3 straws, and one of 4 straws. You will have one straw left.

2 Use the paper clip to make a hanger for the paper cup.

3 As your partner holds the single straw at each end, hang the cup from the middle of the straw. **Predict** how many pennies the straw can support. **Record** your prediction. Then add one penny at a time to the cup. Add pennies until the straw bends sharply. Then **record** the number of pennies that are in the cup.

4 Repeat Step 3 with each bundle of straws.

5 Use the data to make a graph.

Step 3

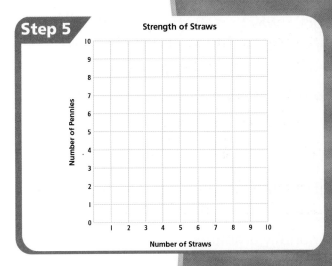

Step 5

Draw Conclusions

1. How are the bundles different from each other?

2. **Standards Link** Which number of straws did your investigation show was the strongest? `S4CS4b`

3. **Inquiry Skill** Using graphs to display data can help scientists interpret the data. What conclusion can you draw from your graph? `S4CS4c`

Independent Inquiry

Use a pan balance to find and record the masses of the pennies in the Investigate. What mass bent the single straw? What mass bent each bundle? **Record** your results, and **display** them in a graph. `S4CS5c`

VOCABULARY
interpret p. 32
scale p. 33

SCIENCE CONCEPTS
▶ how to use data to construct graphs
▶ how to interpret graphs

Focus Skill **MAIN IDEA AND DETAILS**
Look for ways to make and read graphs.

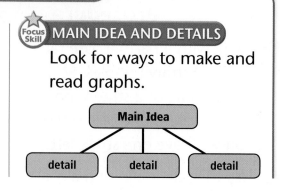

Getting Ready to Graph

When you do a science investigation, you must record your results. A table is a good way to record data in an organized way. Others can read your table easily to get useful information. You can read others' tables easily, too.

When you **interpret**, you analyze data to draw conclusions. To interpret the information in a table, first read the title. It tells you what the table is about. The table on this page shows the average monthly amounts of rain in Helen, Georgia.

Next, read the headings. They tell you what information is given in each part of the table. In the table on this page, the number of centimeters of rain is given for each month of the year.

Study the data, looking for patterns. You might notice here that the amount of rain increases in the winter and decreases in the summer.

Finally, draw conclusions. What is your interpretation of the data? One possible conclusion is that in Helen, January is the rainiest month.

Focus Skill **MAIN IDEA AND DETAILS**
How are tables helpful?

▼ By studying the table, you can see the average rainfall for each month. A scientist might also display the data in a graph to look for patterns.

Average Monthly Rainfall in Helen, Georgia						
Month	January	February	March	April	May	June
Average rainfall (cm)	18.0	16.3	16.3	13.5	16.8	12.5
Month	July	August	September	October	November	December
Average rainfall (cm)	14.2	13.5	14.0	10.9	15.5	15.8

Using a Bar Graph

A bar graph can show the same data as a table. It can be used to compare, at a glance, the data about different events or groups.

Bar graphs can help you interpret results. You don't have to read all the data as you do in a table. Instead, a quick look at a bar graph can give you important information. From the bar graph on this page, it's easy to see that in Helen, the most rain falls during January.

MAIN IDEA AND DETAILS

In what way is a bar graph better than a table?

A **scale** on a graph shows you the size of the units. The scale at the left of this graph is marked in centimeters.

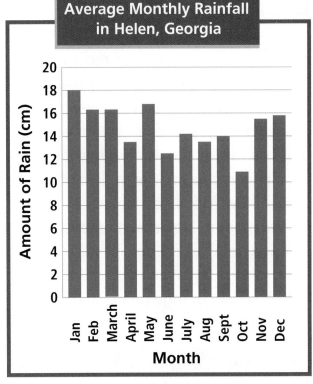

▲ The data in this bar graph is the same as in the table. A bar graph can be used to easily compare the data about different events or groups.

The Tour de Georgia bike race passes through Helen.

Using a Line Graph

In some investigations, data is collected over time. The data can be recorded in a table and displayed in a line graph. Line graphs often show changes over time.

The line at the side or bottom of a graph is called an *axis.* Numbers or labels are along each axis. The middle of a line graph shows points connected by lines. For each point, look down or left to see its value on an axis. Look for patterns. On this page, what can you conclude from the dark orange points and the lines between them?

MAIN IDEA AND DETAILS

What information do line graphs often show?

A scientist collected this information about average high temperatures in Savannah, Georgia. ▼

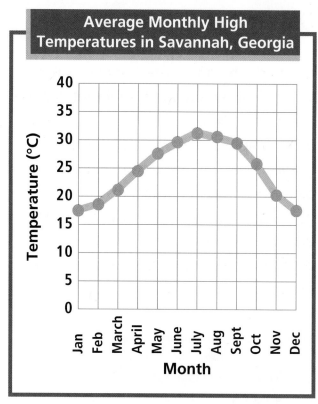

Average Monthly High Temperatures in Savannah, Georgia

▲ A line graph often shows changes over time. The numbers along the *y*-axis of this graph tell you what temperatures are shown. The labels on the *x*-axis tell you the months when temperatures were measured. What patterns do you see?

Average Monthly High Temperatures in Savannah, Georgia	
Month	Temperature (°C)
January	17.2
February	18.3
March	21.1
April	24.1
May	27.4
June	29.8
July	31.2
August	30.8
September	29.4
October	25.8
November	20.1
December	17.4

Using a Circle Graph

Some scientists wanted to classify the animals at a park. They wanted to find out which animal group had the most members. They counted 100 animals in all and recorded their data in a table.

Then they displayed their data in a circle graph to easily compare the animal groups. A circle graph shows data as a whole made up of parts. To read a circle graph, look at the label of each section to find out what is shown. Compare the sizes of the sections, and then draw conclusions.

 MAIN IDEA AND DETAILS

What conclusion can you draw from the circle graph on this page?

The circle graph shows the same data as the table. ▼

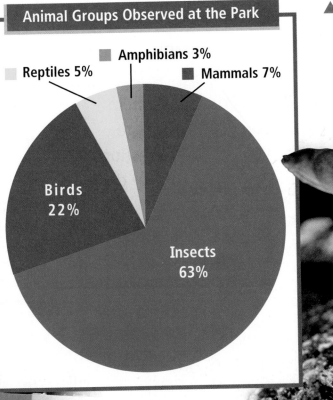

Animal Groups Observed at the Park

Reptiles 5% Amphibians 3% Mammals 7% Birds 22% Insects 63%

Insta-Lab

Make a Pie!
Circle graphs are sometimes called pie charts. You can make your own pie! With your classmates, find a way to classify all your shoes. You might classify them by color, size, or style. Display your data in a circle graph (a pie chart).

| Animal Groups Observed at the Park ||
Animal Group	Number Observed
Mammals	7
Insects	63
Birds	22
Reptiles	5
Amphibians	3

▲ **The table shows how animals in a park were classified.**

katydid

35

Essential Question

How do scientists use graphs?

In this lesson, you learned how to use graphs to organize and display measurements and other data. Graphs make it easier to interpret patterns in data and to draw conclusions.

1. (Focus Skill) **MAIN IDEA AND DETAILS** Draw and complete a graphic organizer that lists the features of bar, line, and circle graphs. **S4CS4**

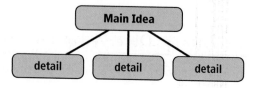

2. SUMMARIZE Use the graphic organizer to write a lesson summary. **S4CS4**

3. DRAW CONCLUSIONS Why is a line graph a good way to display average temperatures in a city by month? **S4CS4c**

4. VOCABULARY Write a definition in your own words for each vocabulary term. **S4CS4**

5. Critical Thinking What is the relationship between tables and graphs? **S4CS4**

6. A fourth-grade class is studying the growth of plants. Over several weeks, the students have measured and recorded the growth of one plant. What would be a good way for them to display their data? Why? **S4CS4c**

CRCT Practice

7. Which of the following BEST displays the relationships between the parts of a whole?

A table

B line graph

C bar graph

D circle graph **S4CS4b**

8. How do graphs help you find answers to your science questions?

A Graphs display data at a glance.

B Graphs measure data.

C Graphs test hypotheses.

D Graphs control variables. **S4CS4**

Write a Report

Suppose you're a scientist who has studied weather. Write a report that tells what kind of data you collected. Show how you recorded your data and how you used graphs.

Label Graphs

Find at least three graphs in newspapers or magazines. Identify and label the major parts of each graph.

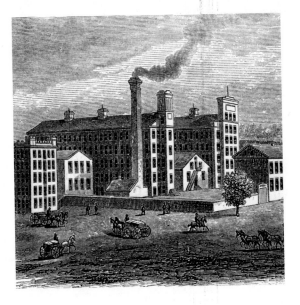

Boomtown

Gather and display data about population changes in Columbus, Georgia, from its founding in 1828. Write a report in which you explain how the city's location on the Chattahoochee River helped it become a thriving cotton-marketing center.

 For more links and activities, go to **www.hspscience.com**

Georgia Performance Standards in This Lesson

Characteristics of Science

S4CS5a Write instructions that others can follow in carrying out a scientific procedure.

S4CS7a Similar scientific investigations seldom produce exactly the same results, which may differ due to unexpected differences in whatever is being investigated, unrecognized differences in the methods . . . or observational uncertainties.

S4CS8a Scientific investigations may take many different forms, including observing what things are like or what is happening somewhere, collecting specimens for analysis, and doing experiments.

S4CS8b Clear and active communication is an essential part of science. . . .

Georgia Fast Fact

Under Pressure

Scientists use this "shake table" to model the strength of buildings during earthquakes. At Georgia Tech, scientists use large rods called *actuators* to repeatedly move a structure back and forth. Scientists analyze the data from these experiments to learn how to make buildings stronger.

Essential Question

What Is the Scientific Method?

scientific method

[sy•uhn•TIF•ik METH•uhd] A series of steps that scientists follow to test hypotheses and to find out answers to their science questions (p. 42)

Earthquake "shake table"

Model 7
Test 8
South

Model 7
Test 8
East

Testing a Straw Model

Start with Questions

You've learned that scientists build models, like the one below, but this is only one of the methods scientists use to answer questions.

- How do scientists form their questions?

- What steps do scientists follow to answer their questions?

Investigate to find out. Then read to find out more.

Prepare to Investigate

Inquiry Skill Tip

When you experiment, you test a hypothesis. You answer science questions by using controlled procedures to gather data. You then analyze the data and draw conclusions.

Materials

- paper clips
- paper cup
- straw model from Lesson 2
- pennies

Make a Data Table

Number of Pennies	Result

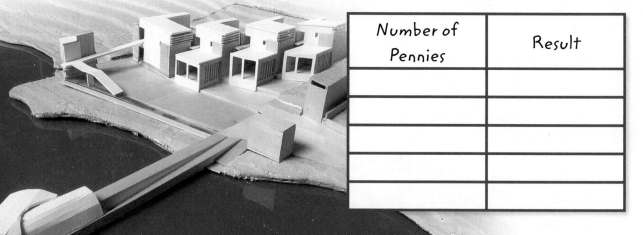

Follow This Procedure

❶ Bend the paper clips to make a hanger for the paper cup.

❷ **Predict** how many pennies your straw model can support. Hang your cup on the model. Add one penny at a time. Was your prediction accurate?

❸ With your group, think of ways to strengthen your model. You might also look for other places on your model to hang the cup. **Record** your ideas.

❹ **Form a hypothesis** about what will make the model stronger. Then **experiment** to see if the results support the hypothesis. Use multiple trials.

❺ Discuss what made your straw model stronger, and **draw conclusions**. **Communicate** your findings.

Draw Conclusions

1. Were you able to increase the strength of your model? How?

2. **Standards Link** Why is it important to follow the procedure as it is described? **S4CS7a**

3. **Inquiry Skill** Scientists **experiment** to test their hypotheses. What did you learn from this experiment? **S4CS8a**

Step 1

Step 2

Independent Inquiry

Will your model support more pennies if their weight is spread across it? Plan and conduct an experiment to find out. Write your experiment's steps as instructions that others can follow. **S4CS5a**

SCIENCE CONCEPTS
▶ what the steps in the scientific method are
▶ how the scientific method helps scientists learn

Focus Skill **MAIN IDEA AND DETAILS**

Look for the steps in the scientific method.

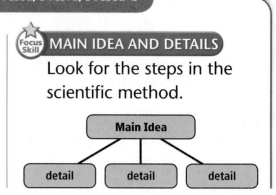

Main Idea

detail detail detail

Observe and Ask Questions

The **scientific method** is a way in which scientists find out how things work and affect each other. The five steps of this method help scientists test ideas. The steps describe how scientists—and you—can find answers to questions.

Observe and Ask Questions After observing the straw models your class built, you might ask these questions:

• Is a cube stronger than a pyramid?

• Are straws more likely to bend if they are placed at an angle?

• Is a shorter straw stronger than a longer one?

• Why do buildings use triangles?

Focus Skill **MAIN IDEA AND DETAILS**

What is the scientific method?

You can find triangle shapes on bridges and other structures. Why is that? ▶

Hypothesize and Experiment

Form a Hypothesis Suppose you want to know whether a pyramid or a cube is stronger. You can form a hypothesis. A *hypothesis* is a scientific explanation that you can test. Here is one hypothesis: Pyramids hold more weight than cubes because triangles are stronger than squares.

Plan an Experiment How can you test your hypothesis? You can think of a plan and write it down as a set of steps. For example, you might hang a cup on each of two models and then add one penny at a time to each cup.

Next, you need to think about all the variables. Make sure you change only one variable on the trials of your test.

In this experiment, both models are made of straws. They are made the same way. The cups will be the same. Only one variable will be tested—the shape of the models.

The complete plan should list all the materials. Then it should list, in order, all the things to do. You should plan to conduct several trials. They help make your data more reliable. If you get about the same result for each trial, your measurements were done well.

Conduct an Experiment Now it's time to conduct, or carry out, your experiment. You should follow the steps in the correct order. In each step, you should record everything you observe, especially any results you didn't expect.

 MAIN IDEA AND DETAILS

How do you plan an experiment?

You can use the scientific method to determine which of these structures is stronger.

Share Your Findings

Draw Conclusions and Communicate Results The final step in the scientific method begins with drawing conclusions. Look at your hypothesis again. Then analyze the observations you recorded. Do the results support your hypothesis? Did the pyramid hold more pennies than the cube?

For this experiment, you could give the results in numbers. You recorded the number of pennies each model supported. For other experiments, you might describe the results in other ways. For example, you might explain that a liquid turned blue or a plant wilted.

Scientists share their results. This allows others to double-check the work. Other scientists should be able to repeat the investigation. If the results aren't the same, they can find and fix any mistakes. This allows scientists to build new ideas with knowledge that is reliable.

Sharing findings of an investigation allows others to learn as well. You can share your findings in a written report or an oral report. Your report should state your hypothesis, list your materials, and describe your procedure. It should include the details of your setup and a diagram. It should end with your results and conclusions.

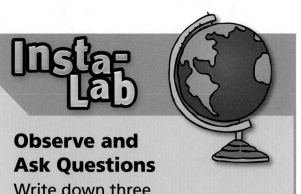

Observe and Ask Questions

Write down three questions about anything you can see from your desk. Discuss the questions with two classmates. Choose one question that none of you can answer. Then plan a way to find an answer.

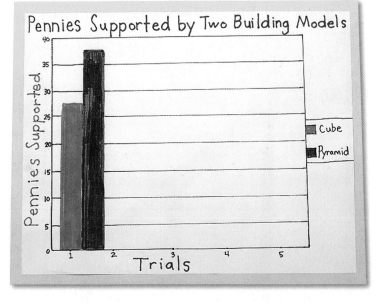

▲ You can display your results in charts, graphs, or diagrams. Each graph should have a title, a key, and clear labels.

▲ Your report should describe your hypothesis, materials, procedure, results, and conclusion. Another person should be able to read your report, repeat your investigation, and get similar results.

In your report, you should tell whether or not the results supported your hypothesis. *Supported* means that the results matched your prediction. The hypothesis was *disproved* if the results were the exact opposite of your prediction.

Your results may not be clear. Maybe they don't support your hypothesis, but they also don't disprove it. That's OK! You should be curious about unusual data. It may show you a new question to investigate.

Unclear results may also lead you to improvements. You may need to measure more carefully. You may not have controlled variables well enough.

Charts, graphs, and diagrams can help you explain your results and conclusions clearly.

 **MAIN IDEA AND DETAILS** Why should a report on an investigation be detailed?

GPS Wrap-Up and Lesson Review

Essential Question

What is the scientific method?

In this lesson, you learned that the scientific method is a way in which scientists find answers to their questions. The five steps of the scientific method help scientists find the correct answers. Repeated trials help show that results are reliable.

1. **(Focus Skill) MAIN IDEA AND DETAILS** Draw and complete a graphic organizer to give details about this main idea: *The scientific method consists of five steps.* `S4CS5–8`

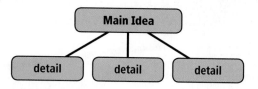

2. **SUMMARIZE** Write a summary of the lesson, beginning with this sentence: *The scientific method helps us gain new knowledge.* `S4CS7–8`

3. **DRAW CONCLUSIONS** Will the scientific method be different 100 years from now? Explain your answer. `S4CS7b`

4. **VOCABULARY** Write a fill-in-the-blank sentence for the vocabulary term. `S4CS8a`

5. **Critical Thinking** State an everyday problem a young person might have that could be solved with the scientific method. `S4CS8a`

6. Suppose you need to know whether short triangles or long ones are stronger. You predict that short ones are stronger, and your results support this. How can you make sure the results are accurate? `S4CS7a`

CRCT Practice

7. When you use the scientific method, what are you testing?
   A instruments
   B experiments
   C hypotheses
   D observations `S4CS8a`

8. In which steps of the scientific method do you predict an outcome and then compare the results with the prediction? `S4CS8a`

The **Big** Idea

 Writing   **ELA4W2**

Write a Report

Choose an investigation you have conducted or observed. Then write a report about it. Describe how each step of the scientific method was followed—or how it should have been followed.

 Math   **M4N4b**

Solve a Problem

A pyramid supports 10 pennies, which weigh 28 grams (1 oz.) total. How much does one penny weigh?

 Social Studies   **SS4E1f**

Super Inventor

Use library resources to gather information about Eli Whitney's invention of the cotton gin. Then make a poster to share your findings. Be sure to tell how this invention changed cotton production in Georgia.

 For more links and activities, go to **www.hspscience.com**

Wrap-Up

Visual Summary

Tell how each picture helps explain the **Big Idea**.

The Big Idea You can answer your science questions by carrying out careful investigations.

Lesson 1 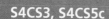 S4CS3, S4CS5c

Inquiry Tools
Scientists use tools to make careful measurements. You can also estimate, or make a good guess about a measurement.

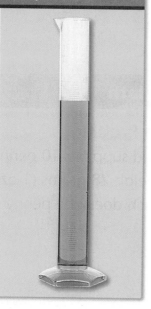

Lesson 2 S4CS1, S4CS2, S4CS6b

Inquiry Skills
Scientists use important skills when they carry out experiments. These skills include observing, inferring, predicting, measuring, and estimating.

Lesson 3 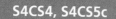 S4CS4, S4CS5c

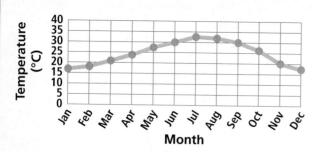

Display Your Data
You can organize measurements in a table and then display them on a graph. Graphs help you interpret data.

Lesson 4 S4CS5a, S4CS7a, S4CS8

The Scientific Method
The scientific method includes observations, inferences, hypotheses, predictions, an experiment plan, and the sharing of results.

Show What You Know

Writing About Inquiry Tools/Research and Report

The inventor of one of the earliest microscopes was Dutch scientist Anton van Leeuwenhoek. Use reference materials to learn about van Leeuwenhoek's life. Write a report that tells what he is famous for and what kinds of things he observed with his microscope. How did van Leeuwenhoek apply the scientific method?

ELA4W3

Georgia Performance Task

Build and Repair

Think of another question about your straw models that you can investigate. For example, you may wish to cut some of the straws and test different substances to see which is best used to repair the break. Or you might test several materials to see which adds the greatest strength and stability when you use it to enclose one of the shapes. Be sure to record your procedure so that others can repeat your experiment.

S4CS3a, 5a

Vocabulary Review

Use the terms below to complete the sentences. The page numbers tell you where to look in the unit if you need help.

microscope p. 8

spring scale p. 11

inference p. 18

hypothesis p. 23

experiment p. 23

scientific method p. 42

1. Forces are measured by a _____.　　**S4CS5c**

2. A _____ is a testable explanation of observations.　　**S4CS8a**

3. When you make an observation and then draw a conclusion, you make an _____.　　**S4CS8a**

4. To observe very small details, you might use a _____.　　**S4CS8c**

5. Scientists find out how things work and how they affect other things by using the _____.　　**S4CS8a**

6. A scientific test in which variables are controlled is an _____.　　**S4CS8a**

Check Understanding

Choose the best answer.

7. What can you measure with the tool shown here? (p. 11)　　**S4CS3**

A balance　　**C** weight

B mass　　**D** volume

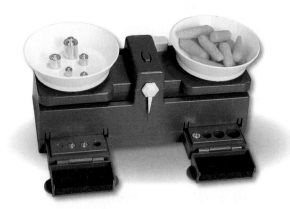

8. MAIN IDEA AND DETAILS Which is the main purpose of the scientific method? (p. 42)　　**S4CS8a**

A to ask questions

B to share information

C to test ideas

D to plan an experiment

9. Why is it important to list enough details in reports about investigations? (p. 44)　　**S4CS8b**

A so that scientists can observe and ask questions

B so that scientists can build new ideas on reliable results

C so that scientists can form a hypothesis

D so that scientists can plan and conduct a simple experiment

10. SEQUENCE Which letter below lists the steps of the scientific method in order? (pp. 42–44) `S4CS8a`

   1. Form a hypothesis.
   2. Ask questions.
   3. Conduct an experiment.
   4. Draw conclusions.
   5. Plan an experiment.

   A 2, 1, 5, 3, 4   **C** 1, 2, 3, 4, 5
   B 1, 2, 5, 3, 4   **D** 5, 4, 3, 2, 1

11. Which inquiry skill is based on describing the ways in which things are alike and different? (p. 20) `S4CS8a`

   A measuring   **C** sequencing
   B summarizing   **D** comparing

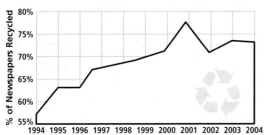

12. Use the graph above to decide what prediction you would make for recycling in 2010. (p. 34) `S4CS4c`

   A It will increase a lot.
   B It will increase a little.
   C It will decrease a little.
   D It will decrease a lot.

13. Some students want to classify and compare plants growing in a forest. They identify 100 plants and record their data. How can they BEST display their data? (p. 35) `S4CS5c`

   A in a table   **C** in a line graph
   B in a report   **D** in a circle graph

14. Why are variables controlled? (p. 24)

   A to know what questions to ask
   B to know what caused the results
   C to plan your investigation
   D to form a hypothesis `S4CS7a`

15. Which characteristic must a hypothesis have? (p. 43) `S4CS8a`

   A It must be a testable statement.
   B It must be a short prediction.
   C It must predict and plan.
   D It must predict and measure.

16. How would experiments be different without tools? (p. 6) `S4CS3`

   A Measuring would be easier.
   B Information could be gathered.
   C The results would not be precise.
   D There would be no change.

Inquiry Skills

17. A model is not the real thing. Why do scientists **use models**? `S4CS4b`

18. Which tool is used to **measure** the mass of water? `S4CS3`

Critical Thinking

19. An experiment is repeated, but the result is different. What are some possible causes? `S4CS7a`

20. You want to find out how water temperature affects the movement of goldfish. Write a hypothesis. Then identify the variables you will control, change, and measure. `S4CS8a`

The Big Idea

What do YOU wonder?

This computer artwork shows sunrise over Earth as seen from space. High clouds in the atmosphere glow in the sun's light.

Chapter 2 Planets and Stars
Chapter 3 Weather

GO online for student eBook
www.hspscience.com

Build a Model Solar System

Our solar system is made up of eight unique planets. It takes Earth about 365.26 days, which we round off to 365 and call one year, to travel around the sun. Do the other planets take the same amount of time to orbit the sun? Plan and conduct an investigation to find out, using a model of the solar system.

Sunrise over Earth

Georgia Performance Standards in This Chapter

Content

S4E1 Students will compare and contrast the physical attributes of stars, star patterns, and planets.

S4E1a, b, c, d

S4E2 Students will model the position and motion of the earth in the solar system and will explain the role of relative position and motion in determining sequence of the phases of the moon.

S4E2a, b, c, d

This chapter also addresses these co-requisite standards:

Characteristics of Science

S4CS3 Students will use tools . . . in scientific activities.

S4CS4 Students will use ideas of system . . . and scale.

S4CS4b

S4CS5 Students will communicate scientific ideas . . .

S4CS5c

S4CS8 Students will understand . . . the process of scientific inquiry.

S4CS8a, c

What's the Big Idea?

We can predict where the sun, the moon, the planets, and the stars will be in the sky.

Essential Questions

Go online for student eBook
www.hspscience.com

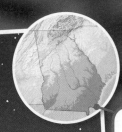

Cumberland Island National Seashore

Dear Emma,

I'm camping with my family on Cumberland Island. Last night, we stayed up to watch the stars and moon over the ruins of the Dungeness Plantation.

It was really neat. There were no city lights, so the stars looked brighter, and we could see more of them. I can't wait to tell you all about it!

Your friend,
Kenny

USA

What changes in the sky have you noticed? Can you distinguish planets from stars? How do these things relate to the **Big Idea?**

Content

S4E2a Explain the day/night cycle of Earth using a model.

S4E2b Explain the sequence of the phases of the moon.

S4E2c Demonstrate the revolution of the earth around the sun and the earth's tilt to explain the seasonal changes.

Characteristics of Science

S4CS5c

LESSON

1

Essential Question

How Do Earth and Its Moon Move?

Georgia Fast Fact

Sunrise and Sunset

Atlanta, Georgia, gets about $14\frac{1}{2}$ hours of daylight in June. In December, Atlanta gets only about $10\frac{1}{2}$ hours of daylight. This is one example of a seasonal change. In the Investigate, you will begin to learn about what causes seasonal changes on Earth.

Atlanta, Georgia

rotate [ROH•tayt] To spin around an axis (p. 60)

axis [AKS•sis] An imaginary line that runs through the center of Earth from the North Pole to the South Pole (p. 60)

revolve [rih•VAHLV] To travel in a closed path (p. 62)

orbit [AWR•bit] The closed path of one object in space around another object; or to move in such a path (p. 62)

moon [MOON] A natural body that revolves around a planet (p. 64)

phase [FAYZ] One of the shapes the moon seems to have as it orbits Earth (p. 64)

Seasons and Sunlight

Start with Questions

As winter approaches, there are fewer hours of daylight. Temperatures become cooler. The leaves of some trees turn brown and die.

- Why are there fewer hours of daylight in winter than in summer?

- Why do temperatures decrease?

Investigate to find out. Then read to find out more.

Prepare to Investigate

Inquiry Skill Tip

When you measure, you make observations using numbers. You can then use these numbers to make accurate comparisons.

Materials

- small 60-watt table lamp
- ruler
- graph paper
- black construction paper
- thermometer

Make an Observation Chart

Lamp Angle	Temperature of Black Paper
straight down	
tilted	

Follow This Procedure

1 Work with a partner. Shine the lamp straight down from a height of 30 cm onto a sheet of graph paper. Draw an outline of the lit area, and label it Step 1.

2 Repeat Step 1 with a new sheet of graph paper, this time placing the lamp at an angle. Label this outline Step 2.

3 Shine the lamp straight onto a sheet of black paper. After 15 minutes, **measure** the temperature of the paper in the lit area. **Record** the temperature on the sheet of graph paper labeled Step 1.

Step 4

4 Now use another sheet of black paper, and angle the light as you did in Step 2. Again, **measure** the temperature of the lit area after 15 minutes. **Record** the temperature on the sheet of graph paper labeled Step 2.

Draw Conclusions

1. How did the area covered by the light change? How did the temperature in that area change?

2. **Standards Link** How is the change in area related to the change in temperature? **S4E2c**

3. **Inquiry Skill** How could scientists **measure** the effect that the sun has on seasons? **S4CS5c**

Independent Inquiry

Try your experiment on the real thing! Choose a sunny spot outdoors, and measure and record its temperature throughout the day. Why do you think it changes?

 S4CS5c

Understand Science

VOCABULARY
rotate p. 60
axis p. 60
revolve p. 62
orbit p. 62
moon p. 64
phase p. 64

SCIENCE CONCEPTS
▶ how the movements of Earth and the sun result in day and night and the seasons
▶ why we have time zones
▶ why the moon appears to change shape

SEQUENCE
Events in a sequence happen in a certain order.

Day and Night

Every day the sun appears to rise in the east. It appears to reach its highest point around noon and to set in the west. After a period of darkness, this process repeats.

This cycle of day and night occurs because Earth **rotates**, or spins on its axis. Earth's **axis** is an imaginary line that passes through the North and South Poles. When a place on Earth faces the sun, it is day in that place. When that place faces away from the sun, it is night.

Our system of time is based on Earth's 24-hour cycle of daylight and darkness. Because of Earth's rotation, sunrise and sunset occur at different times in different places. Long ago, people didn't need to know the exact time. Each place used local time—time based on sunrise and sunset in that place. This changed in the late 1800s. Trains were starting to travel long distances. If each train station had kept its own time, there would have been confusion. People needed to develop standard times.

The sun appears to rise and set, but it actually doesn't. Earth's rotation causes the sun to appear to move.

Time Zones

▲ It's 7 A.M. in Seattle, on the west coast.

▲ Much of the United States is within one of four time zones. Time zone lines aren't perfectly straight, partly because of state boundaries.

▲ In Atlanta, on the east coast, it's 10 A.M.

In 1884, standard times were set up in 24 time zones around the world. Each time zone represents one of the hours in the day. All the places within a time zone have the same time. If you travel east from one time zone to the next, the time becomes one hour later. If you travel west from one time zone to the next, the time becomes one hour earlier.

In the middle of the Pacific Ocean is the International Date Line. If you go west across that line, you travel into the next day. Crossing the line eastward, you travel into the previous day. For example, if it's 3 A.M. Tuesday and you cross the International Date Line while going west, the time becomes 2 A.M. Wednesday, not 2 A.M. Tuesday.

The United States has seven time zones. If you're just about to have dinner at 6 P.M. in Georgia and you call a friend in Oregon, it will be 3 P.M. there. Your friend may be just getting home from school.

Focus Skill SEQUENCE

Describe the sequence of time zones from east to west across the continental United States.

Insta-Lab

Sunrise, Sunset
Use a flashlight and a ball to model day and night. Where on the ball are sunrise and sunset represented?

Earth's Tilt and the Seasons

Night follows day. Spring follows winter. The changes of the seasons, as well as the changes of night and day, occur because of the ways Earth moves.

Earth moves in two ways. You have learned that Earth rotates on its axis. It takes about 24 hours for Earth to make one complete rotation.

In addition to rotating on its axis, Earth **revolves**, or travels in a path around the sun. An object's path in space around another object is its **orbit**. Earth's orbit takes about 365 days, or one year.

Some people think we have seasons because Earth is closer to the sun in the summer than in the winter. This isn't so. It's the tilt of Earth's axis that produces seasons.

As Earth revolves, one part is tilted toward the sun. That part of Earth takes in more energy from the sun in the form of heat. The part that is tilted away from the sun takes in less energy from the sun.

You may know that Earth is divided into Northern and Southern Hemispheres by the equator. The *equator* is an imaginary line going all the way around Earth halfway between the North and South Poles.

In this illustration, Earth's tilt is causing the sun's rays to shine more directly on the Northern Hemisphere than on the Southern Hemisphere. So, the Northern Hemisphere has summer.

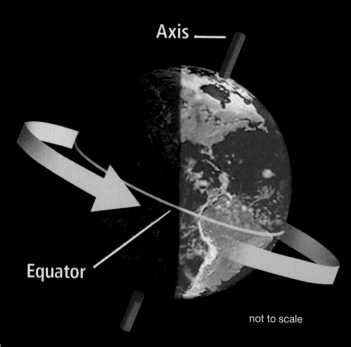

Axis

Equator

not to scale

1 The summer *solstice* (SAHL•stis), about June 21 in the Northern Hemisphere, is the day of the year that has the most hours of daylight. **3** The winter solstice, about December 21, is the day that has the most hours of darkness.

2 On the autumn *equinox* (EE•kwih•nahks), about September 21, and the **4** spring equinox, about March 21, the hours of daylight and darkness are the same. These dates mark the beginning of autumn and of spring.

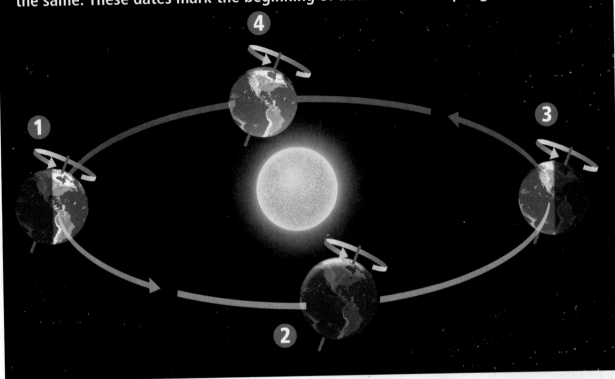

During June, July, and August, the Northern Hemisphere of Earth is tilted toward the sun and the Southern Hemisphere is tilted away. The sun's rays shine more directly on the Northern Hemisphere, which has summer, than on the Southern Hemisphere, which has winter. As Earth continues its orbit, the Northern Hemisphere is tilted away from the sun, causing winter. The Southern Hemisphere is tilted toward it, causing summer. This cycle continues as Earth revolves around the sun.

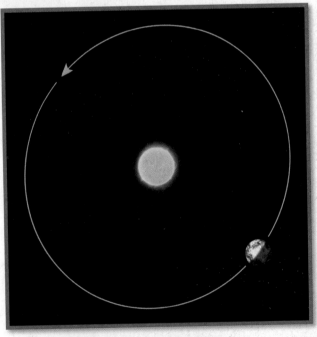

▲ Earth's orbit around the sun is almost a perfect circle.

Focus Skill **SEQUENCE** Which season occurs after the Northern Hemisphere has been tilted away from the sun?

Moon Phases

The **moon** is a small planetlike body that revolves around Earth rather than the sun. As Earth revolves around the sun, the moon revolves around Earth.

The moon appears to shine, but the light you see is actually reflected light from the sun. As the moon revolves around Earth, different amounts of its lit surface can be seen. That's why the moon seems to have different shapes, or **phases**.

The phases of the moon follow the same pattern about every $29\frac{1}{2}$ days.

On one of those days, all of the lit side of the moon can be seen from Earth. When this happens, we say there is a full moon. Then, as the days pass and the position of the moon changes, from Earth we see less and less of the lit side. Finally, we see none of the lit side at all. On that night, the moon is called a new moon.

Focus Skill SEQUENCE What phase of the moon happens after we see less and less of the moon at night?

During the first half of the moon's cycle, the amount of the lit side of the moon seen from Earth waxes, or increases.

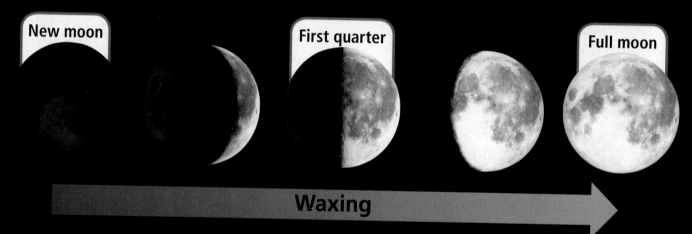

New moon   First quarter   Full moon

Waxing

During the second half of the moon's cycle, the amount of the lit side of the moon seen from Earth wanes, or decreases. Then the cycle begins again.

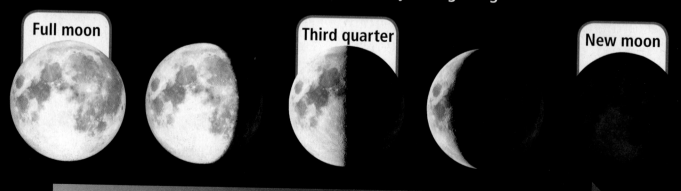

Full moon   Third quarter   New moon

Waning

One half of the moon is always being lit by the sun. Whether people can see all, some, or none of the lit side depends on the positions of the moon and Earth.

During the new moon phase, the lit side of the moon can't be seen from Earth.

The full moon phase occurs about 15 days after the new moon phase.

New Moon to Full Moon

When the moon's orbit brings it between Earth and the sun, its lit side can't be seen from Earth. This phase is called the new moon. Later in the month, when Earth is between the moon and the sun, we see the sun's light reflected from one whole side of the moon. When this happens, we see a full moon.

For more links and animations, go to **www.hspscience.com**

Essential Question

How do Earth and its moon move?

In this lesson, you learned that Earth's rotation causes day and night. Because Earth's axis is tilted, seasonal changes occur as Earth orbits the sun. As the moon orbits Earth, we see different shapes, or phases.

1. (Focus Skill) **SEQUENCE** Draw and complete a graphic organizer to complete the sequence of Earth's seasons, beginning with the *winter solstice*. **S4E2b**

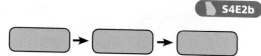

2. SUMMARIZE Write a summary of the lesson. Begin with the sentence *Earth moves in two ways.* **S4E2a, b**

3. DRAW CONCLUSIONS If Earth took 500 days instead of 365 to orbit the sun, how would the seasons be different? Why? **S4E2c**

4. VOCABULARY Use *axis* in a sentence that explains its meaning. **S4E2a**

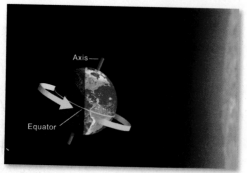

5. Critical Thinking Suppose you see a full moon on the first day of the month. What phase of the moon will you observe in one week? **S4E2b**

CRCT Practice

6. If you live in the Southern Hemisphere, what season do you have in August?
- **A** spring
- **B** summer
- **C** fall
- **D** winter **S4E2c**

7. What causes the moon's phases?
- **A** Earth's orbiting the sun
- **B** Earth's rotation
- **C** the moon's orbiting Earth
- **D** the moon's rotation **S4E2b**

8. How would day and night be different if Earth's axis were not tilted?

The Big Idea

S4E2c

 Writing ELA4W2

Write a Letter

Suppose a friend from the Southern Hemisphere plans to visit you in December. Write a letter in which you explain what kind of clothes to pack and why.

 Math M4N6c

Compare Lengths

An object is 200 centimeters tall. Its shadow is 100 centimeters long at 10 A.M. What fraction compares the object's height to its shadow's length? Will the fraction be greater or smaller just after sunrise?

 Art

The Sun's Positions

Choose an object in your yard. Throughout the year, as the sun rises and sets, draw pictures to show the sun's position relative to this object. Place your drawings on a poster that you can show to your classmates.

 For more links and activities, go to **www.hspscience.com**

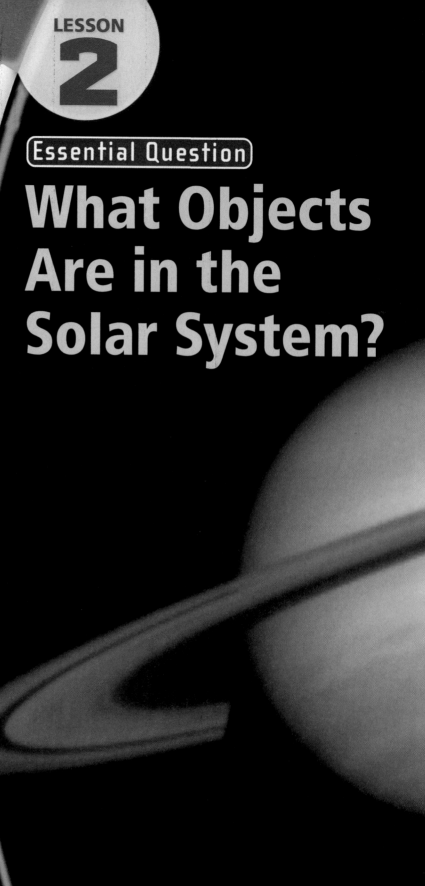

Content

Demonstrate the relative size and order from the sun of the planets in the solar system.

Identify how technology is used to observe distant objects in the sky.

Characteristics of Science

LESSON 2

Essential Question

What Objects Are in the Solar System?

Georgia Fast Fact

Rings Around a Planet

Saturn's rings have fascinated sky gazers since the astronomer Galileo (gal•uh•LAY•oh) first saw them in 1610. We've learned that the rings are made of rock, gas, and ice. Saturn is millions of kilometers from Earth. In the Investigate, you will make a model to help you understand that distance.

solar system [SOH•ler SIS•tuhm] A star and all the planets and other objects that revolve around it (p. 72)

planet [PLAN•it] A large body that revolves around a star (p. 72)

comet [KAHM•it] A ball of rock, ice, and frozen gases that revolves around the sun (p. 77)

Saturn

Distances Between Planets

Guided Inquiry

Start with Questions

An orrery, like the one shown below, is a mechanical device that models the positions and motions of the planets and moons in our solar system.

- How many planets orbit the sun?

- What are the planets' positions in relation to the sun?

Investigate to find out. Then read to find out more.

Prepare to Investigate

Inquiry Skill Tip

There are many ways you can use numbers in science. You can use numbers to estimate and to make comparisons among things or events.

Materials

- 4-m length of string
- tape measure
- 8 markers of different colors

Make a Data Table

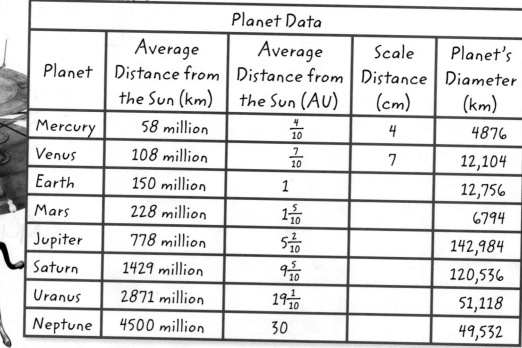

Planet Data				
Planet	Average Distance from the Sun (km)	Average Distance from the Sun (AU)	Scale Distance (cm)	Planet's Diameter (km)
Mercury	58 million	$\frac{4}{10}$	4	4876
Venus	108 million	$\frac{7}{10}$	7	12,104
Earth	150 million	1		12,756
Mars	228 million	$1\frac{5}{10}$		6794
Jupiter	778 million	$5\frac{2}{10}$		142,984
Saturn	1429 million	$9\frac{5}{10}$		120,536
Uranus	2871 million	$19\frac{1}{10}$		51,118
Neptune	4500 million	30		49,532

Follow This Procedure

1. Copy the table on page 70.

2. At one end of the string, make a large knot. This knot will stand for the sun as you **make your model**.

3. An AU (astronomical unit) is Earth's average distance from the sun. In your model, 10 cm will represent 1 AU. Use the tape measure to **measure** Earth's distance from the knot that represents the sun. Use a marker to mark this point on the string. **Record** on the table which color you used for Earth by placing a small dot with the marker next to the planet name.

4. Complete the Scale Distance column of the table. Repeat Step 3 for each planet, using a different color for each.

Draw Conclusions

1. Why do scientists use AUs to measure distances in the solar system?

2. **Standards Link** In your model, how far away from the sun is Mercury? How far away is Neptune? **S4E2d**

3. **Inquiry Skill** How does it help to **use numbers** instead of comparing real distances? **S4CS5c**

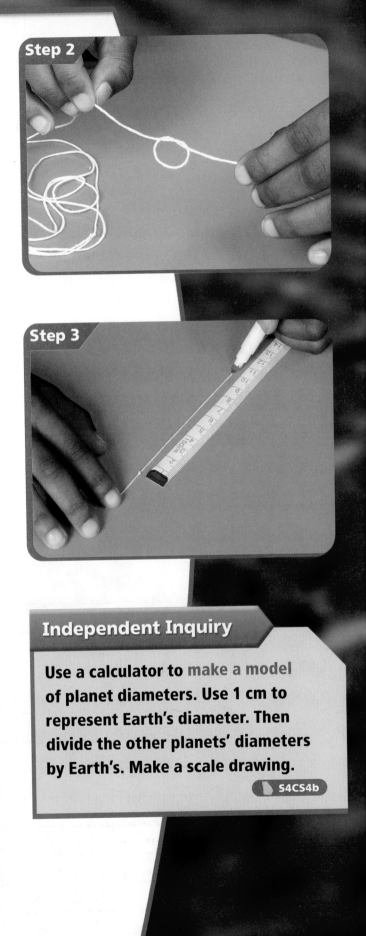

Step 2

Step 3

Independent Inquiry

Use a calculator to **make a model** of planet diameters. Use 1 cm to represent Earth's diameter. Then divide the other planets' diameters by Earth's. Make a scale drawing. **S4CS4b**

Understand Science

VOCABULARY
solar system p. 72
planet p. 72
comet p. 77

SCIENCE CONCEPTS
▶ what makes up our solar system
▶ what the inner and outer planets are

Focus Skill COMPARE AND CONTRAST
Look for phrases such as *by contrast* and *in common*.

alike —— different

Our Solar System

A **solar system** is a group of objects in space that orbit a star in the center, plus the star itself. The sun is the star in the center of our solar system. Everything else in the solar system is small compared to the sun.

Our solar system contains a variety of objects. These include planets, "dwarf planets," moons, and asteroids. A **planet** is a large object that revolves around a star in a clear orbit. A "dwarf planet" also revolves around a star, but its path is not clear of other objects. A moon is a smaller object that revolves around a planet. Asteroids are small and rocky.

In our solar system, there are eight planets. Often, scientists group them as the inner planets and the outer planets. These groups of planets are separated by a ring of asteroids that orbit the sun between Mars and Jupiter.

Focus Skill COMPARE AND CONTRAST

How are moons and planets similar? How are they different?

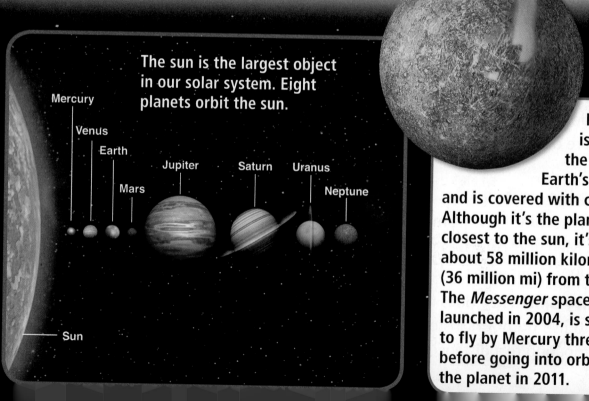

The sun is the largest object in our solar system. Eight planets orbit the sun.

Mercury
Venus
Earth
Jupiter
Saturn
Uranus
Mars
Neptune
Sun

Mercury is about the size of Earth's moon and is covered with craters. Although it's the planet closest to the sun, it's still about 58 million kilometers (36 million mi) from the sun. The *Messenger* spacecraft, launched in 2004, is scheduled to fly by Mercury three times before going into orbit around the planet in 2011.

The Inner Planets

The inner planets are those closest to the sun. They are Mercury, Venus, Earth, and Mars. These planets are alike in many ways. They all have rocky surfaces and are smaller than most of the outer planets. Also, none of the inner planets has more than two moons.

There are also differences among the inner planets. For example, it can be 450°C (840°F) on Mercury—hot enough to melt lead—while Mars's temperature never gets higher than 20°C (70°F).

Earth is the most unusual inner planet. Only Earth has liquid water on its surface and a large amount of oxygen in the atmosphere. This water and oxygen help support life on Earth.

 COMPARE AND CONTRAST

How are the inner planets similar?

Mars is called the Red Planet because it looks fiery red from Earth. Mars is small—its diameter is only half of Earth's. It has huge dust storms that can last for months. Scientists think that at one time, Mars may have had liquid surface water. Many probes have landed on Mars, including *Viking 1* and *2* in 1976, *Pathfinder* in 1997, and the two rovers *Spirit* and *Opportunity* in 2003.

Venus is about the same size as Earth. Venus is the third-brightest object in Earth's sky—only the sun and the moon appear brighter. Clouds of sulfuric (suhl•FYUR•ik) acid make the planet difficult to study from Earth. This radar image shows a surface made up of volcanoes, mountain ranges, highland

Earth is the largest of the inner planets. It's the only planet known to have life and the only one whose surface is mostly water. Earth's distance from the sun helps the planet maintain a temperature that supports life.

The Outer Planets

Beyond Mars, on the far side of the asteroid belt, are the outer planets. They are Jupiter, Saturn, Uranus, and Neptune.

These four planets are huge and made mostly of gases. They have no known solid surface. Their atmospheres blend smoothly into the denser layers of their interiors, very deep beneath the outer layers. For this reason, these planets are often called the gas giants. They all have many moons, and they all are surrounded by rings that are made of dust, ice, or rock.

Because the gas giants have no kr solid surface, a spaceship cannot lar on them. However, the *Pioneer* miss launched in 1972 and 1973, the *Voy* and *2* missions, launched in 1977, a the *Galileo* spacecraft, launched in 1989, flew to the outer planets. *Gal* even dropped a probe into Jupiter's atmosphere in 1995. In 2004, the C spacecraft reached Saturn. From its around Saturn, *Cassini* has given sci a wealth of information about the p famous rings.

Focus Skill **COMPARE AND CONTRAST**

How is Uranus different from the c outer planets?

Jupiter—the largest planet in our solar system—has a diameter that's more than 11 times the diameter of Earth. Jupiter has at least 63 moons. For more than 300 years, a gigantic hurricane-like storm called the Great Red Spot has raged on Jupiter.

Saturn has rings that are visible from Earth through a telescope. Saturn has at least 31 moons. Its atmosphere is mostly hydrogen and helium. Like the other gas giants, Saturn has no known solid surface.

Length of a Year

On any planet, a year is the length of time it takes that planet to orbit the sun. Here is a list of how long a year is on some planets in our solar system, compared to a year on Earth.

Planet Years

Planet	Length of Year (in Earth years)
Mars	1.9
Jupiter	11.9
Saturn	29.5
Neptune	165

If a person has just turned 60 on Earth, about how old is he or she in Saturn years?

Neptune's atmosphere is mainly hydrogen and helium. Neptune is one of the windiest places in the solar system. Winds can reach 2000 kilometers per hour (1200 mi/hr). Neptune has at least 13 moons.

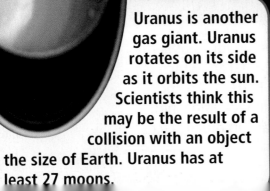

Uranus is another gas giant. Uranus rotates on its side as it orbits the sun. Scientists think this may be the result of a collision with an object the size of Earth. Uranus has at least 27 moons.

Insta-Lab

Planet Sizes

Compare the approximate sizes of planets. Use a large marble to represent Mercury, a table tennis ball to represent Earth, and a basketball to represent Jupiter. Which of the three balls would best represent the size of Venus?

What About Pluto?

Since its discovery in 1930, Pluto has stood apart from the previously discovered planets. For one thing, Pluto is small. It is considerably smaller than Earth's moon. Pluto is made of rock and ice, while the outer planets are made of gases. Pluto's orbit is a long oval that is tilted with respect to the planets. Pluto's orbit sometimes cuts inside the orbit of Neptune.

For these reasons and others, Pluto was reclassified in 2006 as a "dwarf planet." Like the eight planets, a "dwarf planet" orbits the sun and is round.

However, a "dwarf planet's" orbit is not clear of other objects. As a result, "dwarf planets" are found among groups of smaller bodies.

Scientists have identified three "dwarf planets." Ceres is found in the belt of asteroids that orbit the sun between Mars and Jupiter. Eris and Pluto are located beyond the orbit of Neptune in a region that contains many smaller, cometlike objects. Scientists suggest that there may be hundreds of "dwarf planets" in our solar system.

(Focus Skill) **COMPARE AND CONTRAST** How do the planets and "dwarf planets" differ?

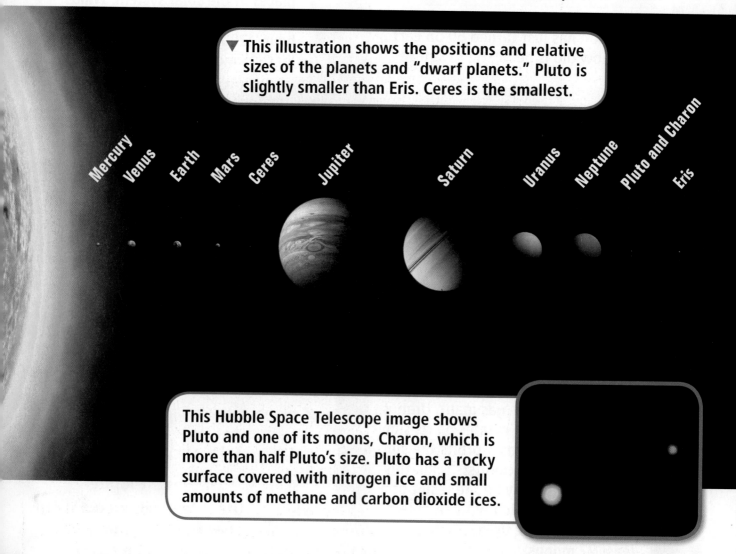

▼ This illustration shows the positions and relative sizes of the planets and "dwarf planets." Pluto is slightly smaller than Eris. Ceres is the smallest.

Mercury   Venus   Earth   Mars   Ceres   Jupiter   Saturn   Uranus   Neptune   Pluto and Charon   Eris

This Hubble Space Telescope image shows Pluto and one of its moons, Charon, which is more than half Pluto's size. Pluto has a rocky surface covered with nitrogen ice and small amounts of methane and carbon dioxide ices.

Small Solar System Bodies

There are many types of small bodies in our solar system. Two of these are asteroids and comets. Although both orbit the sun, comets and asteroids are very different.

Asteroids are bits of rock and metal. Most asteroids are found in the asteroid belt that separates the inner planets from the outer planets. Most are less than 1 kilometer (0.6 mi) across. The largest body in the asteroid belt has a diameter of about 1000 kilometers (620 mi).

By contrast, a **comet** is a ball of rock, ice, and frozen gases. As a comet's orbit brings it close to the sun, the sun's heat may turn some of the frozen matter into gas. That gas, plus the dust that rises with it, then looks like a fiery tail and may be visible from Earth. Most comets are less than 10 kilometers (6 mi) across, but the tails can be as much as 100,000 kilometers (62,000 mi) long.

Focus Skill COMPARE AND CONTRAST

What do comets and asteroids have in common?

Some comets, like Halley's Comet, become well known because their orbits bring them close to Earth.

◀ This is the asteroid Gaspra. Asteroids are harder to see from Earth than comets. A 1991 space probe took the first close-up pictures of an asteroid.

GPS Wrap-Up and Lesson Review

What objects are in the solar system?

In this lesson, you learned about the different objects that make up the solar system. You also learned about the characteristics of each planet, including its size and distance from the sun.

1. **COMPARE AND CONTRAST** Draw and complete a graphic organizer that compares and contrasts the inner planets and the outer planets. **S4E2d**

> alike ——— different

2. SUMMARIZE Write a paragraph in which you describe the solar system. **S4E2d**

3. DRAW CONCLUSIONS Why do you think life hasn't been found on any of the other planets in the solar system? **S4E2d**

4. VOCABULARY Write a sentence using the vocabulary terms *planet* and *solar system.* **S4E2d**

5. Critical Thinking How do scientists use technology to learn about the solar system? **S4E1d**

CRCT Practice

6. What separates the inner planets from the outer planets?

   A Venus

   B comets

   C Earth

   D asteroid belt **S4E2d**

7. What makes Earth different from other planets in the solar system?

   A It is very rocky.

   B It has liquid water.

   C It has the most moons.

   D It has an atmosphere. **S4E1d**

8. How does using numbers help you compare the planets in terms of size and distance from the sun?

S4E2d

Writing

ELA4W2

Write a Paragraph

Use the information in this lesson and from library resources to write a paragraph in which you compare and contrast Earth and the other planets in our solar system.

Math

M4D1a

Make a Bar Graph

Use the table in the Investigate to find the diameters of the planets in our solar system. Make a bar graph that compares the diameters.

Literature

ELA4R1

Planet Fiction

Read a short story about life on another planet or about space travel. Decide whether the story could really happen. Give a brief report to your class about the story.

For more links and activities, go to **www.hspscience.com**

WATER WORLD

Over the years, many people have dreamed of going to Mars. The day when travel to Mars is possible is coming closer. Robot spacecraft have already traveled there. These spacecraft have made amazing discoveries.

One of the most recent spacecraft to journey to the fourth rock from the sun is *Mars Odyssey*. Photos taken by *Mars Odyssey* show that Mars has water. Because it is very cold on Mars, the water is frozen. Most of the water is frozen under the surface of Mars.

Lots of Lakes

Even though lots of ice crystals are mixed in with the Martian soil, Mars doesn't have as much water as Earth. Mars has buried lakes of water, not buried oceans of water. In fact, some scientists think that if you could collect all the water on Mars, it would fill a lake about twice the size of Lake Michigan.

There is evidence that some of the frozen water locked under the surface of Mars might melt every once in a while. Some of the water is only 46 centimeters (18 in.) below the surface. Molten rock deep beneath the surface of Mars might heat the ice. The water may then flow onto the surface.

A Grand Canyon?

Photos taken by *Mars Odyssey* show long, dark streaks on the walls of some canyons. The streaks might indicate areas where water recently flowed down the canyon walls.

Not all scientists agree, however. Many scientists say wind blowing across Mars caused the streaks. Scientists have long

known about powerful wind storms on Mars. Some of those storms blow across the surface for months at a time.

Even if liquid water and life do not exist on Mars today, many scientists still want to explore the red planet. "I'm interested in Mars because it's probably the most fascinating planet in the solar system besides Earth, and probably the only one that could have ever supported other forms of life," said one NASA scientist.

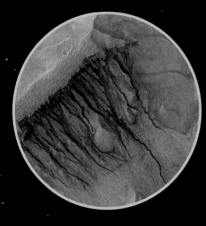

Some scientists say these dark lines were caused by streams of water flowing down a canyon wall.

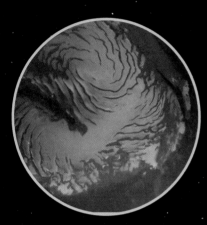

Frozen carbon dioxide covers the North Pole of Mars.

The *Mars Odyssey* spacecraft studies Mars. Photos by the spacecraft show that ice exists on Mars.

Think and Write

1. What would life on Earth be like if Earth had as little water as there is on Mars? **S4E2**

2. How have satellites helped us learn about other planets? **S4E1d**

Find out more. Log on to
www.hspscience.com

LESSON 3

Content

S4E1a Recognize the physical attributes of stars in the night sky such as number, size, color, and patterns.

S4E1b Compare the similarities and differences of planets to the stars in appearance, position, and number in the night sky.

S4E1c Explain why the pattern of stars in a constellation stays the same, but a planet can be seen in different locations at different times.

S4E1d Identify how technology is used to observe distant objects in the sky.

Characteristics of Science

Essential Question

What Can We See in the Sky?

Georgia Fast Fact

Objects in the Sky

This 16-inch reflecting telescope is used to study faraway objects, including star clusters in our own Milky Way Galaxy and other galaxies as well. This telescope is but one of several found at the Hard Labor Creek Observatory, which is home to a number of astronomers from Georgia State University.

Hard Labor Creek Observatory

star [STAR] A huge ball of superheated gases (p. 86)

sun [SUHN] The star at the center of our solar system (p. 86)

constellation [kahn•stuh•LAY•shuhn] A pattern of stars that form an imaginary picture or design in the sky (p. 88)

galaxy [GAL•uhk•see] A huge system of gases, dust, and many stars (p. 88)

universe [YOO•nuh•vers] Everything that exists in space (p. 88)

Make a Telescope

Guided Inquiry

Start with Questions

When you look through a telescope, you can see distant objects in detail. Telescopes help scientists see objects in space that are very far away.

- How does a telescope work?
- How do objects appear when you look through a telescope?

Investigate to find out. Then read to find out more.

Prepare to Investigate

Materials

- modeling clay
- small-diameter cardboard tube
- 1 thin (eyepiece) lens
- 1 thick (objective) lens
- large-diameter cardboard tube

Make an Observation Chart

Object Viewed	Observations

Follow This Procedure

1 Use the clay to fasten the thin lens in one end of the small tube. Set the lens as straight as possible, taking care not to smear the middle of the lens with clay.

2 Repeat Step 1, using the thick lens and the large tube. Slide the open end of the small tube into the large tube. You have just made a telescope.

3 Hold your telescope up, and look through each lens. CAUTION: **Never look directly at the sun.** Slide the small tube into and out of the large tube until what you see is in focus. How do objects appear through each lens? Record your observations.

Draw Conclusions

1. What did you observe as you looked through each lens?

2. **Standards Link** Compare the way that distant objects look when viewed through your telescope and when viewed with your eyes alone. **S4E1d**

3. **Inquiry Skill** Scientists use telescopes to observe objects that are far away. How would you plan and conduct a simple investigation to observe Earth's moon? **S4CS8c**

Step 1

Step 2

Independent Inquiry

Use your telescope to observe the moon at night. List details you can see by using your telescope that you can't see by using only your eyes.

S4CS8c

VOCABULARY
star p. 86
sun p. 86
constellation p. 88
galaxy p. 88
universe p. 88

SCIENCE CONCEPTS
▶ what stars and galaxies are
▶ what constellations are
▶ how stars and planets compare

(Focus Skill) **MAIN IDEA AND DETAILS**
Look for the details that support each main idea.

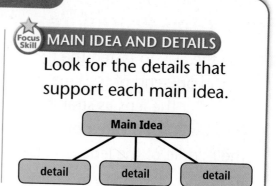

The Sun and Other Stars

You have probably looked up at the stars in the night sky and noticed their different sizes and colors. You may know that a **star** is a huge ball of superheated gases. The **sun** is a star that is at the center of our solar system.

At more than 1 million kilometers (621,000 mi) in diameter, the sun is the largest object in the solar system. It is the source of most of the energy on Earth—without it life could not exist.

From Earth, the sun looks like a ball of light. Like other stars, it is made up of gases, mostly hydrogen and helium.

The sun sometimes has dark spots called sunspots on its surface. They do not give off as much light and heat energy as the rest of the sun's surface. The red streams and loops are solar flares, gases that shoot out from the sun. These hot fountains of gas often begin near a sunspot and extend tens of thousands of kilometers into space. Both sunspots and solar flares last only a few days.

The sun is important to us because of the energy it provides, but it is just one of billions of stars in the universe.

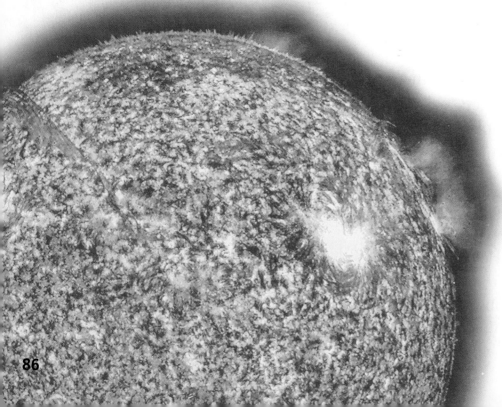

◀ Although they appear fiery, the loops of gases shooting from the sun's surface are cooler than the rest of the sun.

▲ **There are many ways to classify stars. A star can be classified according to its size, its brightness, its temperature, and its color.**

Among all those stars, the sun is average. It's a yellow star of medium size, medium brightness, and medium heat.

One way scientists classify stars is by color. Star colors range from blue, white, and yellow to orange and red. The color of a star is a clue to its surface temperature. Blue stars are the hottest, and red stars are the coolest. Our sun is between the hottest and the coolest stars.

Another way scientists classify stars is by brightness. How bright a star appears depends on two factors. One is how far it is from Earth. The other is how bright it actually is.

Stars go through stages. They form from clouds of spinning dust and gas, which gravity squeezes. When the mass is squeezed enough, changes take place that form a star. The mass of the star then begins to change into light and heat. Over billions of years, most of the mass of the star is converted to light and heat.

MAIN IDEA AND DETAILS What does a star's color tell about the star?

Groups of Stars

Have you ever seen the Big Dipper in the night sky? The Big Dipper belongs to a group of stars called Ursa Major. These stars form a **constellation**, a group of stars that form an imaginary picture in the sky. In ancient times, people often gave names to these imaginary star pictures. Constellations are helpful to people because their patterns serve as landmarks in the night sky. For hundreds of years, sailors have used them to find their way.

Have you seen a bright band of stars on a clear summer night? If so, you were looking at the Milky Way Galaxy, the galaxy in which our solar system lies. A **galaxy** is a huge system of gases, dust, and stars. Galaxies contain billions of stars. Our sun is on the edge of the Milky Way Galaxy. Constellations are made up of stars in our own galaxy. The Milky Way Galaxy is only one of the millions of galaxies in the universe. The **universe** is everything that exists in space.

There are many galaxy shapes. The Milky Way Galaxy is a spiral (SPY•ruhl) galaxy. A barred spiral galaxy has two main arms. Some galaxies look like balls or eggs. Other galaxies have no regular shape.

Focus Skill **MAIN IDEA AND DETAILS**

What are two ways in which people classify groups of stars?

▲ This is a drawing of Orion, a hunter in Greek myths.

◄ This is how the constellation Orion appears in the night sky.

Seasonal Star Positions

Each day, the sun appears to rise in the east, move across the sky, and set in the west. The same is true for stars at night. However, what is actually moving is Earth.

The positions of the stars appear to change with the seasons, too. In winter, you may see Orion clearly in the night sky. A few months later, Orion may no longer be visible.

This, too, is due to Earth's movement. As Earth revolves around the sun, we see different parts of space at different times of the year.

To see Orion in the same place you saw it last winter, you must wait until next winter. It will be visible again when Earth reaches that part of its orbit of the sun.

Where you live determines the constellations you will see. In the Northern Hemisphere, people see different sets of constellations from those people see in the Southern Hemisphere. People who live near the equator can see some constellations of both hemispheres.

Focus Skill **MAIN IDEA AND DETAILS**

Explain why constellations seem to change their locations throughout the year.

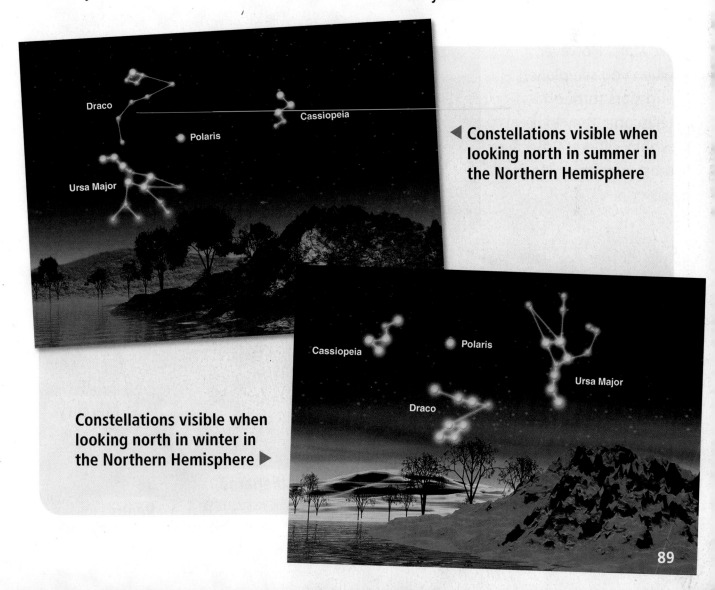

◀ **Constellations visible when looking north in summer in the Northern Hemisphere**

Constellations visible when looking north in winter in the Northern Hemisphere ▶

Watching the Sky

Many ancient cultures have watched the changing night sky. Ancient people named the constellations. The early Greeks identified Mercury, Venus, Mars, Jupiter, and Saturn, which are visible with the unaided eye. The Italian astronomer Galileo Galilei was one of the first people to use a telescope to study the planets and the stars. He discovered Jupiter's four largest moons, and he observed that Venus has phases like the moon does. Later astronomers discovered the planets Uranus and Neptune.

To the unaided eye, planets look very much like stars. However, when you see planets and stars through a telescope, they look slightly different. Because most stars are trillions of kilometers away from Earth, they look like faint dots of twinkling light. Planets shine with a steady light. Jupiter is among the brightest objects in the night sky. Usually, only the moon and Venus are brighter. Mars looks red when seen from Earth, but Uranus and Neptune have a bluish color when seen through a telescope.

Focus Skill **MAIN IDEA AND DETAILS** Which planets can be seen without a telescope?

In the seventeenth century, Galileo used the newly invented telescope to study planets and stars.

The planets shown in this photograph can be seen without a telescope. At lower center is the bright star Aldebaran, in the constellation Taurus.

Jupiter

Saturn

Mars

Mercury

Aldebaran

Venus

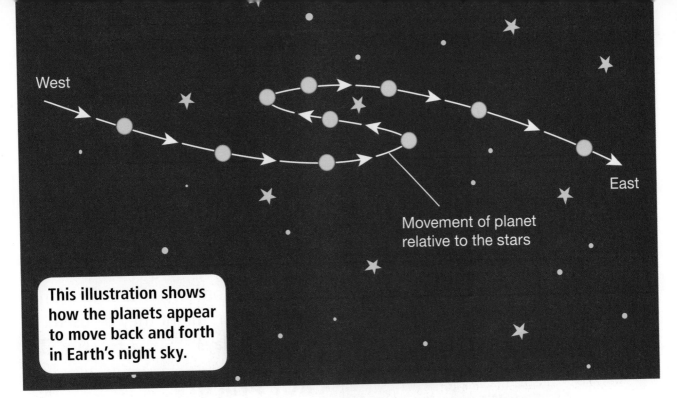

West

East

Movement of planet relative to the stars

This illustration shows how the planets appear to move back and forth in Earth's night sky.

Planets and Stars

Both planets and stars seem to rise in the east and set in the west. However, if you watch a planet every night for several months, you'll notice that it appears to move independently of the stars, which remain in fixed positions relative to one another.

Suppose you watched the planet Mars. First, Mars would appear to move from west to east among the stars. Then, it would reverse direction for a while and travel from east to west. Finally, it would resume its eastward motion. No wonder the early Greeks called these moving bodies *planetai,* the Greek word for "wanderers."

Although the rising and setting of the sun and other stars is due to Earth's rotation, stars do actually move through space. Because the stars are so far away from Earth, it is hard for us to detect their motion. This is why the pattern

of stars in a constellation seems fixed. If you could watch constellations over thousands of years, you would see them slowly change shape.

 **MAIN IDEA AND DETAILS**

Why did the early Greeks call the planets "wanderers"?

Model a Constellation

Use a pencil point or toothpick to poke a "constellation" in a piece of aluminum foil. Use a rubber band to fasten the foil to the end of a paper towel tube. Turn the tube while you look through it. What planetary motion are you modeling as you turn the tube?

Essential Question

What can we see in the sky?

In this lesson, you learned that stars can be classified by size, color, and brightness and that groups of stars can be classified as constellations or galaxies. You also learned that stars and planets differ in appearance, position, and number.

1. (Focus Skill) **MAIN IDEA AND DETAILS** Draw and complete a graphic organizer to give details about stars, how groups of stars are classified, and seasonal star positions. **S4E1a**

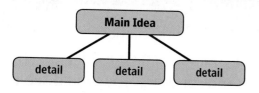

2. SUMMARIZE Write three or four sentences to tell the important facts you learned about stars and planets. **S4E1**

3. DRAW CONCLUSIONS If the sun were a red star or a blue star, how would it be different? **S4E1a**

4. VOCABULARY Use the terms *star*, *galaxy*, and *universe* in a sentence about objects in space. **S4E1**

5. Critical Thinking How were constellations useful to sailors long ago? When might they be useful to sailors today? **S4E1a**

CRCT Practice

6. Which words BEST describe the sun?

 A small star

 B medium-size star

 C large star

 D very large star **S4E1a**

7. Which statement is true?

 A Planets shine with a steady light, while stars twinkle.

 B Stars are the brightest objects in the night sky.

 C Unlike stars, planets are easy to see because they glow with heat energy.

 D Planets do not move in the sky, but stars do. **S4E1b, c**

8. Describe how the planets appear to move among the stars.

S4E1c

 Writing ELA4W2

Write a Description

Observe the movement of star patterns in the sky one night, or tell about a visit to a planetarium. Write a description of what you observe in the sky, or describe what you saw at the planetarium.

 Math M4G1a, c

Complete a Shape

Look for constellations in the night sky, or find pictures of some in a book. Draw the constellations. Outline any geometric shapes, such as squares and triangles, in the star patterns.

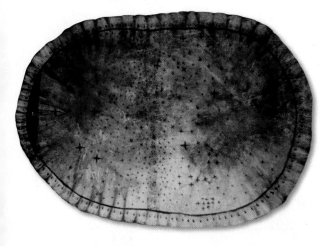

 Social Studies SS4H1

Stories About the Stars

Many American Indian tribes have legends about the stars. Choose an American Indian tribe, and find a story its people tell about the stars. Draw pictures and write captions to go with the story.

 For more links and activities, go to **www.hspscience.com**

Hal McAlister

▶ **HAL McALISTER**
▶ **Professor and astronomer, Georgia State University**
▶ Studies properties of stars

By the time he was in fourth grade, Hal McAlister knew he was going to be an astronomer. While other children were playing baseball, he was studying the stars at an observatory near his home in Tennessee.

Now McAlister is a professor of physics and astronomy. He led the team of scientists that created CHARA. Because CHARA is a group of telescopes, it is more powerful than the Hubble Space Telescope. It can spot an object the size of a nickel from 10,000 miles away!

CHARA is helping McAlister and his team watch stars being born. It helps them measure a star's mass, diameter, surface temperature, energy, and distance from Earth. It is also helping scientists find planets that orbit other stars. Someday, it may help scientists determine the size of the universe.

One goal of this research is to understand how the sun produces energy. "By learning more about the stars, we learn more about our own star and what really gives us life on Earth," McAlister says.

✏️ Think and Write

❶ Why did McAlister want to create such a powerful telescope? `S4CS8c`

❷ How can studying stars help us learn about the sun? `S4E1d`

CHARA links six 1-meter (40-in.) telescopes. The system was built on top of Mount Wilson, in southern California. The atmosphere there is clearer there than in Atlanta, where Hal McAlister lives.

Adriana Ocampo

Have you ever wanted to know more about Earth's neighbors in space? So does Adriana Ocampo. She is a planetary geologist, a scientist who studies rocks on planets, moons, and other solid bodies in space.

▶ **ADRIANA OCAMPO**

▶ **Research scientist for NASA**

▶ Worked on *Viking*, *Voyager*, and *Galileo* missions

Ocampo works at the Jet Propulsion Laboratory in Pasadena, California. She first worked on the *Viking* mission to Mars. She was particularly interested in impact craters, the holes formed when space objects such as asteroids crash into planets and moons. She used photos from the *Viking* mission to help make a map of Phobos, one of the moons that orbits Mars.

Ocampo looks at rocks on Earth, too. She is studying pieces of an asteroid that struck Earth about 65 million years ago. The asteroid may have caused most of Earth's lifeforms, including the dinosaurs, to become extinct. Ocampo is now researching ways asteroids can affect Earth.

An asteroid slammed into Phobos, making this huge dent.

✎ Think and Write

1 How is Phobos like Earth's moon? `S4E2b`

2 Why is it important to study how Earth might be affected by an asteroid? `S4CS8a`

Ocampo compares Earth's surface with the surfaces of other planets, such as Mars.

Wrap-Up

▶ Visual Summary

Tell how each picture helps explain the **Big Idea**.

The Big Idea We can predict where the sun, the moon, the planets, and the stars will be in the sky.

Lesson 1   S4E2a, b, c

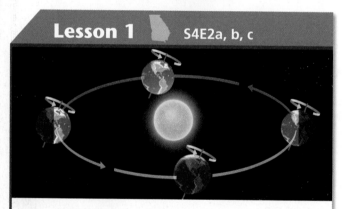

Movement of Earth and the Moon
Earth's rotation causes day and night. The seasons are caused by Earth's orbit and its tilted axis. The moon's cycle of phases repeats about every $29\frac{1}{2}$ days.

Lesson 2   S4E2d, S4E1d

Our Solar System
The solar system includes the sun, Earth and its moon, seven other planets and their moons, and "dwarf planets." Smaller objects such as asteroids and comets are also part of the solar system.

Lesson 3   S4E1a, b, c, d

Watching the Sky
At night, we can see thousands of faraway stars. Over time, we can watch the planets as they move against the background of the constellations. The relative positions of stars in the constellations do not change.

Show What You Know

Chapter Writing Activity

Writing About Space Exploration/Descriptive Writing

Imagine you are a photographer. NASA has hired you to study images taken by cameras that were placed on the sun, the planets, and the moon. The cameras were also carried throughout the solar system on satellites. Write descriptions of the objects you see. Include the features you see on the planets, "dwarf planets," and other bodies such as asteroids and comets.

ELA4W2

Georgia Performance Task

Make Science Center Displays

Work together as a class to set up a science center. Make posters or models for topics covered in the chapter. For example, you could make a poster to show the moon's cycle of phases. You could use a flashlight to show how the sun appears to move across the sky in the summer and winter. You could also display images made using telescopes and other technology. Invite other classes to visit your science center. Explain the displays to the visitors.

S4E1, 2

Vocabulary Review

Use the terms below to complete the sentences. The page numbers tell you where to look in the chapter if you need help.

rotate p. 60   planet p. 72

axis p. 60   comet p. 77

orbit p. 62   star p. 86

moon p. 64   sun p. 86

solar system p. 72   constellation p. 88

1. The star at the center of our solar system is the _____. **S4E1a**

2. The path an object takes around another object is its _____. **S4E2c**

3. A star and a group of objects that orbit it make up a _____. **S4E2c**

4. The imaginary line through both poles of a planet is its _____. **S4E2a**

5. A small mass of rock, ice, and frozen gases that orbits the sun is a _____. **S4E2**

6. A large object that orbits a star is a _____. **S4E2c**

7. An enormous ball of superheated gases in space is a _____. **S4E1a**

8. A group of stars that form an imaginary picture in the sky is a _____. **S4E1a**

9. Earth experiences day and night because it spins, or _____, on its axis. **S4E2a**

10. A natural object that orbits a planet is a _____. **S4E2b**

Check Understanding

Write the letter of the best choice.

11. **MAIN IDEA AND DETAILS** Which is true about stars? (p. 87) **S4E1a**
    A They exist forever.
    B They are all about the same size as our sun.
    C Their color indicates their temperature.
    D They are clouds of spinning dust and gas.

12. **COMPARE AND CONTRAST** How do the inner and outer planets differ? (pp. 73–74) **S4E2d**
    A The outer planets have fewer moons than the inner planets do.
    B The outer planets are smaller than the inner planets.
    C The inner planets are farther from the sun.
    D The inner planets are dense and rocky, while the outer planets are made mostly of gases.

13. Which detail explains why summers at the North Pole are cold? (p. 63) S4E2c

A Winters are long at the poles.

B The North Pole is covered with ice.

C Earth's revolution around the sun slows during the summer.

D The sun's rays are indirect at the North Pole.

14. What does this illustration BEST show? (p. 60) S4E2a

A why Earth has day and night

B why planets orbit the sun

C why the moon has phases

D why Earth has seasons

15. Which statement is true? (p. 91) S4E1b

A Stars appear to be the brightest objects in the sky.

B Each planet keeps its position in the night sky, unlike the stars, which move across the sky.

C It is easier to see planets in our solar system than stars because the planets glow with heat.

D Planets shine with a steady light, while stars appear to twinkle.

16. Suppose there is a full moon tonight. Which phase of the moon will you see in about 15 days? (p. 65) S4E2b

A full moon

B first quarter

C new moon

D third quarter

Inquiry Skills

17. You **used numbers** to understand distances in space. What other ideas in this chapter did using numbers help you understand? S4CS5c

18. How could **measuring** the orbit of a comet help scientists understand when it will next be visible from Earth? S4CS5c

Critical Thinking

19. Give examples of ways in which technology has been used to observe distant objects in the sky. S4E1d

20. Suppose that you have been asked to do a presentation about how Earth moves in the solar system. Write a paragraph in which you explain Earth's cycle of day and night and why Earth has seasons. S4E2c

The **Big Idea**

Georgia Performance Standards in This Chapter

Content

S4E3 Students will differentiate between the states of water and how they relate to the water cycle and weather.

S4E3a, b, c, d, e

S4E4 Students will analyze weather charts/maps and collect weather data to predict weather events and infer patterns. . . .

S4E4a, b, c, d

This chapter also addresses these co-requisite standards:

Characteristics of Science

S4CS1 Students will be aware of the importance of curiosity, honesty, openness, and skepticism in science and will exhibit these traits. . . .

S4CS1a, b, c

S4CS4 Students will use ideas of system, model, change, and scale in exploring scientific . . . matters.

S4CS4c

S4CS5 Students will communicate scientific ideas. . . .

S4CS5c

S4CS8 Students will understand . . . the process of scientific inquiry.

S4CS8a

What's the Big Idea?

The sun's energy causes water and air to move in ways that result in predictable weather patterns.

Essential Questions

Go online for student eBook
www.hspscience.com

Science in Georgia

Jekyll Island

Dear Mykel,

My family and I are staying on Jekyll Island. Of course, I'm practically living on the beach!

The weather is warm and sticky. Luckily, the ocean breezes help to keep me cool, as does the occasional rain shower. I love to watch the rain hit the sand and the waves. I wish you were here to see it, too!

Your friend,
Jasmine

USA

What causes water to move between Earth's surface and the air? How does this relate to the **Big Idea?**

Georgia Performance Standards in This Lesson

Content

S4E3a Demonstrate how water changes states from solid (ice) to liquid (water) to gas (water vapor/steam) and changes from gas to liquid to solid.

S4E3b Identify the temperatures at which water becomes a solid and at which water becomes a gas.

S4E3d Explain the water cycle (evaporation, condensation, and precipitation).

Characteristics of Science

S4CS1c   **S4CS5c**

Essential Question

What Is the Water Cycle?

▶ Georgia Fast Fact

Journey to the Sea

The Altamaha River is formed by the Ocmulgee and Oconee rivers near Lumber City. It flows more than 130 miles from its beginning to its entry into the Atlantic Ocean north of Brunswick. Along North America's eastern shore, the Altamaha is the third largest contributer of fresh water to the Atlantic Ocean. Where does the water in the Altamaha River come from? What happens to it after it reaches the ocean?

Altamaha River, north of Brunswick

Vocabulary Preview

water cycle [WAW•ter SY•kuhl] The constant movement of water from Earth's surface to the atmosphere and back to Earth's surface (p. 108)

water vapor [WAW•ter VAY•per] The gas form of water (p. 108)

evaporation [ee•vap•uh•RAY•shuhn] The process by which a liquid changes into a gas (p. 110)

condensation [kahn•duhn•SAY•shuhn] The process by which a gas changes into a liquid (p. 111)

103

Changing States of Matter

Start with Questions

Even on a cold day, this geyser blasts a cloud of hot water and steam into the air. When water trickles underground, hot rocks turn it into steam. The steam expands—and explodes!

- What are the different forms, or states, of water?

- What causes water to change state?

Investigate to find out. Then read to find out more.

Prepare to Investigate

Inquiry Skill Tip
When you compare, you tell how things are alike and how they are different. For example, you can use numbers to compare objects or events.

Materials

- 2 ice cubes
- plastic spoon
- safety goggles
- glass beaker
- thermometer
- hot plate
- measuring cup
- zip-top plastic bag
- cold water
- balance

Make a Data Table

	Temperature (°C)	Mass (g)	Inference
Bag with ice cubes and water			
Bag of melted ice			
Boiling water			

Follow This Procedure

1. Place the ice cubes in the beaker. Add 1 cup of cold water.

2. Stir with the plastic spoon. Use the thermometer to **measure** and **record** the temperature.

3. Pour the contents of the beaker into the zip-top bag. Seal the bag.

4. Use the balance to **measure** the mass of the bag and its contents. **Record** the **data**.

5. Set the bag in a warm place. Leave it there until the cubes disappear. **Infer** what happened. **Record** your inference.

6. Repeat Step 4.

7. Pour the contents of the bag back into the beaker. Repeat Step 2.

8. CAUTION: **Put on safety goggles.** Your teacher will boil water and measure its temperature. **Record data** and **inferences**.

Draw Conclusions

1. What inferences did you make?

2. **Standards Link** From your data, at what temperatures did the ice melt and the water boil?

   S4E3b

3. **Inquiry Skill** Use your data to **compare** the mass of the bag and its contents before and after the ice melted.

   S4CS5c

Step 4

Step 7

Independent Inquiry

Pour 1 cup of water into each of two different containers. Leave them out until the water disappears. Where did the water go? **Hypothesize** why the water disappeared from one sooner than it did from the other.

 S4CS1c

VOCABULARY

water cycle p. 108
water vapor p. 108
evaporation p. 110
condensation p. 111

SCIENCE CONCEPTS

▶ where water is located on Earth
▶ what processes make up the water cycle

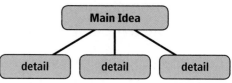

MAIN IDEA AND DETAILS

Look for details about how water moves between the air and Earth's surface.

Main Idea

detail   detail   detail

The Water Planet

Water covers almost three-fourths of Earth's surface. Because of this, Earth is sometimes called the water planet. A little more than 97 percent of Earth's water is found in the oceans. Ocean water is salty. Salt water is also found in some lakes.

The rest of Earth's water is fresh water. Fresh water is water that has very little salt dissolved in it. People need fresh water to live. For instance, we use fresh water for drinking, washing, and growing plants. However, less than 3 percent of all Earth's water is fresh water. Where can fresh water be found?

Most of the fresh water on Earth is frozen in ice caps and *glaciers*. Glaciers are huge sheets of ice. Most glaciers are near Earth's poles. They can also be found in other cold places, such as on mountaintops.

Math in Science
Interpret Data

What percent of Earth's liquid water is fresh water?

Groundwater, 0.5%
Ice, 2.19%
Soil moisture, 0.005%
Atmosphere, 0.001%
Inland lakes, 0.018%
Rivers, 0.000096%
Oceans, 97.3%

◀ From space, Earth looks blue. That's because most of Earth's surface is covered with water.

▲ Glaciers and ice caps are both made of frozen fresh water. However, their water can't be used by many people because glaciers and ice caps are usually far away from cities and towns.

The frozen water in glaciers, though, is almost impossible for people to use. Most of the remaining fresh water is underground. In fact, underground water is the only source of fresh water for many people around the world. To get to this water, people have to pump it up to Earth's surface.

We are most familiar with fresh water that is in the air, soil, rivers, and freshwater lakes. However, only 0.5 percent of all the fresh water on Earth is found in these familiar places.

 MAIN IDEA AND DETAILS

Where is most of Earth's water found?

Insta-Lab

How Much Water?
Fill a 1-L container with water. This represents all of the water on Earth. Add 4 drops of food coloring. Put 28 mL of the water into a small, clear container. This represents all of the fresh water on Earth. From the small container, put 7 mL of the water into another small, clear container. This is all of the liquid fresh water on Earth. Observe how much water is in each container. How important do you think it is to protect our freshwater resources?

The Water Cycle

Water moves constantly through the environment. It moves from Earth's surface to the air and back to Earth's surface again in a never-ending process called the **water cycle**.

Energy from the sun drives the water cycle. When the sun's energy warms water on Earth's surface, some of the water changes from a liquid to a gas.

The gaseous form of water, called **water vapor**, moves into the air. When water vapor cools, it becomes liquid water again. When the liquid water drops are heavy enough, they fall back to Earth.

Water may fall back into the ocean, into lakes or rivers, or onto the ground. When it falls on land, it can soak into the ground or run off the surface into rivers and lakes. Some water can also quickly recycle back to the atmosphere if the sun heats it and it turns into water vapor again.

Science Up Close

For more links and animations, go to **www.hspscience.com**

The Water Cycle

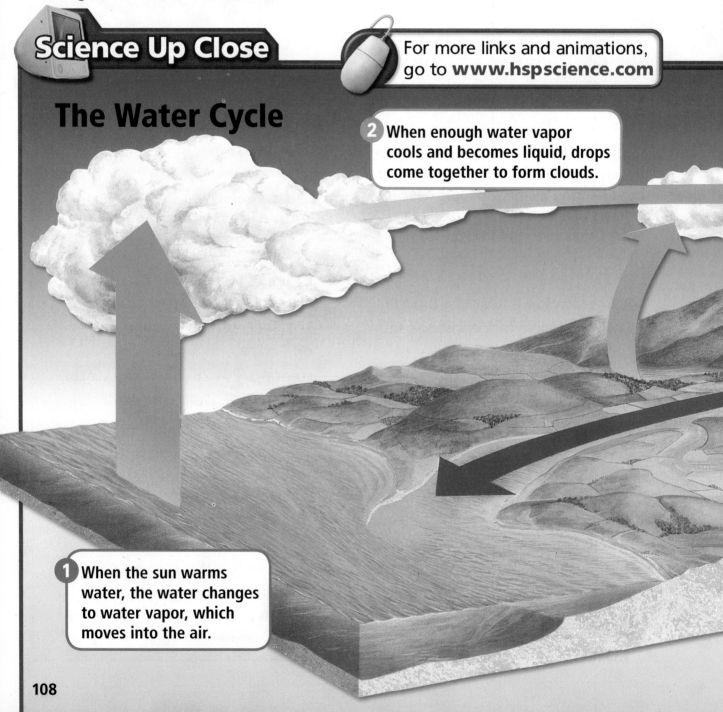

2 When enough water vapor cools and becomes liquid, drops come together to form clouds.

1 When the sun warms water, the water changes to water vapor, which moves into the air.

Most of the water moving through the water cycle comes from the oceans. The sun's energy heats water on the ocean's surface and turns it into water vapor. Winds carry the water vapor over land, where it becomes liquid water and falls as rain, snow, sleet, or hail.

Most rainwater comes from the oceans. So why isn't rain salty? When water in the ocean turns into water vapor, all of the salts dissolved in the water stay in the ocean. When the water vapor in the air cools, it becomes liquid again. Drops of fresh water form and fall to Earth.

Some water drops fall on land. These drops dissolve small amounts of salts and minerals on the land. The water with the dissolved salts and minerals runs off into rivers. Rivers carry the water to the oceans. Over time, all the salts build up in the ocean. That is why the oceans are salty.

Focus Skill MAIN IDEA AND DETAILS How does salt water become fresh water again?

3 In clouds, water droplets join to make larger drops. When the drops become heavy enough, they fall to Earth.

4 Some rain soaks into the ground. Rainwater can also run over the ground and flow into creeks, rivers, lakes, and, in time, back into the ocean.

Ice is water in its solid state.

As ice warms, it becomes liquid water. Ice melts—and water freezes—at 0°C.

Heat Makes a Difference

Evaporation

Suppose it's a hot day. To cool off, you take a swim. When you get out of the water, you dry off with a towel. You lay the towel in a sunny spot. The towel dries. Where did the water go?

The water evaporated. **Evaporation** is the process by which a liquid changes into a gas. Water evaporates because heat changes it from a liquid to a gas, or water vapor. It is hard to see evaporation happening because water vapor is invisible. However, you can infer that water has evaporated when it seems to disappear, like the water in the towel.

A large amount of water evaporates from Earth's oceans, lakes, and rivers every day. Water also evaporates from the soil, from puddles, from plants, and even from your skin as you sweat.

Water vapor mixes with other gases in the air. When the wind blows, the air moves. The water vapor moves with the air. It has become part of the air.

 MAIN IDEA AND DETAILS Where does water go when it evaporates?

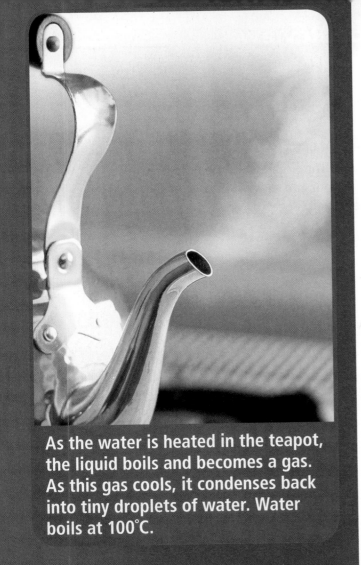

As the water is heated in the teapot, the liquid boils and becomes a gas. As this gas cools, it condenses back into tiny droplets of water. Water boils at 100°C.

Condensation

Air can carry water vapor high into the atmosphere. As air and water vapor move up, they cool. When the water vapor gets cold enough, condensation occurs. **Condensation** is the process by which a gas changes into a liquid.

Air has dust particles in it. When water vapor cools, it condenses, or changes to liquid, on the dust particles. The condensed water and dust particles form clouds or fog. *Fog* is a cloud that forms near the ground.

Clouds that form very high up may be made of tiny ice crystals instead of water droplets. That is because the air is below the freezing point of water.

Clouds stay in the air because the ice crystals and water droplets are tiny. Additional condensation causes the droplets to grow and become heavier. When the drops become too heavy to float, they fall to Earth as rain.

Water may also fall to Earth as snow, sleet, or hail if the air is cold enough for water to freeze. If the air temperature is below freezing, water vapor becomes a solid without becoming a liquid first. This forms snow. Raindrops can form sleet or hail if they freeze as they fall to Earth.

 **MAIN IDEA AND DETAILS**

How do clouds form?

Sweat is evaporating from this boy's face. At the same time, water vapor condenses on his cold drink glass. ▶

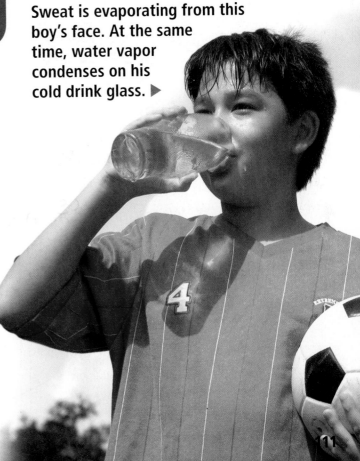

Essential Question

What is the water cycle?

In this lesson, you learned that most water on Earth is salt water. You also learned about the water cycle and how water moves between the oceans and the land by the processes of evaporation and condensation. Water vapor can move from one place to another as fog or clouds and can fall to Earth as rain, hail, sleet, or snow.

1. (Focus Skill) **MAIN IDEA AND DETAILS** Draw and complete a graphic organizer to show the supporting details of this main idea: *Water on Earth is found in many different places.*

 S4E3

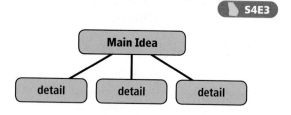

2. SUMMARIZE Draw a diagram that summarizes the water cycle.

S4E3d

3. DRAW CONCLUSIONS Most rainwater comes from the ocean, but rainwater is not salty. Explain.

S4E3d

4. VOCABULARY Write one sentence that uses all the vocabulary terms in this lesson.

S4E3

5. Critical Thinking How can water in an ocean end up in a freshwater lake?

S4E3d

CRCT Practice

6. On which type of day will the most pond water evaporate?

A hot and sunny

B hot and cloudy

C cool and rainy

D cool and cloudy

S4E3d

7. At which temperatures does ice melt and liquid water boil?

A 0°F and 100°F

B 32°C and 212°C

C 0°C and 100°C

D 32°F and 100°F

S4E3b

8. Your glass of ice water has left a ring of water on the table. What conclusion can you draw by examining this evidence?

The **Big** Idea

S4E3a

 Writing ELA4W2

Persuasive Writing

Less than 3 percent of Earth's water is fresh. Write a speech in which you explain to people why it's important to protect Earth's freshwater resources. Present your speech to the class if time permits.

 Math M4N5e

Solve Problems

Suppose that about 550,000 L of water flow through a creek during the spring. If this amount of water is four-tenths (0.4) of all the water that flows through the creek during a year, how much water does the creek carry during a year?

 Social Studies SS4G2a

Water and Culture

The Seminoles are Native Americans who once lived along the Georgia-Florida border. Use library resources to find out why the Suwannee River and the Okefenokee Swamp were important to the Seminole culture.

For more links and activities, go to **www.hspscience.com**

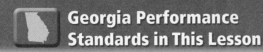
LESSON 2

Content

S4E3c Investigate how clouds are formed.

S4E3e Investigate different forms of precipitation and sky conditions (rain, snow, sleet, hail, clouds, and fog).

Characteristics of Science

S4CS1b   **S4CS8a**

Essential Question

How Do the Oceans and the Water Cycle Affect Weather?

 Georgia
Fast Fact

A Foggy Beginning

Fog covers the base of the cypress trees during sunrise in George L. Smith State Park in Georgia's wiregrass region. Fog is a stratus-like cloud that forms at ground level. Fog also forms on hills and mountains and along coastlines.

George L. Smith
State Park

current [KUR•uhnt] A stream of water that flows like a river through the ocean (p. 118)

weather [WETH•er] The condition of the atmosphere at a certain place and time (p. 122)

humidity [hyoo•MID•uh•tee] A measurement of the amount of water vapor in the air (p. 122)

precipitation [pree•sip•uh•TAY•shuhn] Water that falls from clouds to Earth (p. 122)

The Water Cycle and Weather

Guided Inquiry

Start with Questions

Sudden rainstorms happen all the time. You know to take an umbrella when the forecast says "rain today."

- Where does rain come from?
- What parts of the water cycle are involved?

Investigate to find out. Then read to find out more.

Prepare to Investigate

Inquiry Skill Tip

When you infer, you use what you observe to explain what happened. Inferring is like using clues to solve a mystery. Observing carefully, like finding good clues, can help you infer correctly.

Materials

- graduated cylinder
- zip-top plastic bag
- water
- paper towels
- small plastic cup

Make an Observation Chart

Day	Observation
1	Cup: Bag:
2	Cup: Bag:
3	Cup: Bag:
4	Cup: Bag:

Follow This Procedure

1 Using the graduated cylinder, measure and pour 100 mL of water into the cup.

2 Open the plastic bag, and carefully put the cup inside. Then seal the bag. Be careful not to spill any water from the cup. If you do spill any, wipe it up with a towel.

3 Place the sealed bag near a sunny window. Predict what will happen to the water in the cup.

4 Leave the bag near the window for 3 to 4 days. Observe the cup and the bag each day. Record what you see.

5 Remove the cup from the bag. Measure the water in the cup by pouring it back into the graduated cylinder. By using the numbers you recorded, find any difference in the amount of water poured into the cup and the amount removed from the cup.

Draw Conclusions

1. What did you observe during the time the cup was inside the bag?

2. Standards Link What happened to the water in the cup? How does this relate to rain and clouds? **S4E3c**

3. Inquiry Skill What can you infer about where the water in the bag came from? **S4CS1b**

Step 1

Step 3

Independent Inquiry

Think about the procedure for this Investigate. Which conditions do you think affected the results? How can you tell?

Assume you're going to plan an experiment based on this Investigate. List a variable that you could change. List the variable that you would observe or measure. Then tell which variables you would keep the same.

S4CS8a

VOCABULARY
current p. 118
weather p. 122
humidity p. 122
precipitation p. 122

SCIENCE CONCEPTS
▶ how the ocean affects weather
▶ how the water cycle relates to weather

Focus Skill **CAUSE AND EFFECT**
Look for effects of the water cycle on weather.

cause ⟶ effect

The Oceans Affect Weather

The oceans cover about 70 percent of Earth's surface. During the summer, the oceans absorb much heat from the sun. This absorption keeps the air over the oceans cooler than it would otherwise be. In the winter, the oceans release heat into the air above them, causing the planet to be warmer than it would otherwise be. In this way, the oceans help keep Earth's weather mild. Earth's temperatures would be much more extreme without oceans.

Although the oceans' overall temperature stays steady throughout the year, different parts of the oceans are heated unevenly by the sun. Water on the surface is pushed forward by winds. The result is a **current**, or stream of water, that flows like a river through the ocean. Currents distribute heat over great distances.

The Gulf Stream current flows across the Atlantic Ocean. It begins in the tropics and moves northeast. Part of it then becomes the North Atlantic Current, which carries warm water toward countries in northern Europe.

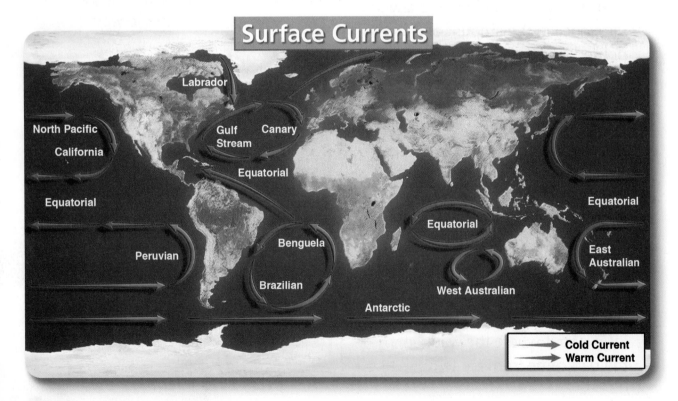

Surface Currents

Labrador

North Pacific
California
Gulf Stream
Canary

Equatorial

Equatorial
Equatorial
Equatorial
Equatorial

Peruvian
Benguela
East Australian

Brazilian
West Australian

Antarctic

→ Cold Current
→ Warm Current

Insta-Lab

Kitchen El Niño

Fill a large container with very warm water. Fill a small cup with very cold water, and add a few drops of food coloring. Use tongs to gently lower the cup straight down into the warm water, below the surface. Observe what happens. How is this similar to what happens during El Niño?

▲ Rain from El Niño events has caused many landslides along the west coast of the United States.

Some currents are deep in the oceans. Off the west coast of South America, winds blow warm surface water away from the land. Deep currents then carry cooler water up toward the surface near the coast. Changing winds can affect these currents. If the winds don't blow the warm surface water away from the coast, the cooler currents won't reach the surface, and coastal water stays warm. This causes El Niño (EL NEEN•yoh), which changes many weather patterns over the Pacific Ocean.

How does this change affect the weather? The amount of rain depends a great deal on the surface temperature of the ocean. Warm water evaporates faster than cool water does. Where the ocean is warm, clouds form and it rains. In most years, the wind pushes the warm water to the west. As a result, Australia gets rain, and the west coast of North America stays dry. During El Niño, the weather pattern reverses. Australia has drier than normal weather. Western North America has wetter than normal weather, with huge amounts of rain on the coast and heavy snows in the mountains.

El Niño also causes portions of the southeastern United States to experience very wet and cool winter and spring seasons. Much of Georgia has a wetter-than-normal winter during an El Niño.

Focus Skill **CAUSE AND EFFECT** How does the Gulf Stream affect northern Europe?

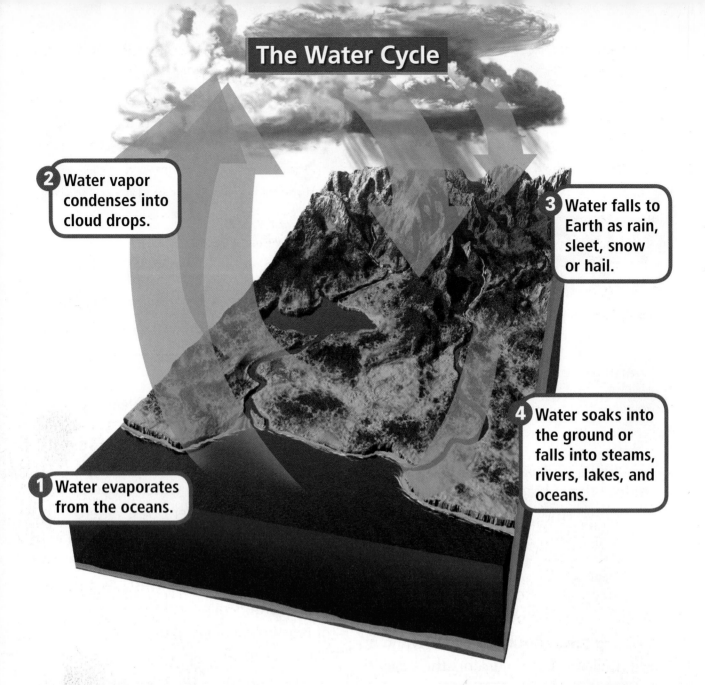

The Water Cycle

2 Water vapor condenses into cloud drops.

3 Water falls to Earth as rain, sleet, snow or hail.

4 Water soaks into the ground or falls into steams, rivers, lakes, and oceans.

1 Water evaporates from the oceans.

Weather Patterns and the Water Cycle

In Lesson 1, you learned that water continuously moves from Earth's surface to the atmosphere and back to Earth in a process called the water cycle. Just as the sun's heat causes currents in the atmosphere and oceans, it also drives the movement of water in the water cycle.

During the water cycle, liquid water is heated and evaporates, becoming water vapor. Water vapor stays a gas as long as it is warm. If the water vapor cools, much of it condenses back into liquid form.

Liquid water falls back to Earth. Some of the water soaks into the ground or runs into streams, rivers, lakes, and oceans. Rivers often carry the water back to the oceans. The cycle starts again as the sun heats the oceans' surface, causing water to again enter the atmosphere.

If the sun heated the atmosphere evenly, the air in the atmosphere would not move in currents. The water that evaporated over an ocean would eventually fall back down over that same area. More evaporation takes place in the tropics than in cooler regions. This means that if air did not move, almost all of the rain on Earth would fall near the equator.

But air in the atmosphere does move in currents. Because it does, water that evaporates from the oceans near the tropics moves long distances on global winds.

The water vapor carried by global winds contains heat. Warm air that flows toward the poles from places near the equator carries a lot of water vapor with it. As the air gradually cools and the vapor condenses, heat energy is released into the atmosphere. In this way, both heat and water are transported through the water cycle. This process helps balance temperatures in the atmosphere. The tropics lose some heat and water vapor while cooler regions gain heat and moisture.

Focus Skill CAUSE AND EFFECT In addition to providing water for precipitation, what effect does the water cycle have on weather?

Heat Transfer Through the Water Cycle

Global winds carry warm water vapor from the tropics to cooler regions. There, heat is released to the atmosphere as the water vapor condenses.

121

Clouds

You have begun to see that **weather** is the condition of the atmosphere at a particular time and place. Much of what you may call weather is actually part of the water cycle. Some areas of the atmosphere have more water vapor than other areas. The amount of water vapor in the air is called **humidity**. A large amount of water vapor in the air is high humidity. A small amount of water vapor in the air is low humidity.

Humidity depends partly on the air's temperature. Warm air can have more water vapor in it than cold air can. Suppose you're on an island near the equator. The air over the island is warm. The humidity is high because the air contains a lot of water that has evaporated from the ocean.

Clouds form in air that is relatively high in humidity. As warm air is forced up, it cools. Some of the water vapor begins to condense on dust and other particles in the air. As more and more water condenses, a cloud forms. A cloud is basically dust and condensed water.

The water that forms in clouds returns to Earth as precipitation. **Precipitation** (pree•sip•uh•TAY•shuhn) is water that falls from the atmosphere to Earth's surface.

CAUSE AND EFFECT

What causes clouds to form?

Types of Clouds

CUMULUS CLOUDS
Cumulus (KYOO•myuh•luhs) clouds are puffy. They indicate fair weather, but as a cumulus cloud grows, rain can develop.

STRATUS CLOUDS
Stratus (STRAT•uhs) clouds form low in the atmosphere. They usually cover the sky. Heavy precipitation does not usually fall from stratus clouds, but moderate rainfall or snowfall is possible.

CIRRUS CLOUDS
Cirrus (SIR•uhs) clouds form high in the atmosphere, where the air is very cold. They are made mostly of ice crystals.

How Precipitation Forms

Energy from the sun

Water Particles

Evaporation Heat from the sun causes evaporation. When water evaporates from the ocean, salts are left behind.

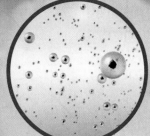

Condensation As water vapor rises into the air, it begins to lose heat. The water vapor turns back into a liquid, or condenses, on small pieces of dust in the air. This forms clouds.

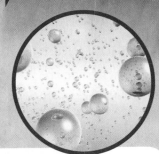

Precipitation Inside clouds, small water droplets form larger droplets. In time, these larger droplets become raindrops that fall to Earth. The water in raindrops is fresh water.

Precipitation

Precipitation falls only from certain types of clouds. Light drizzle may fall from *stratus* clouds. Rain as well as most other forms of precipitation fall from *cumulonimbus* clouds.

Snow forms when water vapor turns directly into ice crystals. Sleet and hail form when liquid water passes through freezing-cold air.

Water vapor doesn't always form precipitation as it condenses. Have you ever seen dew on the ground after a cool night? Dew forms because the ground loses heat more quickly than the air does. As the ground cools, water vapor in the air directly above the ground condenses. If the air is cold enough, frost forms.

A similar weather condition can form fog. Fog is a stratus-like cloud that forms when water vapor condenses into small water droplets near ground level.

 **CAUSE AND EFFECT** What causes different types of precipitation?

Essential Question

How do the oceans and the water cycle affect weather?

In this lesson, you learned that ocean currents can change weather patterns and that the water cycle provides moisture for cloud formation and precipitation.

1. (Focus Skill) **CAUSE AND EFFECT** Draw and complete this graphic organizer to show what causes rain, snow, and fog to form. **S4E3e**

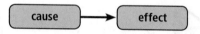

cause → effect

2. SUMMARIZE Fill in the blanks. The sun causes water to _____ from the ocean. As air cools, water vapor _____, forming clouds. When cloud drops get too heavy, water falls as _____. **S4E3c**

3. DRAW CONCLUSIONS What affects the kind of precipitation that will fall? **S4E3e**

4. VOCABULARY Describe how the terms in each pair are related: *evaporation* and *condensation*; *cloud* and *fog*; *rain* and *snow*. **S4E3c, e**

5. Critical Thinking You see cirrus clouds in the sky. Will it rain soon? Explain your answer. **S4E3e**

CRCT Practice

6. You heat an ice cube, and it melts. What will happen to the water if you continue to apply heat?
  A It will condense.
  B It will freeze.
  C It will evaporate.
  D It will precipitate. **S4E3c**

7. Which two things form in similar ways?
  A frost and dew
  B snow and sleet
  C frost and sleet
  D rain and dew **S4E3e**

8. Explain how weather is related to the water cycle. **S4E3**

The **Big** Idea

Write a Report

Suppose you're going to be on a sailing ship traveling along the coast of Georgia. Research the types of weather you might encounter during different seasons. Write a report detailing the different types of weather you can expect on your trip.

Interpret Data

Use library resources to find the types and amounts of precipitation for six cities in different areas of the United States. Use one or more graphs to display your data. What conclusions can you draw about snowfall amounts by comparing your data to a map?

Make a Diorama

Use a shoe box and craft materials of your choice to make a diorama of the water cycle. Decide how you will show underground water storage, evaporation, condensation, and precipitation. Display your diorama.

 For more links and activities, go to **www.hspscience.com**

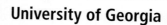

University of Georgia

The CLIMATOLOGY RESEARCH Laboratory

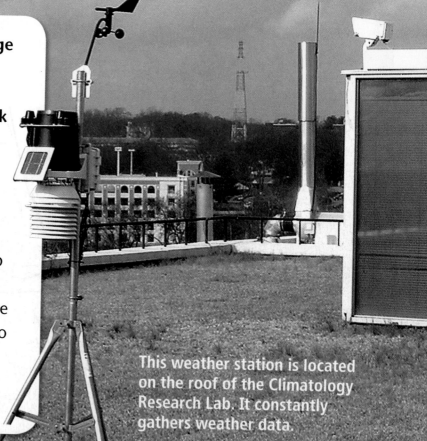

Do you know the average high temperature in Americus in January? What does the sky over Athens look like right now?

The Climatology Research Laboratory (CRL), at the University of Georgia, can answer those questions. This lab fills a rooftop room of the Geography-Geology Building. The lab staff gathers information about the weather and climate from one or more weather stations outside. The staff also collects data from the atmosphere, from the ocean, and from Earth's surface all over the world.

This weather station is located on the roof of the Climatology Research Lab. It constantly gathers weather data.

Unidata

The Climatology Research Lab is part of Unidata. Unidata is a group of more than 160 labs that collect and analyze data from weather satellites, aircraft in flight, radar, and forecasters on the ground. As soon as the weather anywhere in the world changes, Unidata spreads the information.

Sometimes, students and researchers at the CRL use Virtual Weather Station software to make graphics based on their forecasts. These graphics help them understand weather events. Researchers use the software to look for unexpected changes in the weather, such as winter storms in Idaho and tornadoes in Texas.

Researching Weather

The lab also researches ways in which weather and climate affect people. For example, one study examined the *heat island* that surrounds the city of Atlanta. This blanket of heat actually increases the number of thunderstorms over the city compared to areas nearby.

Other CRL research has focused on powerful windstorms called *derechos*. Researchers have studied how and when derechos form and what kinds of damage they cause. These and other studies carried out at the CRL are helping scientists understand more about weather and its causes.

Think and Write

1. Why is it important for the CRL to gather weather information from around the world? `S4E4c`

2. All weather stations should measure and record their findings and observations accurately. Why? `S4CS1a`

This special photograph shows daytime surface temperatures in metropolitan Atlanta. Blue shows cool temperatures and red shows warm ones. White represents especially hot temperatures.

Content

Characteristics of Science

Georgia Fast Fact

A Blanket of Ice

Ice covers suburban Atlanta after a January 2000 ice storm. During a severe ice storm, about 45,000 kilograms (99,000 lb) of ice can pile up on a 15-meter (50-ft) tree! Ice also forms on power lines, causing them to break and leaving residents without electricity. In the Investigate, you will use collected weather data to predict future weather.

LESSON 3

Essential Question

How Is Weather Predicted?

128

suburbs of Atlanta

meteorology [mee•tee•uh•RAHL•uh•jee] The study of weather (p. 132)

barometer [buh•RAHM•uht•er] An instrument for measuring air pressure (p. 132)

anemometer [an•uh•MAHM•uht•er] An instrument for measuring wind speed (p. 132)

hygrometer [hy•GRAHM•uht•er] An instrument for measuring humidity (p. 132)

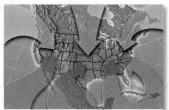

air mass [AIR MAS] A large body of air that has similar temperature and humidity throughout (p. 134)

front [FRUHNT] A place where two air masses meet (p. 135)

climate [KLY•muht] The pattern of weather an area experiences over a long period of time (p. 138)

Measuring Weather Conditions

Guided Inquiry

Start with Questions

When you look out a window, you can see if it is sunny or cloudy or if the wind is blowing. But none of these observations are measurements of the weather.

- How do you think weather is measured?

- Is it hard to measure weather?

Investigate to find out. Then read to find out more.

Prepare to Investigate

Inquiry Skill Tip

You gather data by making observations and measurements. You'll use the data table to record data on the weather each day for five days. Try to gather your data at the same time each day.

Materials

- weather station

Make an Observation Chart

Weather Station Daily Record					
Date					
Time					
Temperature					
Rainfall or snowfall					
Wind direction and speed					
Cloud conditions					

Follow This Procedure

1 Place the weather station in a shady spot, about 1 m above the ground. Be sure the rain gauge will not collect runoff from the buildings or trees. Put the wind vane where wind from any direction can reach it.

2 **Record** the amount of rain or snow, if any.

3 **Record** the wind's speed and the direction it's blowing from.

4 **Observe** and **record** the cloud conditions. Draw a circle, and shade part of it to show the fraction of the sky that's covered with clouds.

5 **Record** the temperature.

6 Repeat Steps 2–5 each day for five days. Make a line graph showing how the temperature changes from day to day.

Draw Conclusions

1. Compare weather conditions you observed on two different days.

2. **Standards Link** What do you think caused changes in the weather? **S4E4c**

3. **Inquiry Skill** Scientists learn about the weather by **gathering and recording data**. From the data you gathered, what might you infer about the weather for tomorrow? **S4CS4c**

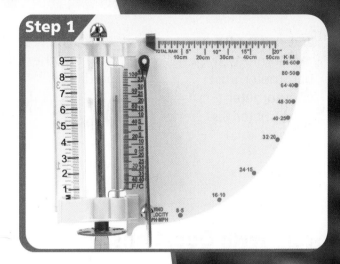

Step 1

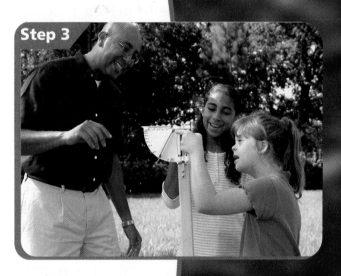

Step 3

Independent Inquiry

Think about the data you recorded during this investigation. What inferences and predictions, if any, can you make about tomorrow's weather by using clues in today's weather data?

Plan and conduct an investigation to find out if specific **observations** can help you **predict** weather. You should search for patterns in the weather data you've already recorded.

 S4CS4c   **S4CS8a**

VOCABULARY
meteorology p. 132
barometer p. 132
anemometer p. 132
hygrometer p. 132
air mass p. 134
front p. 135
climate p. 138

SCIENCE CONCEPTS
▶ how weather can be predicted
▶ how to read weather maps
▶ how to distinguish weather and climate

Focus Skill MAIN IDEA AND DETAILS
Look for details about how weather is measured and predicted.

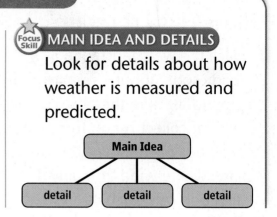

Measuring Weather

The study of weather is **meteorology**. To study weather, scientists must first measure it. *Meteorologists,* scientists who study weather, use many measuring instruments. The measurements taken with these weather instruments can be used to make weather *forecasts,* or predictions of future weather.

For example, you may know that cold air is denser—and thus exerts more pressure—than warm air. A rising barometer reading, which indicates increasing air pressure, often occurs just before colder air arrives. Since cold air usually has less water in it than warm air does, a rising barometer also means lower humidity and less chance of rain.

Weather Instrument		Measures
	Thermometer	A thermometer measures air temperature. If the air cools down during the day or warms up in the evening, this change is a sign that rain may fall soon.
	Barometer	A **barometer** measures the air pressure, which is also called *barometric pressure.* A change in the air pressure often means the weather is about to change.
	Anemometer	An **anemometer** measures wind speed. Like a change in air pressure, a change in wind speed may mean that the weather is about to change.
	Hygrometer	A **hygrometer** measures humidity. An increase in humidity often means it's about to rain.

In the past, people relied on simple observations to help them forecast the weather. Sayings such as "Red sky at night, sailors' delight" helped people remember what their observations might predict about the weather.

In contrast, a falling barometer reading often indicates the presence of warmer, more humid air and a greater chance of rain. Just as you did in the Investigate, meteorologists use *rain gauges* to measure rainfall amounts.

Wind is another weather factor that should be considered. Several instruments can be used to measure wind. Anemometers measure wind speed. Both *windsocks* and *wind vanes* measure wind direction. Information about wind speed and direction is important because wind often brings changes in the weather. Knowing which direction the wind is blowing from helps forecast the weather. For example, if it's winter and a wind starts blowing from the south, you can predict that the weather will soon be warmer.

People can also predict weather changes, although less accurately, just by observing the sky. For example, the clouds in the sky can tell you a lot about the weather. There's an old saying that goes "Red sky at night, sailors' delight. Red sky in the morning, sailors take warning." A red sky in the morning occurs when the rising sun reflects off clouds coming from the west. This often means it will rain later in the day. A red sunset means that no storms are approaching from the west, so the next day should be sunny.

Different cloud types are also associated with different types of weather. For example, cirrus clouds and small cumulus clouds mean fair weather is ahead. Large, gray cumulus clouds mean rain is probably on the way.

Focus Skill **MAIN IDEA AND DETAILS**

How can rising air pressure lead to a prediction about temperature?

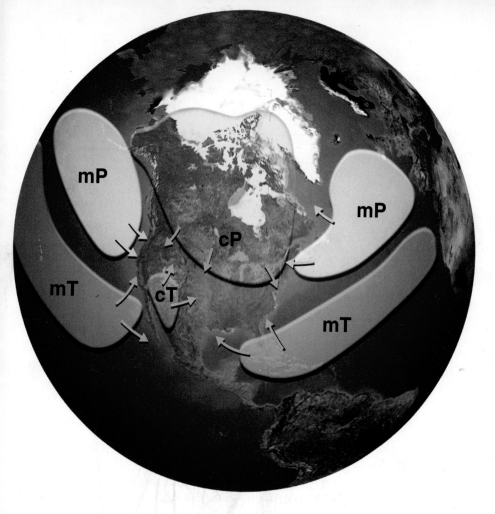

◀ A continental air mass forms over land, so it is dry. A maritime air mass forms over water, so it is humid. A polar air mass forms over a cold area, so it is cold. A tropical air mass forms over a warm area, so it is warm.

Air Masses

The sun heats Earth's atmosphere unevenly. The uneven heating causes the air to move. Air doesn't move around Earth randomly. Instead, air moves in regular, large air masses. An **air mass** is a large body of air that has the same temperature and humidity throughout.

Air masses can be warm or cold. They can also be humid or dry. What determines the characteristics of an air mass? An air mass takes on the characteristics of the region over which it forms. For example, an air mass that forms over the Pacific Ocean near the equator will be humid and warm. An air mass that forms over northern Canada will be dry and cold.

Look at the map above. Four kinds of air masses affect weather in the United States. Continental polar air masses (cP) bring cool, dry weather. Continental tropical air masses (cT) bring hot, dry weather. Maritime polar air masses (mP) bring cold, humid weather. Finally, maritime tropical air masses (mT) bring warm, humid weather.

When the weather changes in an area, the air mass over the area is changing. That is, the current air mass is being replaced by a different air mass. Changing air masses produce winds. Air masses generally move from west to east across the United States.

 **MAIN IDEA AND DETAILS** What kind of air mass causes hot, humid weather?

Fronts

The border where two air masses meet is called a **front**. Most weather changes occur along fronts. For example, if a cold, dense air mass pushes into a warm, light air mass, the warm air is forced up. As that air moves up, it cools. Water vapor in the air condenses, and clouds form.

There are two main kinds of fronts, cold fronts and warm fronts. A cold front forms where a cold air mass moves under a warm air mass. The warm air mass is less dense, so it is pushed up and cooled. When a warm, moist air mass is suddenly cooled, much of the water vapor in the air mass condenses rapidly. This fast cooling and condensation causes heavy rain, thunderstorms, or snow. Cold fronts usually move quickly, so the storms they bring do not last long.

A warm front forms where a warm air mass moves over a cold air mass. As the warm air slowly slides up and over the cold air, stratus clouds form ahead of the front. They produce rain or snow that can last for hours.

Focus Skill **MAIN IDEA AND DETAILS** What kind of weather does a cold front bring?

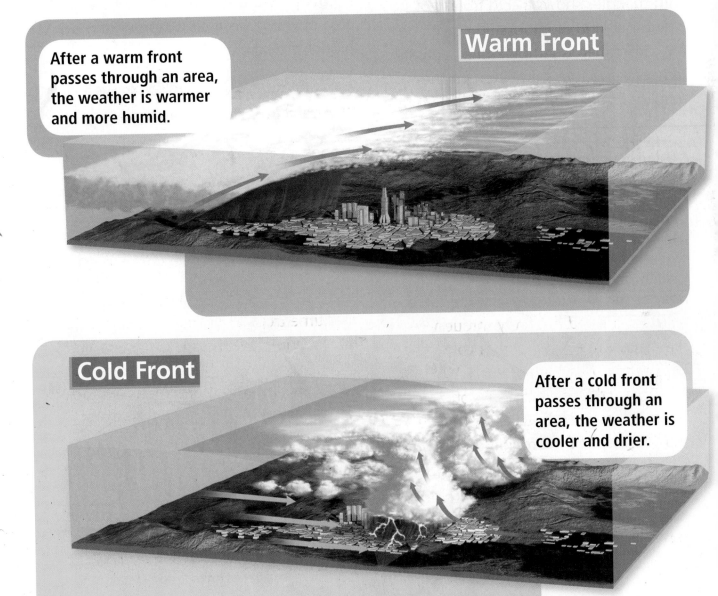

Warm Front

After a warm front passes through an area, the weather is warmer and more humid.

Cold Front

After a cold front passes through an area, the weather is cooler and drier.

Weather Maps

Have you ever used a street map to find someone's house? Another kind of map you can use is a weather map. A weather map gives information about what the weather is like in an area.

Weather maps use symbols to show the weather. A sun symbol means it's sunny in the area. The symbol of a cloud with rain means it's raining in the area. Fronts are also shown on weather maps. The symbol for a warm front is a red line with half circles on the side of the direction the front is moving. A blue line with triangles shows a cold front.

Another kind of information given on a weather map is temperature. Separate temperatures may be written on the map, or temperatures may be shown by colors. The map's key explains what each of the symbols means.

Other information you may see on a weather map includes the high and low temperatures for that day, the wind speed and direction, and the air pressure. High- and low-pressure systems may be indicated on a weather map as well. A high-pressure system is symbolized by an *H*. High-pressure systems form where an area of cool, dense air is surrounded on all sides by lower-pressure air. A low-pressure system is symbolized on a weather map by an *L*. Low-pressure systems form where an area of warm, light air is surrounded by higher-pressure air.

Focus Skill **MAIN IDEA AND DETAILS** How is a warm front shown on a weather map?

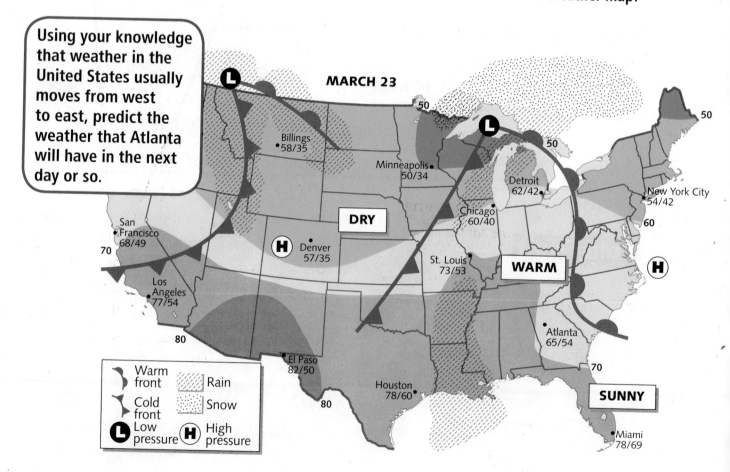

Using your knowledge that weather in the United States usually moves from west to east, predict the weather that Atlanta will have in the next day or so.

MARCH 23

Billings 58/35

Minneapolis 50/34

Detroit 62/42

New York City 54/42

San Francisco 68/49

DRY

Chicago 60/40

Denver 57/35

St. Louis 73/53

WARM

Los Angeles 77/54

El Paso 82/50

Atlanta 65/54

Houston 78/60

SUNNY

Miami 78/69

Warm front
Cold front
Low pressure (L)
Rain
Snow
High pressure (H)

◀ Doppler radar uses radio waves to detect wind and the movements of rain, snow, and ice. This Doppler image shows a hurricane approaching Georgia.

Forecasting Weather

The information presented on a weather map is collected from different weather stations. A weather station is a place where many different instruments measure the weather. Meteorologists use weather-station data, along with data from weather satellites and other special weather instruments, to make forecasts.

Weather forecasts depend on many variables. One variable is wind direction. For example, if the wind is blowing from the north, look at a weather map to find what the weather is like just north of your location. Probably, your area will soon have the weather that's just north of you now.

Another variable to think about when forecasting the weather is air pressure. If you see a low-pressure system on a weather map, you can predict stormy weather in that area. A high-pressure system, on the other hand, usually means the weather will be fair.

Weather predictions for the near future are usually quite accurate. However, very small changes in temperature and air pressure can cause big changes in weather patterns over a few days. Because very small changes can affect weather systems, it still isn't possible to accurately predict the weather very far into the future.

 MAIN IDEA AND DETAILS If a high-pressure system is moving into your area, what kind of weather can you expect?

Weather Patterns and Climates

Weather in most locations occurs in regular patterns. For example, on most days, it's cool in the morning and warmer in the afternoon. The air warms up as the sun's energy heats Earth. When the sun sets, the air begins to cool off again.

Over a longer time, there are seasonal patterns. Every year, much of the United States has different weather during winter, spring, summer, and fall.

Like daily patterns, seasonal weather patterns are driven by the sun. Fall and winter are cool in the United States because the Northern Hemisphere receives sunlight that is less direct and for fewer hours. Spring and summer are warmer because the Northern Hemisphere receives sunlight that is more direct and for more hours.

The pattern of weather an area experiences over a long time is called **climate**. Recall that weather is the condition of the atmosphere at a particular time. Climate is the average of weather conditions over many years. Average temperature and precipitation are the main features of climate.

Because the sun heats Earth unevenly, areas close to the equator get more energy from the sun than areas closer to the poles do. As a result, the farther a place is from the equator, the colder its climate is. How wet or dry a climate is usually depends on how close a place is to large bodies of water. Therefore, coastal areas are often wetter than areas in the interior of a continent.

MAIN IDEA AND DETAILS

Why does much of Earth experience seasons?

Earth takes a year to revolve around the sun. Because Earth is tilted on its axis, the intensity of sunlight reaching the Northern Hemisphere and the Southern Hemisphere varies during the year. This causes the seasons. ▶

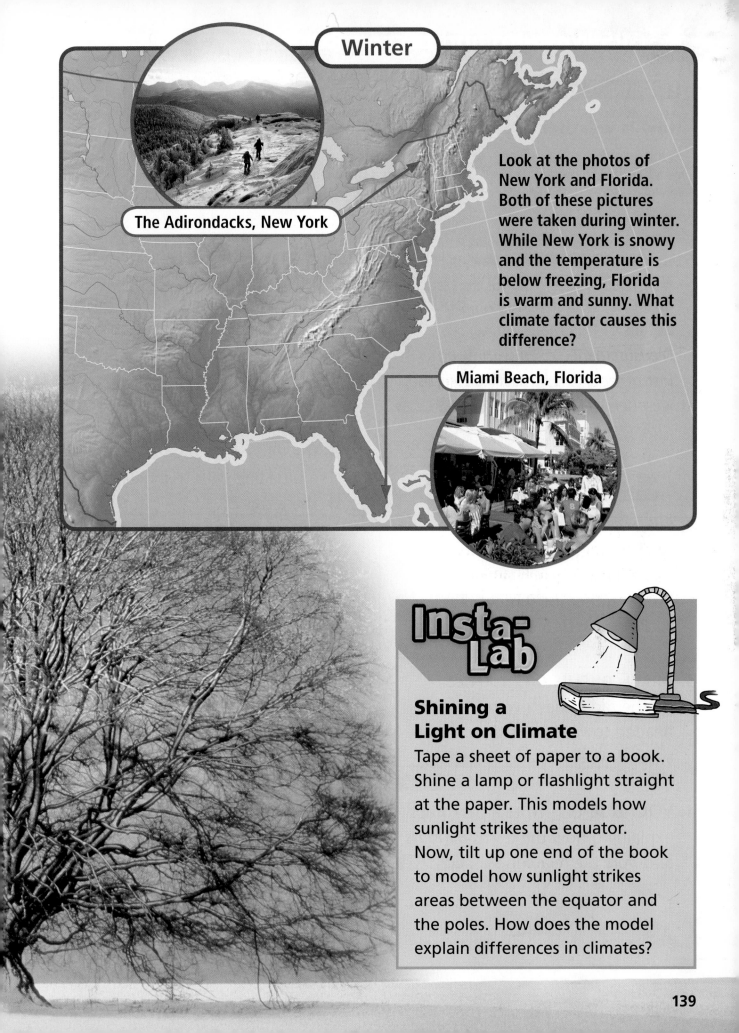

Winter

The Adirondacks, New York

Look at the photos of New York and Florida. Both of these pictures were taken during winter. While New York is snowy and the temperature is below freezing, Florida is warm and sunny. What climate factor causes this difference?

Miami Beach, Florida

Insta-Lab

Shining a Light on Climate

Tape a sheet of paper to a book. Shine a lamp or flashlight straight at the paper. This models how sunlight strikes the equator. Now, tilt up one end of the book to model how sunlight strikes areas between the equator and the poles. How does the model explain differences in climates?

Essential Question

How is weather predicted?

In this lesson, you learned how to use weather maps and weather data to predict weather. You also learned that weather forecasts depend on variables such as air masses and fronts.

1. **(Focus Skill) MAIN IDEA AND DETAILS** Draw and complete this graphic organizer to show three supporting details of this main idea: *Measurements taken with weather instruments can be used to forecast weather.* S4E4a

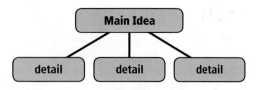

2. **SUMMARIZE** Make a list of the types of data shown on weather maps. Next to each type of data, list a weather instrument that could be used to gather that data. S4E4a, b

3. **DRAW CONCLUSIONS** You hear on the radio that a warm front is headed toward your town. What type of weather can you expect? S4E4c

4. **VOCABULARY** Write a paragraph explaining how the terms *air mass* and *front* are related. S4E4b

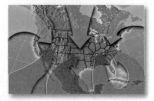

5. **Critical Thinking** Compare and contrast weather and climate. S4E4d

CRCT Practice

6. On a weather map, cold fronts are indicated by
   A a red line with half circles.
   B the letter *L*.
   C a blue line with triangles.
   D the letter *H*. S4E4b

7. How are air masses related to the uneven heating of Earth's surface?
   A Air masses cause uneven heating.
   B Air masses are the result of uneven heating.
   C Air masses help uneven heating.
   D There is no relationship. S4E4b

8. The humidity in an area rapidly increases as the air temperature falls below freezing. What type of weather will the area experience soon? S4E4

The **Big** Idea

 Writing ELA4W2, 3c

Write a Report

Cut a weather map from a local newspaper. Use the weather map to write a report for the evening weather forecast on a local radio station. Be sure to use the correct vocabulary for the weather you are describing. Read your report aloud to the class.

Rainfall Totals

Month	Amount (in.)
January	4.26
February	4.71
March	2.53
April	2.35
May	2.17
June	1.93

 Math M4N5c

Adding Decimals

Study the table, which gives monthly rainfall amounts for Athens, Georgia, from January to June. What is the total amount of rainfall in Athens during this six-month period? Do you see a pattern in the data?

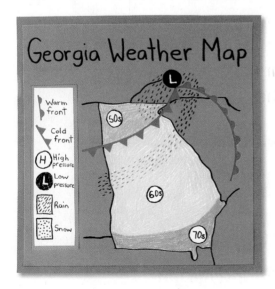

 Art

Draw a Weather Map

Find a weather report for your area of the state. Use the information in the weather report to make a weather map of this part of the state. Include fronts and high-pressure or low-pressure systems. Be sure to use the correct symbols when making your weather map.

 For more links and activities, go to **www.hspscience.com**

On the LOOKOUT

Weather forecasters have a tough job. Millions of people rely on weather forecasts to make their plans. When a weather forecast is wrong, you know that the weather experts will hear about it.

Weather forecasting isn't easy. Forecasters can't simply guess. They have to rely on data from different sources and use computers to be as accurate as possible.

Pictures from Space

Satellites are some of the most important tools that weather forecasters use. Satellites orbit about 35,000 kilometers (21,750 miles) above Earth. They give forecasters a view of clouds from above and also show where the clouds move.

One pair of weather satellites, called GOES, is used by the National Weather Service. The satellites send weather data and pictures to forecasters on the ground. Forecasters can use these satellite images to track the movements of storms.

Doppler Radar

Doppler radar also helps forecasters figure out whether snow, sleet, hail, or rain is falling from clouds. The radar provides color-coded images that identify all the different types of precipitation.

The various colors show the intensity of the precipitation. Both light blue and dark blue colors usually indicate areas of light precipitation. Areas of red colors and pink colors usually indicate strong or severe thunderstorms.

Reliable Technology

Weather balloons have been used by forecasters for many years. The balloons show forecasters what is happening high in the atmosphere.

✎ Think and Write

❶ Why do you think the National Weather Service still uses weather balloons? S4CS8c

❷ Why are accurate weather forecasts important to people and to businesses? S4CS8c

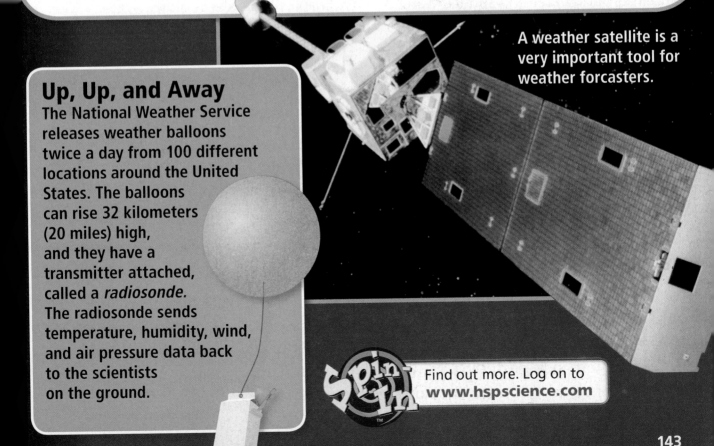

A weather satellite is a very important tool for weather forcasters.

Up, Up, and Away
The National Weather Service releases weather balloons twice a day from 100 different locations around the United States. The balloons can rise 32 kilometers (20 miles) high, and they have a transmitter attached, called a *radiosonde.* The radiosonde sends temperature, humidity, wind, and air pressure data back to the scientists on the ground.

Spin In

Find out more. Log on to www.hspscience.com

Visual Summary

Tell how each picture helps explain the **Big Idea**.

The Big Idea The sun's energy causes water and air to move in ways that result in predictable weather patterns.

Lesson 1 — S4E3a, b, d

The Water Cycle
Most of Earth's water is salt water in the oceans. Fresh water is found as ice and in groundwater and surface water. The sun's energy drives the continual movement of water in the water cycle.

Lesson 2 — S4E3c, e

Currents, Clouds, and Precipitation
Ocean currents distribute heat. Air currents carry water vapor from the tropics to cooler regions. Water vapor condenses to form clouds, from which different types of precipitation fall.

Lesson 3 — S4E4a–d

Predicting Weather
Tracking air masses helps predict weather. Temperature and pressure changes indicate moving air masses. Precipitation usually happens along fronts. Scientists use technology to help make weather predictions.

Show What You Know

Write a Water Essay/Informational Writing

Write an essay about how a drop of water can change states through the processes of evaporation, condensation, and freezing. Include specific information about the three processes. Also, explain how these processes are related to the formation of rain, sleet, snow, hail, and fog.

ELA4W2

Forecast Broadcast

Plan and produce a weather broadcast. You will need to write a script and make maps using current weather data. Be sure to include a local forecast and a national forecast. If possible, videotape the broadcast. You can also present it to your class as a live broadcast.

S4E4b, c

Vocabulary Review

Use the terms below to complete the sentences. The page numbers tell you where to look in the unit if you need help.

water vapor p. 108   hygrometer p. 132

condensation p. 111   air mass p. 134

precipitation p. 122   front p. 135

barometer p. 132   climate p. 138

1. Water that falls from the air to Earth is _____. **S4E3d**

2. The average of weather conditions in an area over many years is _____. **S4E4d**

3. When water boils, it enters the air as _____, the gas form of water. **S4E3d**

4. A large body of air that has the same temperature and humidity is an _____. **S4E4b**

5. The border between two air masses is a _____. **S4E4b**

6. Water vapor becomes liquid water during the process of _____. **S4E3d**

7. Air pressure is measured with a _____. **S4E4a**

8. Humidity is measured with a _____. **S4E4a**

Check Understanding

Choose the best answer.

9. **MAIN IDEA AND DETAILS**
   Where is most of Earth's water located? (p. 106) **S4E3d**
   A in lakes
   B in rivers
   C in the oceans
   D in the ground

10. In the water cycle, what happens just before water condenses in clouds? (p. 108) **S4E3d**
    A Water falls as rain.
    B Water evaporates.
    C Water vapor changes to a gas.
    D Water dissolves salt in the ocean.

11. How does the process occurring on the outside of the glass in the picture below relate to weather? (p. 111) **S4E3c, d**
    A Water freezes along fronts.
    B Water evaporates to form winds.
    C Water flows in ocean currents.
    D Water condenses to form precipitation.

12. What type of weather does El Niño bring to the west coast of North America? (p. 119) **S4E3, 4**

 A dry weather   **C** wet weather

 B mild weather   **D** sunny weather

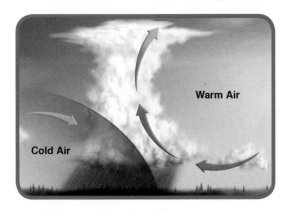

Warm Air

Cold Air

13. What is shown in the picture above? (p. 135) **S4E4b**

 A tornado

 B hurricane

 C cold front

 D warm front

14. What type of weather would most likely occur if a cold front moved into your area? (p. 135) **S4E4b**

 A stormy weather

 B warm weather

 C sunny weather

 D cloudy weather

15. **CAUSE AND EFFECT** Fog or dew can form when (p. 123) **S4E3e**

 A clouds descend to Earth's surface.

 B air masses collide along a front.

 C the ground loses heat more slowly than the air does.

 D water vapor in humid air directly above the ground condenses.

16. Ice melts and water boils at (pp. 110–111) **S4E3b**

 A 0°F, 32°F.   **C** 0°C, 100°C.

 B 0°F, 212°F.   **D** 32°C, 100°C.

Investigation Skills

17. On a weather map, you see the symbol for a low-pressure system near the area where you live. **Infer** how the weather is about to change.

S4CS4c

18. What two instruments are most important for **measuring** a region's weather? Explain your answer.

S4CS3

Critical Thinking

19. Draw a picture of the type of cloud that may cause drizzle and a picture of the type that may cause thunderstorms. Label your drawings.

S4E3c, e

20. Several factors affect weather changes. Explain what causes air pressure in an area to change. **S4E4b**

The **Big** Idea

Use the diagram below to answer question 1.

1. Where would the sun be?

A. to the left of Earth because Earth's left side is in daylight

B. to the left of Earth because the Northern Hemisphere is having summer

C. to the right of Earth because Earth's right side is in darkness

D. to the right of Earth because the Southern Hemisphere is having summer

S4E2a   S4CS4b

2. A drawing of the moon is shown below.

Which phase is shown, and why?

A. new moon, because it looks bright

B. first quarter, because the new moon has just passed

C. full moon, because the entire side of the moon facing Earth is lit

D. full moon, because the sun has lit the whole surface of the moon

S4E2b

3. Which of these is the correct order of the planets, starting from the sun and moving outward?

A. Venus, Mercury, Earth, Mars, Jupiter, Saturn, Uranus, Neptune

B. Mercury, Venus, Earth, Mars, Jupiter, Saturn, Uranus, Neptune

C. Mercury, Venus, Earth, Mars, Jupiter, Saturn, Neptune, Uranus

D. Mercury, Venus, Mars, Earth, Jupiter, Saturn, Uranus, Neptune

S4E2d

4. Which statement is accurate?

A. All stars have rocky cores.

B. You can see all eight planets in our solar system without a telescope.

C. The planets seem to wander through the constellations.

D. All stars are the same size and have the same color.

S4E1b

5. Which of the following is true?

A. The inner planets are all huge.

B. The planets gradually increase in size the farther they are from the sun.

C. The planets gradually decrease in size the farther they are from the sun.

D. The inner planets are much smaller than the outer planets.

S4E2d

Use the diagram below to answer question 6.

6. How would the seasons be different if Earth rotated as shown above?

A. There would be no seasons.

B. The seasons would be shorter.

C. There would be no night and day.

D. The climate would be warmer at the North Pole and at the South Pole. `S4E2c` `S4CS4b`

7. Which is true about stars?

A. Their color indicates their temperature.

B. They are clouds of spinning gas.

C. They are all the same size as our sun.

D. They are permanent bodies in space. `S4E1a`

8. Why does the pattern of stars in a constellation not change?

A. The stars in a constellation revolve around Earth together.

B. The stars in a constellation rotate very slowly on their axes.

C. Stars appear not to move because they are so far away from Earth.

D. Earth's gravity holds the stars in place. `S4E1c`

Use the diagram below to answer question 9.

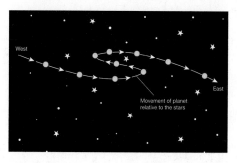

9. What does this illustration BEST show?

A. why planets orbit the sun

B. why Earth has seasons

C. why the pattern of stars in a constellation remains the same

D. why planets are seen in different locations at different times `S4E1c`

10. Why is the Hubble Space Telescope valuable for studying objects outside our solar system?

A. We have already learned a great deal about everything inside our solar system.

B. This telescope can take clearer pictures than telescopes on Earth.

C. It is the biggest telescope we have.

D. It can be repaired by robots. `S4E1d`

Use the drawing to answer question 11.

11. Which change of state is shown above?

A. solid to liquid
B. liquid to solid
C. liquid to gas
D. gas to liquid   ▸ **S4E3a**

12. Ice is forming on a pond. Inside, a pan of water on a stove is starting to boil. What is the temperature of the water in each instance?

A. 32°C; 212°C   C. 32°C; 100°C
B. 10°C; 212°C   D. 0°C; 100°C
               ▸ **S4E3b**

13. Warm air cools as it moves upward. What will likely happen to the water vapor in the air?

A. It will turn into hail.
B. It will absorb energy.
C. It will condense and form clouds.
D. It will continue to evaporate.
               ▸ **S4E3c**

14. Look at the diagram of the water cycle shown below.

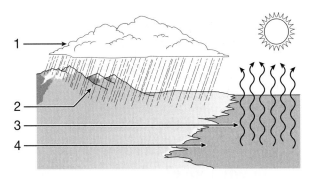

What is happening to the water at the arrow labeled 2?

A. The water is freezing.
B. The water is condensing.
C. The water is evaporating.
D. The water is falling as precipitation.   ▸ **S4E3d**

15. On a chilly day, low, gray clouds cover the sky. Your friend says that dark clouds always indicate that a big thunderstorm is coming. What should you tell your friend?

A. Cumulus clouds bring fair weather, not thunderstorms.
B. Stratus clouds usually do not bring heavy rain.
C. Cirrus clouds bring snow, not rain.
D. It's too cold for a thunderstorm.
    ▸ **S4E3e**   ▸ **S4CS6a**

16. Which is NOT true of sleet and snow?

A. They both fall from cumulonimbus clouds.

B. They are both solid substances.

C. They both form as liquid water freezes.

D. They are both forms of precipitation.

`S4E3e`

17. Falling air pressure indicates that a storm is on the way. Which instrument could help you decide whether to cancel a picnic?

`S4E4a`

A.

C.

B.

D.

18. As the sun rises, the sky around it looks reddish. What does this tell you about today's weather?

A. It probably won't rain.

B. It's likely to rain.

C. A cold front is coming.

D. The air pressure is rising.

`S4E4c`

Use the weather map below to answer question 19.

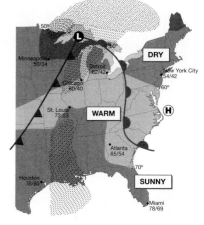

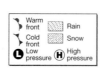

19. Study this weather map. What is the weather likely to be in Detroit tomorrow?

A. hot and rainy

B. cold and snowy

C. cool and rainy

D. warm and sunny

`S4E4b` `S4CS4b`

20. Which statement is true?

A. Climate is the average of the conditions of the atmosphere over many years.

B. Weather is the average of the conditions of the atmosphere over many years.

C. Climate can change quickly.

D. When the Northern Hemisphere receives direct sunlight, the climate gets colder.

`S4E4d`

UNIT B PHYSICAL SCIENCE

What do YOU wonder?

This photograph shows each stage of a gymnast's movement. The camera recorded tiny changes in her position. How do you know the gymnast moved?

GO online for student eBook www.hspscience.com

Test the Shape and Size of Sails Sailboats have large sails that catch the wind, which causes the boats to move. The sails can be many shapes and sizes. What kind of sail is able to catch the most wind and make a boat move the fastest? Plan and conduct an experiment to find out.

A gymnast on a balance beam

4 Sound and Light

Georgia Performance Standards in This Chapter

Content

S4P1 Students will investigate the nature of light using tools such as mirrors, lenses, and prisms.

S4P1a, b, c

S4P2a, b Students will demonstrate how sound is produced by vibrating objects and how sound can be varied. . . .

S4P2a, b

This chapter also addresses these co-requisite standards:

Characteristics of Science

S4CS4 Students will use ideas of system . . . and scale.

S4CS4c

S4CS6 Students will question scientific claims. . . .

S4CS6a

S4CS7 Students will be familiar with the character of scientific knowledge and how it is achieved.

S4CS7a

S4CS8 Students will understand important features of the process of scientific inquiry.

S4CS8a, d

What's the Big Idea?

Sound and light are forms of energy that interact with matter in ways that enable us to see and hear the things around us.

Essential Questions

GO online for student eBook
www.hspscience.com

Turner Field, Atlanta

Dear Ron,

My dad, my little sister, and I recently went to our first Atlanta Braves game at Turner Field.

The roar of the crowd was deafening! I don't think I've ever heard anything so loud. I wonder how far the sound travels? The stadium lights were so bright that it seemed like daytime on the field. I can't wait to go back!

Your friend,
Darnell

USA

What exactly is light? How does sound travel? How does this relate to the **Big Idea?**

155

Content

LESSON 1

Essential Question

What Is Sound?

Georgia Fast Fact

A Grand Instrument

A musician plays a piano by pressing one or more of its 88 keys. The keys operate levers that cause small, padded hammers to strike tightly stretched metal strings, which then vibrate and produce tones. Whether a tone is high or low depends mostly on the length of the strings. These vary in length from 15 to 200 centimeters (6 to 80 inches). The thin sheet of wood that lies just below the strings also vibrates, reinforcing the sounds produced.

vibration [vy•BRAY•shuhn] A back-and-forth movement of matter (p. 160)

volume [VAHL•yoom] The loudness of a sound (p. 161)

pitch [PICH] How high or low a sound is (p. 162)

frequency [FREE•kwuhn•see] The number of vibrations per second (p. 162)

Making Sound

Guided Inquiry

Start with Questions

Perhaps you or someone in your family plays a musical instrument.

- What causes the sounds you hear?

- How do musical instruments produce both high and low sounds?

Investigate to find out. Then read to find out more.

Prepare to Investigate

Inquiry Skill Tip

Whenever you identify the variable to be tested, you identify and isolate the factor that affects the outcome of an investigation.

Materials

- 2 pieces of string, 100 cm long
- 2 metal spoons
- meterstick

Make an Observation Chart

Length of String	Observations
75 cm	
50 cm	
25 cm	

Follow This Procedure

1. Tie one end of each piece of string to one of the spoons.

2. Wrap the other end of each piece of string around your index fingers. Each finger should be wrapped with one string. Gently place those fingers in your ears.

3. Let the spoon hang freely. Have a partner **measure** the string lengths between your fingers and the spoon. Wrap more string around your fingers until the lengths are 75 cm each.

4. Have your partner gently tap the spoon with the other spoon. **Record** your observations.

5. Repeat Steps 2, 3, and 4, but shorten the string lengths to 50 cm.

6. Repeat Steps 2, 3, and 4, but shorten the string lengths to 25 cm.

Step 1

Step 4

Draw Conclusions

1. What did you hear in Step 4 of the activity?

2. **Standards Link** Did the sound change when you shortened the strings? If so, how? **S4P2b**

3. **Inquiry Skill** Before scientists conduct an experiment, they must **identify the variable** to be tested. What variable did you test in this activity? **S4CS8a**

Independent Inquiry

Plan and conduct a simple experiment to find out if the sound changes with plastic objects instead of metal spoons. **S4CS8a**

VOCABULARY
vibration p. 160
volume p. 161
pitch p. 162
frequency p. 162

SCIENCE CONCEPTS
▶ what makes sounds vary
▶ how sounds travel

MAIN IDEA AND DETAILS
(Focus Skill)

Look for the characteristics of sound.

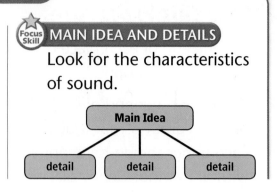

Sound Energy

Have you ever been to a Native American powwow? People dance and celebrate to the rhythm of a drum. The drum may be big—about 1 m (3 ft) in diameter. The sound gets very loud and can be heard far away.

Sound is a form of energy that travels through the air. Sound is made when something vibrates. A **vibration** is a back-and-forth movement of matter. When a drummer hits a drum's head, it moves back and forth very quickly. These movements are vibrations. They cause the air nearby to vibrate, making the sound energy that you hear.

Musical instruments make sounds in various ways. Some, like drums, vibrate when they're hit. A stringed instrument vibrates when the player plucks the strings or draws a bow across them. A woodwind instrument, like a clarinet, has a thin wooden reed attached to it. When the player blows into the instrument, the reed vibrates.

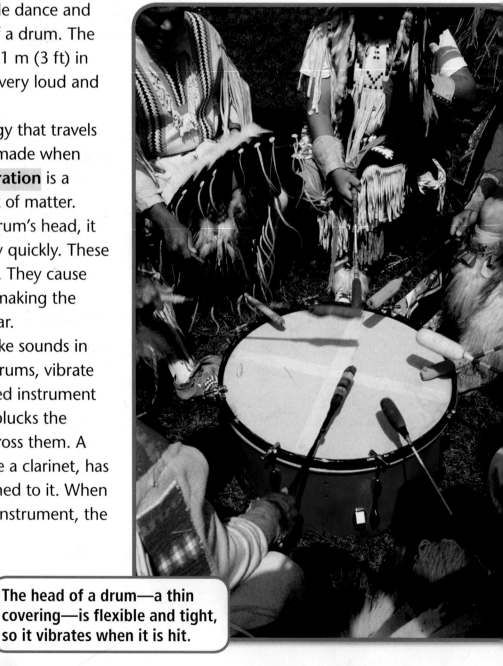

The head of a drum—a thin covering—is flexible and tight, so it vibrates when it is hit.

How Loud Are Some Sounds?

Sound	Decibel Level
Whisper	20 dB
Quiet radio	40 dB
Conversation	60 dB
Dishwasher	80 dB
Jackhammer	100 dB
Thunderclap	120 dB

Why do factory workers and jackhammer operators wear ear protection?

◄ **These representatives at the United Nations are wearing headsets so they can listen to speeches in their own languages. Each person can adjust the volume of the sound for comfort and clarity.**

RMANY

Some sounds are louder than others. If the drummers at the powwow hit the drum gently, the sound is soft. If they hit the drum harder, the sound gets stronger and louder. The loudness of a sound is called the **volume**. Can you think of a sound with a low volume and a sound with a high volume?

When a drummer hits a drum harder, more energy is transferred to the drum and to the sound. The more energy a sound has, the greater its volume is.

The volume of a sound is measured in units called *decibels* (DES•uh•buhlz),

abbreviated *dB*. The softest sound a human can hear is 0 dB. A high-decibel sound is loud and has a lot of energy. Have you ever heard a sound that made your ears ring? Sounds above 100 dB can cause pain and can damage a person's ears. That's why people who work around loud sounds wear ear plugs or other ear protection.

MAIN IDEA AND DETAILS

Describe the ways in which three types of musical instruments make sound.

Sound Waves

Sound travels through the air as waves. When a jackhammer strikes the sidewalk, the sidewalk vibrates and pushes on the air directly above it. Molecules of air are *compressed,* or squeezed together. The compressed air pushes on the air next to it. This passes the compression along, like a wave at the beach.

You already know that some sounds are higher than others. If you've ever listened to a brass band, for example, you know that a trumpet makes a higher sound than a tuba does. The **pitch** of a sound is how high or how low it is. In the Investigate, you found that changing the length of the strings altered the pitch of the sound you heard. That's because the length of the strings affected how fast they vibrated. A shorter string vibrates faster. There are more vibrations per second. The number of vibrations per second is the **frequency** of a sound.

A sound with a high frequency has a high pitch. A sound with a low frequency has a low pitch. Small objects often vibrate at higher frequencies than large objects do. In the Investigate, shortening the strings made them vibrate at a higher frequency. A trumpet is smaller than a tuba, so the trumpet makes sound waves with higher frequencies.

Sound travels in compression waves. In a similar way, when this spring is compressed and then released, the compression moves along the spring as a wave. After the wave has moved through it, the spring returns to its original position.

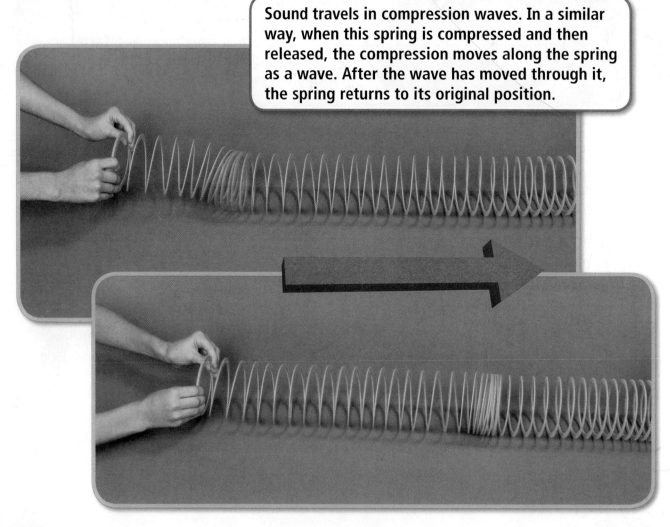

▲ If you shout toward a hard surface, such as a cliff, you may hear an echo of your voice. The echo isn't as loud as the original sound because the surface absorbs some of the energy.

Sound waves move out in all directions from an object that makes a sound. When a sound wave hits something, some or all of the energy is absorbed. Soft surfaces absorb more sound energy than hard surfaces. A sound that hits a hard surface bounces back—not much of it is absorbed. A sound that bounces off a surface is called an *echo.* If you stand at the foot of a cliff and shout, you may hear an echo of your voice. Some caves and canyons are famous for the echoes they produce.

 MAIN IDEA AND DETAILS

How do sounds travel?

Playing the Glasses
You can make a sound by tapping on a drinking glass. If you put water in the glass, the pitch of the sound changes. Use water and several glasses to make different notes. How does adding water to the glasses affect the pitch of the sounds you make?

Sound Transmission

Have you ever set up a line of dominoes and then knocked them down? The first domino pushes over the second and so on. The wave of energy moves down the line, but the individual dominoes do not. Sound has energy just like the dominoes. Waves can carry energy a long distance. The energy travels from place to place, but the matter that carries the energy stays where it is. Sound waves move through air because particles in the air vibrate right where they are.

When you talk to a friend, vibrations move from you to your friend through the air. But the air doesn't have to move to your friend. If it did, a breeze blowing in your face would prevent your friend from hearing your words because they'd be blown back to you!

How Sound Reaches You

Molecules of air carry sound waves from the source to the listeners.

The sound moves through the air as compression waves.

When the performer sings, she produces vibrations that compress the air.

Air is not the only matter that can carry sound waves. Any kind of matter can be made to vibrate and carry sound. Matter that carries sound waves is called a *medium.* Sound waves can't travel without a medium. That's why there's no sound in space, which has no air or other suitable medium.

The speed of sound depends on the medium through which it's moving. The speed doesn't depend on how loud or soft the volume is or how high or low the pitch is. All sounds travel through a certain kind of medium at the same speed.

If the medium changes, the speed of sound changes. Sound moves faster in warm air than in cold air. It travels faster in solids and liquids than it does in gases.

Focus Skill MAIN IDEA AND DETAILS

In reference to sound traveling, what is a medium?

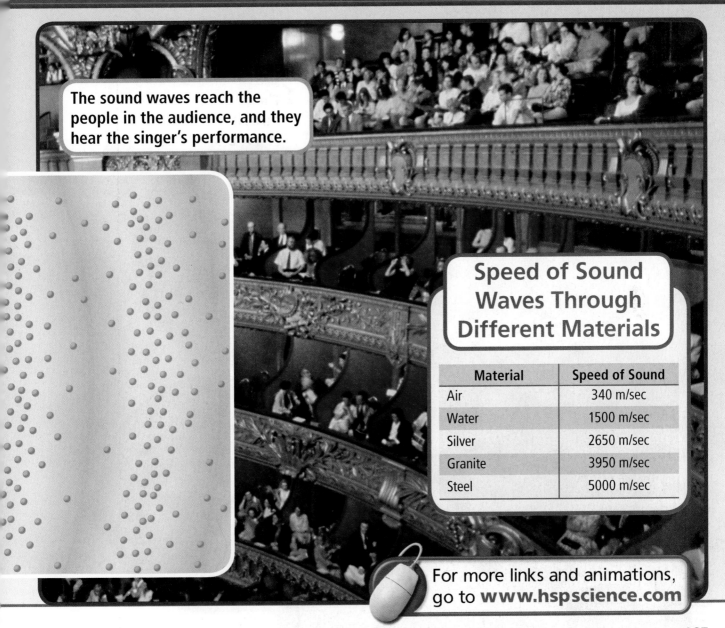

The sound waves reach the people in the audience, and they hear the singer's performance.

Speed of Sound Waves Through Different Materials

Material	Speed of Sound
Air	340 m/sec
Water	1500 m/sec
Silver	2650 m/sec
Granite	3950 m/sec
Steel	5000 m/sec

For more links and animations, go to **www.hspscience.com**

Animals and Sound

People can hear sound over a wide range of frequencies. The highest sounds that people can hear have frequencies of about 20,000 vibrations per second.

Many animals can hear sounds that are outside the range of human hearing. Dogs can hear sounds with higher frequencies than people can hear— frequencies of 25,000 vibrations per second.

Bats have better hearing than most other animals. They can hear sounds with frequencies as high as 100,000 vibrations per second. Bats can also produce sounds with that frequency.

As a bat flies, it produces many short, high-frequency sounds. These bounce off objects in the bat's path, and the bat hears the echoes. The echoes help the bat fly at night by giving it information about its surroundings. They also help the bat hunt. Echoes that bounce from insects give information to the bat about where to find its next meal.

People, dogs, and bats have parts of their ears on the outside of their bodies. But snakes and birds have no outside ears. Grasshoppers pick up vibrations in several ways. A membrane near the large hind leg senses vibrations in the air. Hairlike structures on the body sense vibrations in the ground.

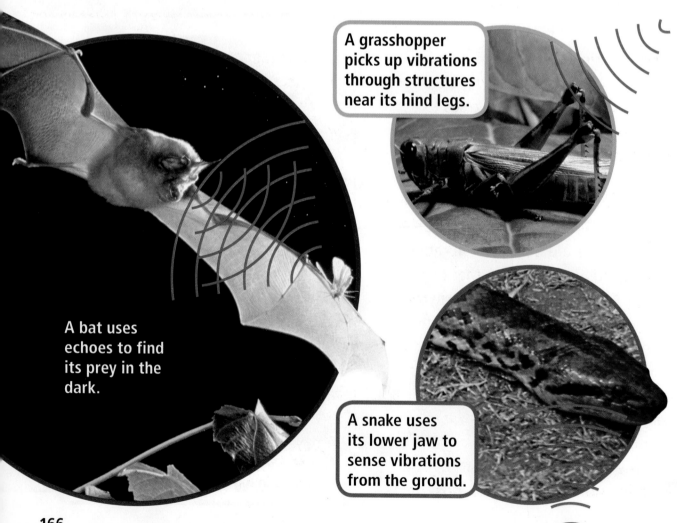

A grasshopper picks up vibrations through structures near its hind legs.

A bat uses echoes to find its prey in the dark.

A snake uses its lower jaw to sense vibrations from the ground.

Elephants communicate using low-pitched rumbles that humans cannot hear.

Special technology helps scientists study low-frequency sound waves.

Many animals communicate by making noises. Wolves howl. Dolphins use whistles and clicking noises to communicate with other dolphins.

Elephants communicate using a variety of noises—roars, trumpets, bellows, cries, snorts, and rumbles—over a wide frequency range. Some of the sounds they produce are below 20 vibrations per second, which means that humans cannot hear them. Elephants use these low-pitched sounds to communicate with other elephants that are as far as several kilometers away. Other animals, including the giraffe and rhinoceros, also communicate by using low-frequency sounds.

Some whales produce both high-pitched and low-pitched sounds that humans cannot hear. The blue whale produces low-frequency sound waves that can travel for thousands of miles, which means that blue whales on the other side of the ocean can hear these calls. Whales are thought to use high-frequency sounds to communicate and to help them find their way.

Some scientists think that noises made by humans and their machines during shipping, oil drilling, and the operation of submarines may interfere with the whales' signals. This is unfortunate because it could disrupt behaviors such as feeding and migration and might even cause permanent hearing loss.

Focus Skill MAIN IDEA AND DETAILS What are two ways in which animals sense vibrations?

Essential Question

What is sound?

In this lesson, you learned that vibrating objects produce sound and that waves carry sound energy through a medium. You also learned about features of sound such as frequency, or pitch.

1. (Focus Skill) **MAIN IDEA AND DETAILS** Draw and complete a graphic organizer to give details that explain how frequency and volume are used to describe sound. **S4P2a, b**

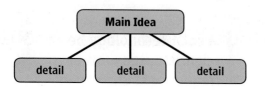

2. SUMMARIZE Fill in the blanks. Sound is _____ you can hear. Sound travels through the air as _____ waves. Sound waves must travel through a _____. **S4P2a**

3. DRAW CONCLUSIONS Why does carpet make a room seem quiet? **S4P2a**

4. VOCABULARY How do vibrations produce sound? **S4P2a**

5. Critical Thinking A xylophone is a musical instrument you play by striking bars of different length. As you move from the longer bars to the shorter bars, the pitch of the sound rises. Explain why. **S4P2b**

CRCT Practice

6. What happens to a sound if the frequency of the vibrations increases?

  A The volume decreases.

  B The pitch increases.

  C The sound echoes.

  D The sound gets louder. **S4P2b**

7. The harder you strike a drum, the greater the sound's

  A pitch.

  B medium.

  C volume.

  D frequency. **S4P2a**

8. Explain the following statement: Sound waves carry energy, not matter. **S4P2**

The **Big** Idea

 Writing ELA4W2

Write a Paragraph

Imagine that you're playing the piano. Your brother says he doesn't understand why some strings produce higher notes than other strings. Write a paragraph to help your brother understand.

 Math M4D1a

Construct a Graph

Research the speed at which sound travels through different materials. Make a bar graph to show your data. Be sure to include the materials listed in the Science Up Close.

 Social Studies IPS 2, 7

The Sound Barrier

A vehicle that travels faster than the speed of sound is said to break the sound barrier. Find out what kinds of vehicles have broken the sound barrier. Make a time line to show your findings.

 For more links and activities, go to **www.hspscience.com**

A SOUND IDEA

For six years, Joanne Peterson lived in a silent world. Because she was deaf, Peterson could see—but not hear—her son play the piano. Thanks to a recently developed bionic ear, Peterson can hear again.

Electrical Impulses

Peterson was one of the first Americans to use the device. Unlike traditional hearing aids, which amplify sounds, the bionic ear changes sounds into electrical impulses. The bionic ear is also called a *cochlear implant.*

The first step is to surgically implant part of the bionic ear into the back of a patient's head. The doctors actually attach an electrode and tiny wires that connect to nerves. Those nerves are connected to the part of the brain that controls hearing.

The user wears a microphone that captures speech and sounds. The microphone is attached to a computer processor. The processor converts the sound into electrical impulses. Those impulses are sent to the surgical implant inside the user's head.

A young child with a cochlear implant.

The implant then delivers the electrical impulses, through the tiny wires, to the nerves that are connected to the part of the brain that controls hearing. The brain is able to translate the impulses into sounds, allowing the user to hear.

Hearing Again

Doctors say the people who benefit the most from the bionic ear are those whose hearing is so bad that they cannot hear a telephone ring.

"I adore [the bionic ear]. At first it was a major shock to the system, to my head," said Cassie Bunker, who also regained hearing with the bionic ear. She thought, "I'm hearing things."

She Longed to Hear Music

"He played Beethoven," Peterson said after listening to her son play the piano. "I thought that was so pretty to sit and listen to."

 Think and Write

1. How is the bionic ear different from traditional hearing aids? **S4CS6a**

2. Describe the steps that enable a person to hear using a bionic ear.

S4P2a

 Find out more. Log on to **www.hspscience.com**

Content

 S4P1a Identify materials that are transparent, opaque, and translucent.

S4P1b Investigate the reflection of light using a mirror and a light source.

Characteristics of Science

S4CS4c   **S4CS8a**

LESSON 2

Essential Question

What Is Light?

Georgia Fast Fact

Look to the Lighthouse

The Tybee Island light station, established in 1736, is one of three active lighthouses along the Georgia coast. Its 1000-watt bulb gives off a continuous white light. A special lens concentrates the light so that it can be seen from over 19 kilometers (12 miles) away. This welcoming light has guided ships entering the Savannah River for over 270 years.

Tybee Island lighthouse

reflection [rih•FLEK•shuhn] The bouncing of light off an object (p. 180)

refraction [rih•FRAK•shuhn] The bending of light as it moves from one material to another (p. 181)

translucent [trans•LOO•suhnt] Allowing only some light to pass through (p. 182)

transparent [trans•PAR•uhnt] Allowing light to pass through (p. 182)

opaque [oh•PAYK] Not allowing light to pass through (p. 183)

The Path of Reflected Light

Guided Inquiry

Start with Questions

When the surface of water is smooth, it acts just like a mirror. The reflection you see is called an image.

- What does light do when it strikes a mirror?

- How does light travel away from the mirror?

Investigate to find out. Then read to find out more.

Prepare to Investigate

Inquiry Skill Tip

When you predict what will happen in an investigation, don't just guess. Based on your observations and what you already know, decide what is the most reasonable thing that will happen.

Materials

- ruler
- masking tape
- small mirror
- protractor
- 3 pushpins of different colors
- piece of corrugated cardboard, 10 cm × 10 cm

Make a Data Table

Angle	Measure (in degrees)
Between left line and mirror	
Between right line and mirror	

Follow This Procedure

1. Lay the cardboard flat, and use tape to stand the mirror vertically at one end of the cardboard. Push two of the pins into the cardboard, about 5 cm in front of the mirror.

2. Position yourself so your eyes are level with the pins. Align yourself so that your view of one pin lines up with the reflection of the other pin. Push a third pin into the cardboard, at the edge of the mirror, right in front of the reflection. The first pin, the third pin, and the reflection of the second pin should appear to be in a straight line.

3. Draw lines on the cardboard to connect the third pin with the others. These lines show how the light from the second pin traveled.

4. Draw a line along the front of the mirror, and then remove the mirror. Measure and record the angle between each line and the edge of the cardboard.

Draw Conclusions

1. What do the two angles represent?

2. **Standards Link** Compare the two angle measures. `S4P1b`

3. **Inquiry Skill** Suppose you know the angle at which light hits a mirror. Predict the angle at which the light will reflect. `S4CS4c`

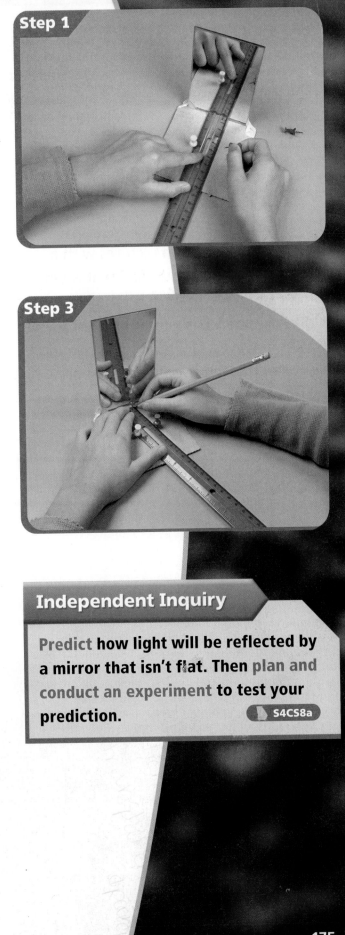

Step 1

Step 3

Independent Inquiry

Predict **how light will be reflected by a mirror that isn't flat.** Then plan and conduct an experiment **to test your prediction.** `S4CS8a`

VOCABULARY
reflection p. 180
refraction p. 181
translucent p. 182
transparent p. 182
opaque p. 183

SCIENCE CONCEPTS
▶ what kinds of light waves there are
▶ how matter affects light

Focus Skill **MAIN IDEA AND DETAILS**
Look for ways that light can be changed.

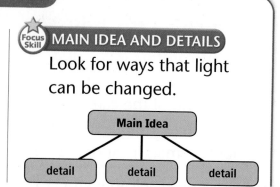

Light Energy

Have you ever taken pictures with a camera? Did you know that light is what allows an image to form on the film? Light, like sound, is a form of energy that travels in waves. However, unlike sound, light can travel through empty space. All waves carry energy. When the waves reach an object, some of the energy can be absorbed by that object. For example, light energy that strikes film in a camera causes a chemical change, enabling a picture to be made.

Light is one small part of a range of energy known as the *electromagnetic spectrum.* The waves that make up the electromagnetic spectrum differ in their frequencies.

Electromagnetic Spectrum

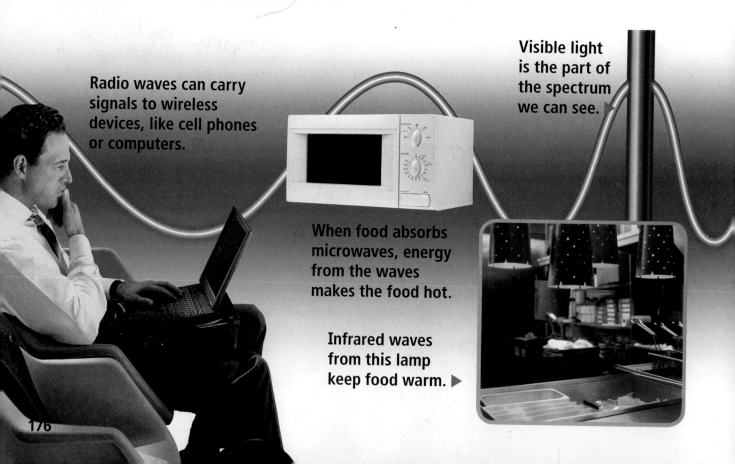

Radio waves can carry signals to wireless devices, like cell phones or computers. ▽

When food absorbs microwaves, energy from the waves makes the food hot.

Infrared waves from this lamp keep food warm. ▶

Visible light is the part of the spectrum we can see. ▶

The part of the spectrum that humans can see is called *visible light.* Radio waves have lower frequencies than visible light waves. X rays have higher frequencies.

Waves with high frequencies carry more energy than waves with lower frequencies. High-energy waves pass through matter more easily. You know that light doesn't pass through your body. But other forms of waves, such as X rays, do, at least partially. Has a dentist ever taken an X-ray image of your teeth? You hold a piece of film in your mouth, and the dentist points an X-ray machine at your jaw. X rays go from the machine, through your jaw, and to the film.

Did you notice that your teeth are white on the X ray, but everything else is dark? When X rays pass through your jaw, your teeth absorb more of the X-ray energy than the rest of your mouth does. The result is that different amounts of energy reach the film in different places.

On the film, the X-ray energy causes changes that can be seen. The different amounts of energy in different places make a picture of your teeth on the film.

Focus Skill MAIN IDEA AND DETAILS

What types of waves are found in the electromagnetic spectrum?

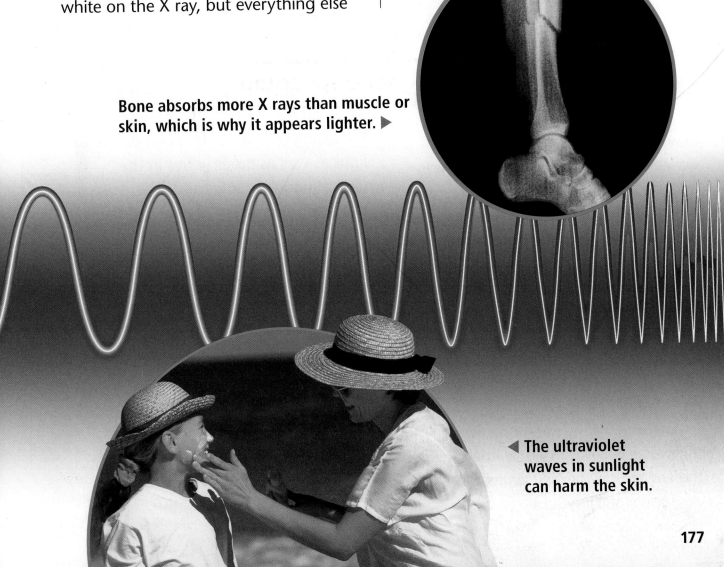

▶ Bone absorbs more X rays than muscle or skin, which is why it appears lighter.

◀ The ultraviolet waves in sunlight can harm the skin.

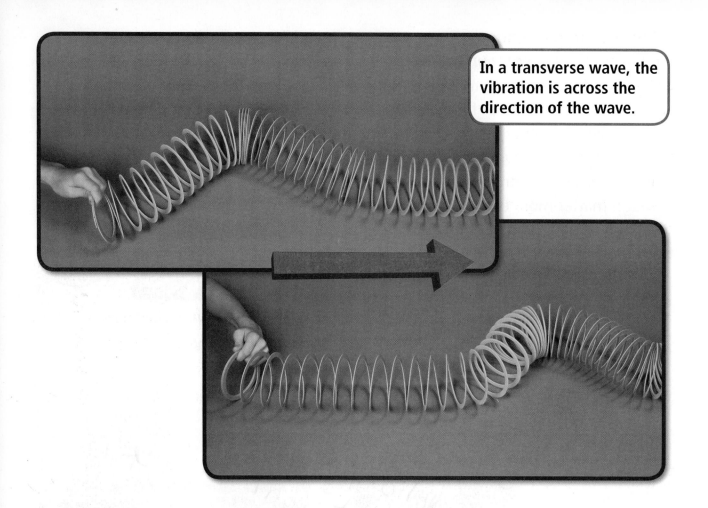

In a transverse wave, the vibration is across the direction of the wave.

Light Waves

Many scientists think that light travels in waves. Unlike sound waves, light waves do not travel as compressions in matter.

Have you watched waves at the ocean or on a lake? While the water moves up and down, it does not move forward or backward. Light moves like ocean waves.

If you hold one end of a rope and shake it up and down, you make a wave that moves along the rope. But the vibration is across that direction, forming an S shape. This kind of wave is called a *transverse* wave. Like compression waves, transverse waves carry only energy. After the energy has traveled away from you, the rope is still in your hand.

Since light waves do not need matter, light can travel through empty space. For example, the sun gives off visible light as well as other waves in the electromagnetic spectrum. These waves travel through space and reach Earth.

Light travels very fast. Scientists have not found anything faster. Light waves move thousands of times faster than sound waves. Light is so fast that sunlight takes only about 8 minutes to travel the distance to Earth—about 150 million km (93 million mi).

You feel the energy in light when you stand in sunlight. Your body absorbs the energy, and you feel it as heat. If you absorb too much of that energy, it harms your skin and you get a sunburn.

The light from a light bulb doesn't have as much energy as sunlight. You can't get a sunburn from standing under an ordinary lamp. A light bulb gives off heat because an electric current heats up the filament, or wire, inside the bulb. This makes the filament give off light.

A light bulb gives off light in all directions. A laser, though, gives off light in a narrow beam. Inside a laser, light waves line up, like the members of a band marching in step in one direction. When the waves exit the laser, they don't spread out. The concentrated light is very powerful—and dangerous. Never look into any bright source of light.

Focus Skill MAIN IDEA AND DETAILS What characteristics do light waves have?

Laser

The light energy from lasers is so concentrated that factories use lasers to cut steel.

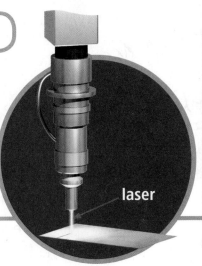

laser

Light Bulb

The light from an ordinary light bulb spreads out in all directions. The energy you get from the bulb decreases as you move away.

Absorption and Reflection

Have you ever seen frosted glass? Some light passes through it, but you can't see objects clearly through the glass.

When light hits an object, the object affects the path of the light. An object can absorb light, make it bounce off, or let it pass through.

Some of the light energy that hits an object is absorbed. Objects of different colors absorb different amounts of light. Dark objects absorb more light energy than light-colored objects do. This difference is the reason light-colored clothes keep you cooler on a bright summer day.

Objects don't absorb all the light that hits them. Some of the light bounces off. **Reflection** is the bouncing of light from a surface. The reflected light that reaches your eyes from an object enables you to see the object.

Usually, light scatters in many directions as it is reflected. A smooth surface, however, reflects light in a predictable pattern. You see the pattern as an image on the reflecting surface. This is what happens when you see the sky reflected by the smooth windows of a building or when you see yourself in a mirror. Your image in a mirror looks just like you— except for one thing. It's backward. Images in a mirror are reversed from left to right.

Focus Skill MAIN IDEA AND DETAILS

Why can you see your image in a calm lake but not when you look at the ground?

All the light hitting a mirror from one direction is reflected in a single new direction. The new direction of light is related to the old direction in a definite way.

The glass used in this building is coated with chemicals that reflect light like a giant mirror.

▲ When a beam of light enters water, it slows down. If it hits the surface at an angle, the light bends.

▲ A beam of light doesn't bend if it enters water straight on.

Refraction

Have you ever used a net to catch a fish in a tank? You probably had a hard time telling where the fish was. That's because your eyes were fooled by the direction the light came from.

Light reflecting from the fish passed through the water, into the air, and to your eye. When the light moved from the water to the air, its speed changed. The change in speed made the beam of light bend. This bending of light as it moves from one material to another is called **refraction** (rih•FRAK•shuhn).

Refracted light can make a solid object seem to be in two parts. For example, if you place a pencil in a glass that is half full of water, you will notice that the pencil appears to be broken. Your eye has been fooled, but how? Light from the part of the pencil that is above the

water reaches your eye on one path. Light from the part of the pencil that is under the water reaches your eye on a different path. As a result, you see the pencil in two separate parts.

 **MAIN IDEA AND DETAILS**

Why does light bend when it moves from one material to another?

You look at the flower through two materials—air and water. The water refracts light, causing the stem to look bent.

Translucent, Transparent, and Opaque

You know that some light passes through frosted glass. Materials that allow some light to pass through are **translucent** (trans•LOO•suhnt). Because these materials absorb or scatter some of the light that strikes them, you can't see through them clearly. A frosted light bulb is translucent. Light passes through the glass, but you can't clearly see what's inside the bulb. Wax paper, tissue paper, and some plastics are translucent. So are some kinds of window shades.

With the shades up, though, you can look through clear glass windows to see what's outside. You get a clear view because almost all the light that strikes the glass passes through. The glass is transparent. A **transparent** material allows most of the light that hits it to pass through it. Most glass, water, and plastic wrap are transparent. Transparent objects don't scatter light as translucent objects do, but they do cause light to bend.

The frosted marbles are translucent.

The clear marbles and the vase are transparent.

Can you see through a metal door? Of course not. The reason is that this material absorbs or reflects all the light that strikes it. No light passes through. Materials that don't allow any light to pass through them are **opaque** (oh•PAYK). Metals are opaque. So is wood. Most of your body is opaque. Plants, clay pots, soil, bricks, chairs, walls, and floors are opaque. Even your best friend is opaque! You can't see through any of these things.

MAIN IDEA AND DETAILS Give one example each of translucent, transparent, and opaque materials.

The stones are opaque.

Math in Science
Interpret Data

The table shows an amount of light leaving a source. It also shows the amount that gets through three different materials—A, B, and C. Which material is translucent? Which is transparent? Which is opaque?

Material	Light from Source	Light Through Material
A	100	55
B	100	0
C	100	95

Look At and Through
Hold sheets of plastic wrap, aluminum foil, and wax paper up to the light. Try to see through each. Which is opaque? Which is translucent? Which is transparent?

Essential Question

What is light?

In this lesson, you learned that visible light is part of the electromagnetic spectrum. You also learned how light behaves and how to classify materials as transparent, translucent, and opaque.

1. **Focus Skill** MAIN IDEA AND DETAILS Draw and complete a graphic organizer to give details about this main idea: *Light waves change when they hit objects.* **S4P1b**

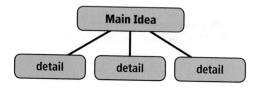

2. **SUMMARIZE** Write a summary of this lesson by using the lesson's vocabulary terms. **S4P1a, b**

3. **DRAW CONCLUSIONS** Is the glass in a stained-glass window transparent, translucent, or opaque? Explain your answer. **S4P1a**

4. **VOCABULARY** Draw diagrams to illustrate *reflection* and *refraction.* **S4P1b**

5. **Critical Thinking** Which has more energy—microwaves or X rays? Explain your answer. **S4P1**

CRCT Practice

6. Which happens to light when it strikes a mirror?
  A It bends.
  B It is absorbed.
  C It bounces off.
  D It makes a shadow. **S4P1b**

7. Unlike sound waves, light waves
  A carry energy.
  B must travel through matter.
  C travel as compression waves.
  D travel as transverse waves.
  S4P1

8. Why can you see your image reflected in a mirror but not in a brick wall? **S4P1b**

The **Big** Idea

Make Connections

Descriptive Writing

Think about a time when you have seen a lake, a pond, or even a puddle reflect a scene. Write a paragraph that describes the scene and its reflection.

 Math   M4N6, M4P5a

Draw Fractions

Material A blocks half of the light that strikes it. Material B blocks two-thirds of the light, and Material C blocks three-sixths of the light. Shade fraction bars or draw pictures to show the fraction of the light that is blocked by each material.

 Health

Sunscreens

Find out how sunglasses protect the eyes. Make a poster to teach others what you learn.

 For more links and activities, go to **www.hspscience.com**

Machelle Pardue

▶ **MACHELLE PARDUE**

▶ **Professor, Emory Eye Center and researcher at the Atlanta VA Medical Center**

▶ Studies diseases of the eye

The eye is an amazing and complex organ. How well we see depends on how healthy our eyes are. Machelle Pardue has always been interested in science. Throughout her schooling, Dr. Pardue has studied how we see.

Dr. Pardue studies a part of the eye called the *retina*. After light passes through the lens of the eye, it travels to the back of the eye, where the retina is located. The retina contains millions of cells that sense light and color. When an image falls on the retina, these cells respond by sending electrical signals to the brain. If there are problems with the retina, the brain may have trouble figuring out the image.

One type of eye disease occurs when the cells of the retina that detect light begin to die. Dr. Pardue is studying how to keep these cells from dying by using small amounts of electricity to stimulate parts of the eye. She is also doing research to see whether a substance made by the liver can keep retinal cells from dying. Dr. Pardue's work could help save the eyesight of many people.

 Think and Write

1 How is Dr. Pardue's work related to light? **S4P1**

2 Why might scientific research on the retina help older adults? **S4CS8d**

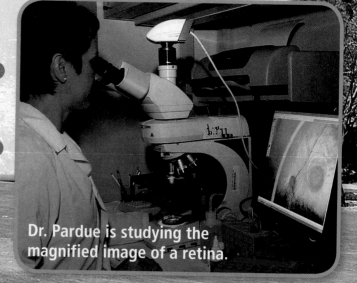

Dr. Pardue is studying the magnified image of a retina.

Lewis Latimer

Lewis Latimer was an inventor. He invented one of the first air conditioners. He also made the drawings that Alexander Graham Bell used when Bell applied for a patent for the telephone.

Latimer is best known for his work with electricity and lighting. While working for the United States Electric Lighting Company, Latimer developed a process for making a carbon filament that lasted longer than the filaments invented by Thomas Edison. Latimer's process helped make electric lights practical for everyday use. Latimer also supervised the installation of electric lighting in New York, Philadelphia, and other cities.

In 1883, Latimer began working for the Edison Electric Light Company. Latimer was an invaluable member of Edison's team. In fact, he wrote the first textbook about Edison's system of electric lighting.

▶ **LEWIS LATIMER**
▶ **Engineer and inventor**
▶ Developed a process for making inexpensive and long-lasting carbon filaments for the electric light bulb

 Think and Write

❶ Why do we need light to see?

❷ How did Latimer's work change how people live?

S4P1

S4CS8d

Today, the filaments in light bulbs are usually made of tungsten.

187

Content

 S4P1c Identify the physical attributes of a convex lens, a concave lens, and a prism and where each is used.

Characteristics of Science

S4CS7a   **S4CS8a**

How Do Objects Bend Light?

Georgia Fast Fact

Colors in Sunlight

These marathon runners are cooling off in a spray of water in which a rainbow can be seen. Rainbows form when the sun shines on water droplets in the air. The droplets separate light so that you can see colors. The colors are always in the same order, from red at the top to violet at the bottom.

Peachtree Road Race in Atlanta

concave lens [kahn•KAYV LENZ] A lens that is thicker at the edges than in the middle (p. 194)

convex lens [kahn•VEKS LENZ] A lens that is thicker in the middle than at the edges (p. 194)

Making Rainbows

Start with Questions

A rainbow that appears after a shower or storm is beautiful. You have probably seen many rainbows.

- What causes a rainbow?
- Why does a rainbow have different colors?
- Can you make a rainbow?

Investigate to find out. Then read to find out more.

Prepare to Investigate

Inquiry Skill Tip

Before you carry out an investigation, predict what will happen. To make a prediction, use what you already know and things you have observed.

Materials

- scissors
- 1 sheet each of black, white, and red paper
- masking tape
- prism
- crayons

Make an Observation Chart

Prism Observations	
Paper Color	Colors Observed
White	
Red	

Follow This Procedure

1. Cut a narrow slit in the sheet of black paper.

2. Tape the paper to the lower edge of a window. Close the blinds to let a narrow beam of sunlight shine through the slit.

3. Place the prism in the beam of light. Slowly turn the prism until you see colors.

4. Place a sheet of white paper under the prism. Use the crayons to **record** what you observe.

5. **Predict** what you will see on the red paper. Then, using the red paper, repeat Steps 3 and 4.

Draw Conclusions

1. How does a prism change sunlight?

2. **Standards Link** How does the shape of a prism differ from the shape of a piece of window glass?
   S4P1c

3. **Inquiry Skill** Scientists compare the results of an investigation with their prediction. Was your **prediction** correct for the red paper? If not, how was the result different from your prediction?
   S4CS7a

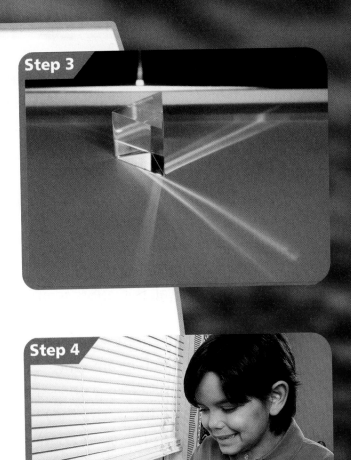

Step 3

Step 4

Independent Inquiry

Think about how the light looked on the red paper. Make a **prediction** about what you would see if you used blue paper. Try it! Did you **predict** correctly?

Compare your observations for the red paper and the blue paper. **Draw a conclusion** that explains the observations.
S4CS8a

VOCABULARY
concave lens p. 194
convex lens p. 194

SCIENCE CONCEPTS
▶ what causes light to separate into colors
▶ how lenses cause light to bend

Focus Skill CAUSE AND EFFECT
Look for information that explains how lenses and prisms bend light.

cause ➔ effect

Light and Color

In the Investigate, you saw that light from the sun contains all the colors seen in a rainbow. As light enters a prism, the light waves change directions. Each color refracts by a slightly different amount, and so takes a slightly different path. As the light waves leave the prism, they change directions again. The changes in direction cause the colors to separate. When this happens, you can see each color.

Opaque objects appear to be colored because they reflect different waves of light to your eye. A red object reflects red light waves. It absorbs the other colors in the light. A blue object reflects blue light waves. A white piece of paper reflects all the colors in the light. When all the colors reach your eye together, you see white. Objects that absorb all light waves appear black.

Transparent objects, such as glass, are different. Suppose you are looking through a piece of red glass. As sunlight strikes the glass, only the red light waves pass through to reach your eye. The red glass absorbs the other light waves. Why does blue glass appear blue?

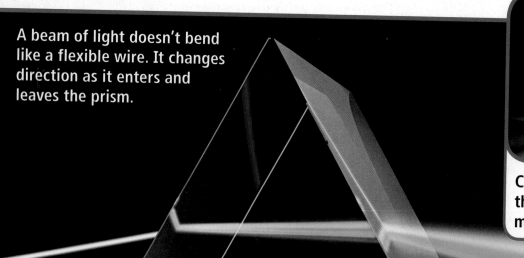

A beam of light doesn't bend like a flexible wire. It changes direction as it enters and leaves the prism.

Clear objects with sides that aren't parallel can make rainbows.

Why Rainbows Form

Light from the sun contains all colors. When there is rain, sunlight passes through drops of water in the air. The light waves refract as they enter and leave each water drop. Each color bends in a slightly different way. This separates the white light into its component colors.

A drop of water is like a tiny prism.

The rainbow contains all the colors the eye can see. The colors blend from one to another. The order of the colors is red, orange, yellow, green, blue, and violet.

For more links and animations, go to **www.hspscience.com**

Rainbows may form any time water droplets are in the air. The droplets act like tiny prisms. As sunlight enters a droplet, each color of light bends by a different amount. Violet light bends the most, red light bends the least, and the rest of the colors appear in between. The colors further separate as they leave the droplet. We see the light from many droplets as a rainbow. Red light comes from droplets higher in the air, and violet light comes from lower droplets.

Focus Skill CAUSE AND EFFECT

What causes light to split into colors when it passes through a prism?

Lenses

A *lens* is a curved, transparent object that refracts light. If you examine a hand lens, which magnifies objects, you'll notice that the glass in the lens is curved. It isn't all the same thickness. The shape of the curve affects how the light bends. A **convex lens** is thicker in the middle than at the edges. As light waves move into the lens, they bend toward the thickest part—the middle. A convex lens makes light waves come together. Objects appear to be larger through a convex lens. They may also appear to be upside down. A convex lens can also be used to make an image on a screen.

A **concave lens** is thicker at the edges than in the middle. As light waves enter the lens, they bend toward the thickest part—the ends. A concave lens makes light waves spread out. An object seen through a concave lens appears to be smaller. Objects seen through a concave lens are always upright.

Focus Skill **CAUSE AND EFFECT**

What causes light to bend differently in concave and convex lenses?

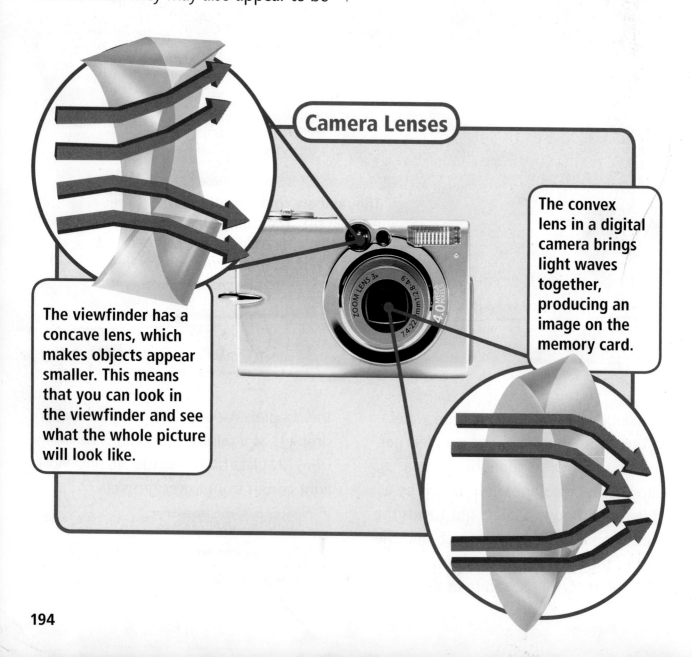

Camera Lenses

The viewfinder has a concave lens, which makes objects appear smaller. This means that you can look in the viewfinder and see what the whole picture will look like.

The convex lens in a digital camera brings light waves together, producing an image on the memory card.

194

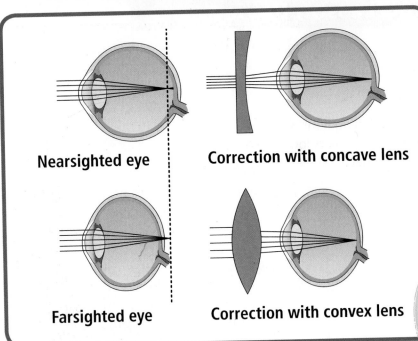

Nearsighted eye

Correction with concave lens

Farsighted eye

Correction with convex lens

▲ The dashed line shows where light is focused in a nearsighted eye and a farsighted eye. Corrective lenses enable light to focus on the retina so that vision is normal.

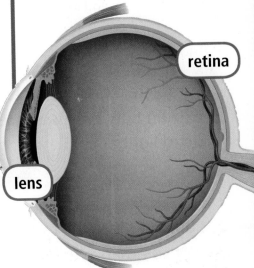

▼ Light enters the eye and is refracted by the lens so that it falls on the retina, which curves around the back of the eye.

retina

lens

Vision

Each of your eyes contains a convex lens. The lens curves on both sides, like a magnifying glass. Muscles in your eye change the thickness of the lens as you look at things close to you or far away from you. The lens focuses the light on the *retina* at the back of your eye. Because the lens is convex, the image that falls on the retina is upside-down! Your brain has learned to "flip" the image to make it look right-side-up.

Some people have trouble seeing because of the shape of their eyes. If the eyeball is too long, the light focuses in front of the retina, and the person is *nearsighted.* Concave glasses or contact lenses fix this problem by spreading the light so that the image forms farther

back. If the eyeball is too short, the image forms behind the retina. The person is *farsighted.* Convex glasses or contact lenses fix this by bending the light more.

Focus Skill CAUSE AND EFFECT What causes an image to form behind the retina?

Insta-Lab

Water Lens
Fill a test tube completely with water, and then close it with a stopper. Hold the filled test tube over some writing. How does your "water lens" change what you see? What kind of lens is it?

GPS Wrap-Up and Lesson Review

How do objects bend light?

In this lesson, you made a rainbow by bending light with a prism. You learned that convex lenses make small objects look larger and concave lenses make large objects look smaller. The lenses in your eyes let you see and focus on objects near and far.

1. **Focus Skill** CAUSE AND EFFECT Copy and complete a graphic organizer to explain how prisms and lenses bend light. **S4P1c**

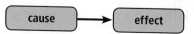

2. **SUMMARIZE** Write three sentences that summarize the lesson.

S4P1c

3. **DRAW CONCLUSIONS** Why don't rainbows form when light passes through a window? **S4P1c**

4. **VOCABULARY** Use the terms *convex lens* and *concave lens* to describe the lenses in a camera. **S4P1c**

5. **Critical Thinking** Do objects look larger or smaller when you look at them through the side of a water-filled glass? Explain. **S4P1c**

CRCT Practice

6. White light can be separated into different colors by using a

A mirror.　　　**C** concave lens.

B convex lens.　　**D** prism.

S4P1c

7. Which is true of a concave lens?

A Its center is thicker than its edges.

B It makes an image on a screen.

C It spreads light rays apart.

D It magnifies objects. **S4P1c**

8. Explain the different ways in which prisms, lenses, and mirrors affect light waves.

The Big Idea

S4P1

 Writing — ELA4W2

Write a Paragraph

Imagine that you are a beam of light. Write a paragraph to explain how you travel from an object to a person's eyes. Tell how you make that object appear to be the color that people see. Write your paragraph so that someone younger than you can understand it.

 9 ÷ 3 Math — M4M2a

Measure an Angle

You will see a rainbow only if the sun is less than 42 degrees above the horizon. Draw a straight line to represent the horizon. Then use a protractor to draw a picture of the sun at an angle of 42 degrees above the horizon.

 Social Studies — IPS 6, 8

An American Inventor

Benjamin Franklin, a leader during the American Revolution, was also an inventor. Find out what Benjamin Franklin did to help people who had problems with both far-away and close-up vision.

 For more links and activities, go to **www.hspscience.com**

Wrap-Up

▶ Visual Summary

Tell how each picture helps explain the **Big Idea**.

The Big Idea Sound and light are forms of energy that interact with matter in ways that enable us to see and hear the things around us.

Lesson 1 S4P2a, b

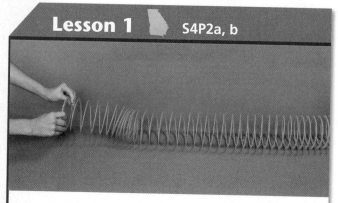

Sound
Sound travels away from a vibrating object in compression waves. Sound waves can't travel without a medium. Characteristics of sound include volume and frequency.

Lesson 2 S4P1a, b

Light
Light moves away from a source as transverse waves. Objects can absorb, reflect, and refract light. Materials can be classified by how much light passes through them.

Lesson 3 S4P1c

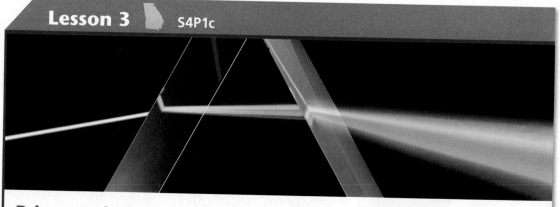

Prisms and Lenses
Light is refracted as if passes through prisms and lenses. A prism separates light into its component colors. A lens's shape determines how it will bend light. Lenses can be used to correct vision.

Show What You Know

Describing Diagrams/Informational Writing

Draw a diagram that shows what light does when it strikes an opaque object. Write a sentence that describes the diagram. Write another sentence to describe what you see when you look at an opaque object. Then draw diagrams and write about what light does when it strikes translucent and transparent objects.

ELA4W2

Georgia Performance Task

Light and Color

Perform an experiment to compare the amount of light energy that is absorbed by materials of different color. Find a sunny location indoors or out and place four colors of construction paper over four thermometers. The colors of paper should range from light to dark. Record the temperature increase for each color of paper at regular intervals. Graph your results, and summarize your findings in a brief report. Use the concepts of reflection and absorption to account for the observed temperature changes.

S4P1a

Vocabulary Review

Use the terms below to complete the sentences. The page numbers tell you where to look in the chapter if you need help.

volume p. 161   **transparent** p. 182

pitch p. 162   **opaque** p. 183

refraction p. 181   **concave lens** p. 194

translucent p. 182   **convex lens** p. 194

1. A sound with a high frequency has a high _____. [S4P2b]

2. A material that does not allow any light to pass through is _____. [S4P1a]

3. Light rays are bent and brought together by a _____. [S4P1c]

4. The loudness of a sound is also known as _____. [S4P2a]

5. Water and plastic wrap are materials that are _____. [S4P1a]

6. A lens that is thicker at the edges than at the middle is a _____. [S4P1c]

7. The bending of light as it moves from one material to another is _____. [S4P1]

8. Wax paper is _____. [S4P1a]

Check Understanding

Write the letter of the best choice.

9. **MAIN IDEA AND DETAILS** Which of the following is a characteristic of sound waves? (p. 165) [S4P2a]

   A A medium is necessary for the waves to travel.

   B The waves are transverse.

   C Different types can be compared on the electromagnetic spectrum.

   D They travel faster than other waves.

10. **MAIN IDEA AND DETAILS** What must happen in order for a sound wave to form? (p. 160) [S4P2a]

    A An electric current must flow.

    B A certain frequency must be reached.

    C Matter must vibrate.

    D Volume must be absorbed.

11. What is the result of someone hitting a drum harder than before? (p. 161) [S4P1c]

    A The number of decibels increases.

    B Pitch decreases.

    C Frequency increases.

    D The number of vibrations decreases.

12. Which of the following surfaces would bounce back almost all the light waves that hit it? (p. 180) `S4P1b`

A a white wall

B a piece of plastic wrap

C a stained-glass window

D a mirror

13. When we see a colored object, what are we really seeing? (p. 180) `S4P1b`

A light that has been absorbed

B light that has not been absorbed

C light that has been refracted

D light that has not been refracted

14. Which of these musical instruments makes sounds with the lowest frequencies? (p. 162) `S4P2b`

A

B

Note: instruments not to scale

C

D

15. A hand lens is a (p. 194) `S4P1b`

A prism.

B convex lens.

C translucent lens.

D concave lens.

16. What kind of image does this lens produce? (p. 194) `S4P1c`

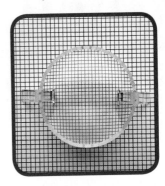

A a distorted image

B a larger image

C a reflected image

D a smaller image

Inquiry Skills

17. Rick is making sound waves by using strings of 12 different lengths. **Identify** the tested **variable**. `S4CS8a`

18. **Predict** whether light and sound would be observed by somebody watching an explosion that occurs in space. Explain. `S4CS5`

Critical Thinking

19. Elephants can detect sources of underground water by using their feet. How is this possible? `S4P2a`

20. Shakira can see and hear an approaching thunderstorm. Would Shakira see the lightning first or hear the thunder first? How will her observations change as the storm gets closer? `S4P1, 2`

The Big Idea

5 Forces and Motion

Georgia Performance Standards in This Chapter

Content

S4P3 Students will demonstrate the relationship between the application of a force and the resulting change in position and motion on an object.

S4P3b, c, d

This chapter also addresses these co-requisite standards:

Characteristics of Science

S4CS3 Students will use tools and instruments for observing, measuring, and manipulating objects. . . .

S4CS4 Students will use ideas of system, model, change, and scale in exploring scientific and technological matters.

S4CS4b

S4CS5 Students will communicate scientific ideas and activities clearly.

S4CS5a, b

S4CS8 Students will understand important features of the process of scientific inquiry.

S4CS8a

What's the Big Idea?

Forces act on and change the motion of objects in measurable ways.

Essential Questions

Go online for student eBook www.hspscience.com

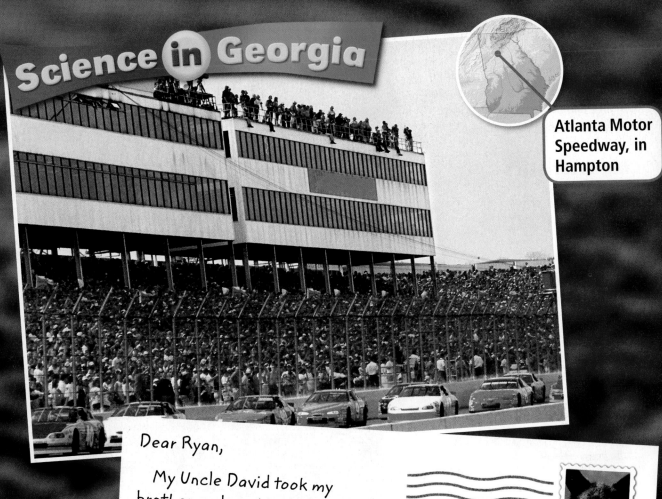

Atlanta Motor Speedway, in Hampton

Dear Ryan,

My Uncle David took my brother and me to our first NASCAR event last weekend.

Did you know that these cars reach speeds of over 190 mph? I noticed that the drivers slowed down on the curves to keep from losing control. Think of the damage they'd cause if they hit another car at these speeds!

Your friend,
Shauna

USA

What did Shauna observe about the cars' motion? How do her observations relate to the **Big Idea?**

203

Content

S4P3 Students will demonstrate the relationship between the application of a force and the resulting change in position and motion on an object.

Characteristics of Science

S4CS4b **S4CS5a**

LESSON

1

Essential Question

How Is Motion Described and Measured?

Georgia Fast Fact

Higher Speed Means Higher Risk

On a highway, cars often go as fast as 120 kilometers per hour (75 mi/hr). High-speed accidents are much more deadly than low-speed ones. A driver is 15 times as likely to die in a crash that takes place at 80 kilometers per hour (50 mi/hr) than in one that takes place at 40 kilometers per hour (25 mi/hr). In the Investigate, you'll describe moving at a very low speed.

Atlanta

position [puh•ZISH•uhn] The location of an object (p. 208)

motion [MOH•shuhn] A change of position of an object (p. 208)

speed [SPEED] The measure of an object's change in position during a unit of time (p. 210)

Walk This Way

Start with Questions

Suppose you were at the park watching the girls in the swings shown in the picture below.

- Are the girls moving? If so, how do you know?

- What kinds of words do we use to describe how things move?

Investigate to find out. Then read to find out more.

Prepare to Investigate

Inquiry Skill Tip

When scientists share the results of an experiment, they tell exactly how they carried out the experiment so that others can check the results. When you communicate, you share ideas. You must explain your ideas clearly so that others can easily understand them.

Materials

- paper
- pencil

Make an Observation Chart

Record of Walk

Follow This Procedure

1. Choose a location in your school. A person going there from your classroom should have to make some turns.

2. As you walk to the location, **record** the way you move. Include the distance you walk, where you turn, any landmarks you see, and how fast you move.

3. Return to the classroom. Use your notes to write detailed directions to the location. Don't name the location. Your partner should follow the directions.

4. Get feedback from your partner about how well your directions worked. Use the feedback to improve your directions. Then follow the improved directions.

5. Switch roles with your partner, and repeat Steps 1–4.

Draw Conclusions

1. How did the feedback help you to improve your directions?

2. **Standards Link** How did your partner know how far and how fast to walk and where to turn? **S4P3**

3. **Inquiry Skill** Tell why your revised directions and a good experiment plan are examples of clear **communication**. **S4CS5a**

Step 2

Step 3

Independent Inquiry

Draw a map to your location. Trade maps with a new partner. **Compare** using a map to using written directions. **S4CS4b**

SCIENCE CONCEPTS
▶ how to define motion
▶ how to measure speed

Focus Skill **COMPARE AND CONTRAST**
Look for similarities and differences between motion and speed.

| alike | | different |

Changing Position

Where are you located right now? Are you *at* your desk? *Under* a light? To the *right* of a door, or *2 meters (about 6 ft) away from* the board? Words such as these describe your position. **Position** is the location of an object.

Every object has a position. The position of your nose is the center of your face. How would you describe the position of the doorway in your classroom? These positions don't change.

But sometimes an object's position does change. When it does, the object is in motion. **Motion** is a change of position of an object.

There are many kinds of motion. You can walk forward or backward. An elevator goes up and down. A pendulum swings from side to side. Things may move quickly or slowly. They may follow a straight, curved, or circular path. But whenever something moves, its position changes.

◀ The soccer players are in constant motion. Their positions are always changing.

The still pictures don't show the actual motion of the boats, but you can tell that the boats moved. How do you know? Without even thinking about it, you interpret an object's change of position as motion. ▶

In the boat race pictures, have the boats in the second picture moved from where they were in the first picture?

You can tell that the boats have moved, because their positions have changed. In the first picture, the boats were close to the docks. They were to the right of the man with the flag. In the second picture, the boats have moved past the man with the flag. The docks can't be seen anymore.

You sensed the boats' motion by looking at the shore and assuming it was still. In other words, you used the shore as your *frame of reference.* Relative to the shore, the boats have moved.

You can change your frame of reference. You might say you're not moving when you're sitting at your school desk. But change your frame of reference to the solar system. Now you realize that you're spinning and moving around the sun with Earth. You're moving at about 1000 kilometers per hour (600 mi/hr)!

COMPARE AND CONTRAST

How are the boat and the shore different frames of reference for the rowers?

209

Measuring Motion

How fast can you run? If you run faster than your friend, your speed is greater. **Speed** tells you how the position of an object changes during a certain amount of time.

You can use words like *fast* and *slow* to describe speed. Fast-moving objects change their position quickly. Slow-moving objects change their position slowly. But you can be more exact if you use numbers and units, such as 10 meters per second or 5 miles per hour.

To find an object's speed, you need to measure two things. You need to measure distance. This distance is the change in the object's position. You also need to measure the time it takes the object to move through the distance.

Once you have both the distance and time measurements, you can find the object's speed with this formula:

speed = distance ÷ time

In other words, find speed by dividing the movement distance by the time it takes to move that distance.

For example, suppose you're going by car to a campground for a vacation. You travel 225 kilometers in 3 hours. You can find your speed this way:

225 km ÷ 3 hr = 75 km/hr

So, speed tells you how far an object can move in a certain amount of time.

◀ In a close race, times can be nearly the same. Judges use precise stopwatches to measure time in tenths or hundredths of a second to determine who is fastest.

To know speed, you must know two other things—distance and time. In a race, the distance is the same for all the runners, but their times vary.

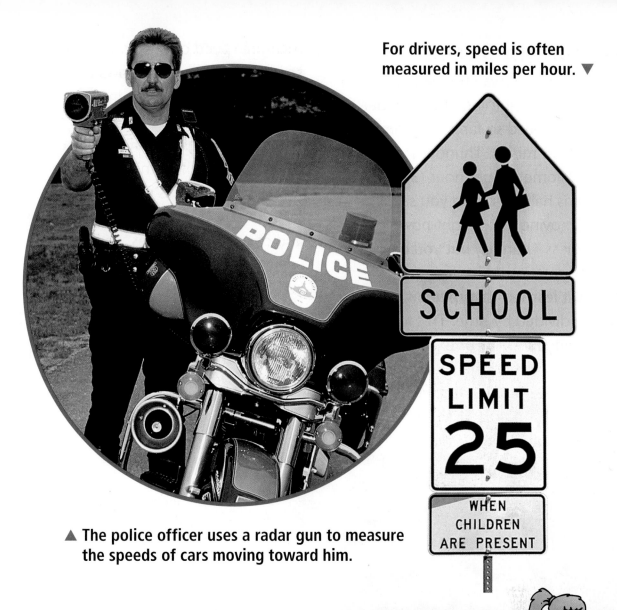

For drivers, speed is often measured in miles per hour. ▼

▲ The police officer uses a radar gun to measure the speeds of cars moving toward him.

Suppose a certain insect moves 100 centimeters per second (40 in./sec). This means that in 1 second, it can travel 100 centimeters (40 in.). Does that seem fast? It is fast, for an insect. An insect that moves this fast probably has wings!

Speed tells you only how quickly or slowly an object moves. It doesn't tell you the direction of the motion.

COMPARE AND CONTRAST

Which travels faster—a bicycle that travels 24 kilometers in 1 hour or a bicycle that travels 48 kilometers in 2 hours?

Insta-Lab

Fast Walk, Slow Walk

Compare walking speeds. Mark off a distance of at least 10 m. Walk that distance twice while measuring the time. Cover the distance first in 10 seconds and then in 15 seconds. How do you determine how quickly you need to walk?

211

Comparing Speeds

Suppose you're watching a horse race between Lightning and Thunder. Lightning's speed so far is 55 kilometers per hour (34 mi/hr). Thunder's speed so far is 60 kilometers per hour (37 mi/hr). The race is half over. Can you say which horse is moving faster right now? You might guess Thunder, but you need more information to be sure.

You just learned that speed is total distance divided by time. This formula gives *average* speed. For example, you learned how to find the average speed during a three-hour car trip. You can also measure speed over a shorter time. The speedometer of a car shows the car's speed moment by moment.

Now let's go back to the horse race. Thunder has a greater average speed so far. However, Lightning could be moving faster at this moment. To be sure, you have to watch the race closely and compare the horses' positions. If Lightning is catching up with Thunder, you know Lightning is running faster now.

 **COMPARE AND CONTRAST**

How is speed at one moment different from average speed?

Can you tell from the pictures whether the horse in front was running faster? Explain.

Displaying Data About Speed

To compare speeds, it is often helpful to display data about speed in tables or graphs. For example, the table on this page gives world-record speeds for different kinds of vehicles. Notice how the table is organized. The category, or type, of vehicle is listed in the first column. The specific vehicles and their speeds are given in the second column.

Which type of graph would you choose to compare speeds? A bar graph is best. Bar graphs are used to display data in categories. The bar graph below compares the average speeds of different kinds of animals, including humans. By comparing the lengths of the bars, you can easily see that the cheetah has the fastest speed.

Focus Skill COMPARE AND CONTRAST

Explain the similarities and differences between using a table to compare speed data and using a bar graph.

World's Fastest Vehicles	
Car	*Thrust SSC*, 1228 km/hr (763 mi/hr)
Plane	*X43-A*, more than 10,800 km/hr (6710 mi/hr)
Boat	*Spirit of Australia*, 511 km/hr (317 mi/hr)

▲ This table shows world-record speeds for cars, planes, and boats.

Math in Science
Interpret Data

Assuming that a human being could run at a steady sprinting rate, how far would the human travel in 3 hours?

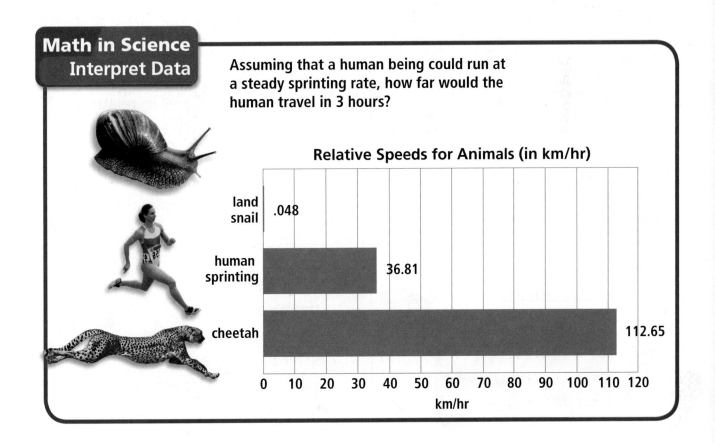

Relative Speeds for Animals (in km/hr)

	km/hr
land snail	.048
human sprinting	36.81
cheetah	112.65

Essential Question

How is motion described and measured?

In this lesson, you learned how to describe an object's motion and how to use distance and time measurements to calculate its speed. You also learned how to use tables and graphs to compare the speeds of objects.

1. **(Focus Skill) COMPARE AND CONTRAST** Draw and complete a graphic organizer to compare and contrast the motion of a person who is driving a car with the motion of a person who is walking on the sidewalk. **S4P3**

    [alike]——[different]

2. **SUMMARIZE** Use lesson vocabulary to write a lesson summary. **S4P3**

3. **DRAW CONCLUSIONS** A top spins in place without changing its location. Is it moving? Tell why or why not. **S4P3**

4. **VOCABULARY** Write one question for each of the terms *position, motion, speed.* Trade questions with a partner, and answer your partner's questions. **S4P3**

5. **Critical Thinking** What does it mean to say that the average speed of a car is 35 miles per hour? **S4P3**

CRCT Practice

6. What is the speed of a dog that runs 9 meters in 3 seconds?

    A 3 meters per second

    B 9 meters per second

    C 12 meters per second

    D 27 meters per second **S4P3**

7. A person riding a snowmobile down a slope moves in relation to the trees. Which term BEST describes the trees?

    A speed   **C** position

    B distance   **D** frame of reference **S4P3**

8. Describe the measurements you would need to make in order to find an object's speed at a given point in time. **S4P3**

The **Big Idea**

Make Connections

 Writing ELA4W2

Informational Writing

Write a paragraph about how you experience motion. Describe examples of each of these kinds of motion: forward, backward, back-and-forth, side-to-side, and rotating.

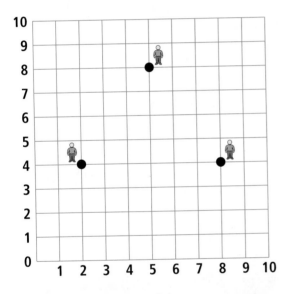

 Math M4G3b, G1a

Ordered Pairs

The points on the coordinate grid show where three different students are standing. When the points are connected, they form a triangle. Identify the ordered pair for each point. Then classify the triangle by measuring and comparing its angles.

 Social Studies IPS 1, 11

Multicultural Studies

Compare the numbers of bicycles and cars in other countries with the numbers of these vehicles in the United States. Write a brief report explaining your findings.

 For more links and activities, go to **www.hspscience.com**

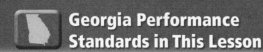
Content

S4P3b Using different size objects, observe how force affects speed and motion.

S4P3c Explain what happens to the speed or direction of an object when a greater force than the initial one is applied.

Characteristics of Science

S4CS3 **S4CS5b**

Georgia Fast Fact

Forces in Action

These cyclists are racing around a track known as a velodrome. The sides of the velodrome are angled, which changes the forces acting on the cyclists. The angled sides allow them to go faster than 50 kilometers per hour (30 mi/hr)! In the Investigate, you'll see how a force changes the motion of an object.

LESSON 2

Essential Question

How Do Forces Affect Motion?

Stone Mountain velodrome from the 1996 Summer Olympics

velocity [vuh•LAHS•uh•tee] The measure of the speed and direction of motion of an object (p. 220)

acceleration [ak•sel•er•AY•shuhn] Any change in the speed or direction of an object's motion (p. 221)

force [FAWRS] A pull or push of any kind (p. 222)

inertia [in•ER•shuh] The property of matter that keeps an object at rest or keeps it moving in a straight line (p. 224)

Which Way the Ball Blows

Guided Inquiry

Start with Questions

The whale thrusts the performer into the air with great force.

- In which direction does the performer move?
- How does the performer's speed change?

Investigate to find out. Then read to find out more.

Prepare to Investigate

Inquiry Skill Tip

During an investigation, scientists collect data by making measurements. When you measure an object, you compare it to a standard measure, such as a centimeter or a liter.

Materials

- ruler
- straw
- table tennis ball
- masking tape, 10-cm strip

Make an Observation Chart

Step	Observations
#2	
#3	
#4	

Follow This Procedure

1 Put the strip of tape on a table or your desktop. Place the table tennis ball at one end of the tape.

2 Blow through the straw onto the ball. Blow gently and steadily. Make the ball roll along the tape. Observe whether the ball rolls in the direction in which you blow.

3 Return the table tennis ball to the end of the tape. Blow on the ball at a right angle to the tape. Observe whether the ball rolls in the direction in which you blow.

4 Roll the ball gently. Blow on the ball in a direction different from where the ball is rolling. Observe what happens.

Draw Conclusions

1. In what direction did you blow to make the ball roll along the tape? To make it roll at right angles to the tape?

2. **Standards Link** What did you observe when you blew on the moving ball in Step 4? **S4P3c**

3. **Inquiry Skill** What tools could you use to measure the motion of the ball? **S4CS3**

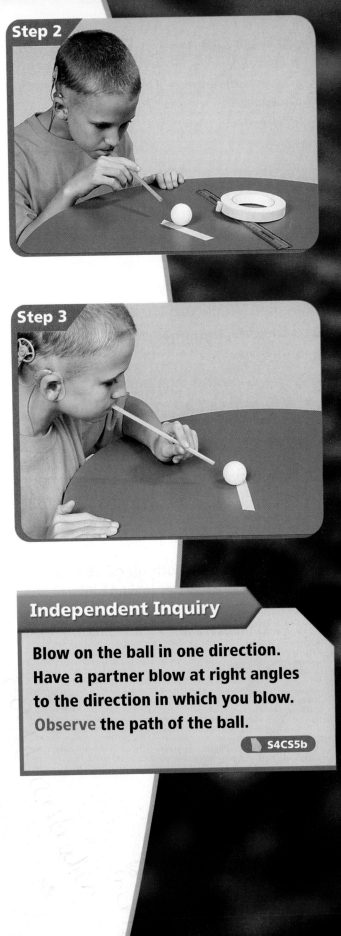

Step 2

Step 3

Independent Inquiry

Blow on the ball in one direction. Have a partner blow at right angles to the direction in which you blow. Observe the path of the ball.

S4CS5b

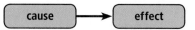
VOCABULARY
velocity p. 220
acceleration p. 221
force p. 222
inertia p. 224

SCIENCE CONCEPTS
▶ how velocity relates to acceleration
▶ how forces cause acceleration

Focus Skill **CAUSE AND EFFECT**
Look for ways in which forces cause acceleration.

cause ➔ effect

Velocity

If you were asked to describe the motion of a bird, a bike, or a train, you'd probably tell how fast it was going. You'd probably also mention its direction. When you tell both the speed and the direction of an object, you give its **velocity**.

To describe the direction part of velocity, you can use compass directions or words such as *right, left, up,* and *down.* For example, suppose you're riding a bicycle at 30 kilometers per hour (19 mi/hr) toward the west. Your speed is 30 kilometers per hour. But your velocity is 30 kilometers per hour, west.

Two objects with the same speed have different velocities if they are moving in different directions. While your velocity is 30 kilometers per hour, west, your friend's velocity might be 30 kilometers per hour, north.

▼ Velocity includes both speed and direction. A rocket's velocity is at least 11 kilometers per second (7 mi/sec), up. These riders' velocity is 24 kilometers per hour (15 mi/hr), east.

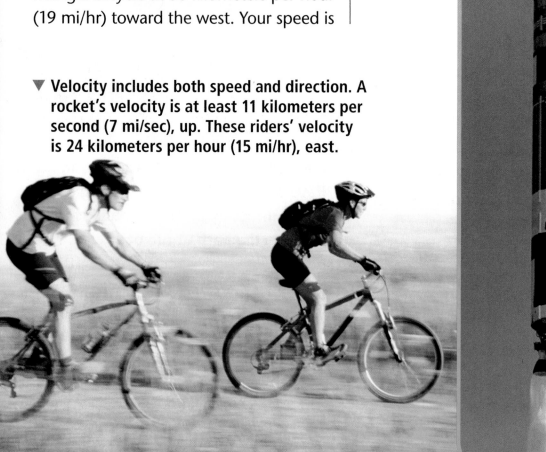

▼ Acceleration may be a change in speed, direction, or both. This boat is changing direction. This skier is changing both speed and direction.

Changing Velocity

Like your bicycle, objects don't always move steadily in one direction. They stop and start, slow down and speed up, and turn. These changes are examples of acceleration. **Acceleration** is any change in the speed or direction of an object's motion. So acceleration is any change of velocity.

Think about what happens to your bicycle when you ride it. It accelerates when it speeds up and rolls away from a stop sign. It also accelerates when it slows to a stop at a stop sign. Slowing down is acceleration, just as speeding

up is. If the bicycle moves in a circle at a constant speed of 10 kilometers per hour (6 mi/hr), is it accelerating? Yes, it is. It is always turning in the circle—changing direction—so it is always accelerating.

You can measure acceleration. The larger the change in speed, the larger the acceleration. Getting a car up to top speed is a larger acceleration than doing so for your bicycle. Stopping a large jet plane that is moving at top speed is a larger acceleration than doing so for a car.

 **CAUSE AND EFFECT** What is one change that causes an acceleration?

More Force, More Acceleration

When forces push or pull in the same direction, they simply add up. Suppose you double the force on an object by pushing it twice as hard. Then you double its acceleration as well.

▲ The athletes push the sled, and it accelerates.

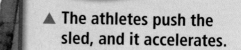

◀ More athletes push this sled with more force. Its acceleration is greater than that of the sled shown above.

Force and Acceleration

Push a door, and it moves. Pull the door, and it moves the other way. Pushes and pulls of all kinds are **forces**. Forces are measured in newtons (N).

Forces change motion. If a soccer ball is still, it stays still until a force moves it. If you kick the soccer ball, it keeps moving in the same direction until a force changes its motion. Any change of speed or direction requires a force. In other words, *forces cause acceleration.*

The direction in which an object moves depends on the direction of the force that is used on the object. You used a force on the table tennis ball in the Investigate. The ball rolled in the direction in which you blew.

What if there's more than one force? In that case, the forces work together. You saw this in the Independent Inquiry. The ball rolled in a direction between the direction of your force and the direction of your partner's force. Two forces of the same size but opposite in direction will cancel each other out. Forces that cancel each other out are called balanced forces.

▲ This sled is pulled by six dogs. The sled with more dogs is pulled harder. It accelerates more than the other sled.

◀ One dog pulls this sled.

For more links and animations, go to **www.hspscience.com**

How does the size of a force affect acceleration? If you tap a basketball with your finger, it may roll a little. You've used a small force. But if you kick the ball hard, it takes off. You've used a large force. A larger force results in a larger acceleration. For example, a windmill's blades are turned by the wind. A gentle breeze turns them slowly. A strong wind spins them so fast that they're a blur!

CAUSE AND EFFECT

What causes the speed or direction of objects to change?

Insta-Lab

Spring-Scale Follow the Leader

You will need a spring scale and a box. Hook the scale to the box. Drag the box. What happens when the scale shows a large reading? What happens when it reads zero?

Mass and Acceleration

Which would you rather move by pushing—a bicycle or a car? Pushing the bicycle would take much less force. You'd need to push the car much harder to get it moving.

The acceleration of an object depends on its mass. It takes more force to accelerate a large mass than to accelerate a small mass. This is because all matter has inertia. **Inertia** is the property of matter that keeps it moving in a straight line and keeps unmoving matter at rest. A truck has more inertia than a motorcycle. It needs a bigger engine, because more force is needed to get it moving quickly.

The more mass an object has, the more inertia it has. And the more inertia an object has, the harder it is to change its motion.

Focus Skill **CAUSE AND EFFECT** Why is it harder to get a loaded wheelbarrow moving than it is for an empty one?

Which ball accelerates more when you throw it—the basketball or the tennis ball? Why?

Momentum

Just as it's easier to push a bicycle than a car, it's easier to stop a bicycle than it is to stop a car when both are moving with the same velocity. *Momentum* is a property of motion that describes how hard it is to slow down or stop an object. Momentum also describes how an object will affect something that it bumps into. Momentum depends on both mass and velocity. You can find momentum by using this formula:

momentum = mass × velocity

In the example, the car has greater inertia because it has far greater mass than the bicycle. The car will be much harder to stop or slow down. Also, if the car bumps into something, it will cause more damage than the bicycle would.

Objects with different masses can have the same momentum if the object with less mass has a greater velocity. Consider two football players. One is big and heavy, and the other is small and light. Suppose the large player runs slowly and the smaller player runs quickly. Each player could be equally hard to stop. And each player could have an equally crushing effect on the other team!

Focus Skill **CAUSE AND EFFECT** What two factors determine an object's momentum?

A big truck moving at a fast speed has a lot of momentum. How much momentum does this small car have?

Essential Question

How do forces affect motion?

In this lesson, you learned that unbalanced forces cause objects to accelerate, or change their speed or direction. The greater the force acting on an object, the greater its acceleration. You also learned that an object's mass affects the amount of force that is needed to change its motion.

1. **CAUSE AND EFFECT** Draw and complete a graphic organizer in order to tell how a force can change the motion of an object. **S4P3b, c**

2. SUMMARIZE Write a summary of this lesson. Begin with this sentence: *I use forces every day.* **S4P3b, c**

3. DRAW CONCLUSIONS Describe the acceleration of a downhill skier. **S4P3**

4. VOCABULARY Describe an everyday situation in which you might notice forces. Use the terms *velocity, acceleration, force,* and *inertia.* **S4P3b, c**

5. Critical Thinking A polar bear walks toward the North Pole. It walks 15 kilometers in 1 hour. What is its velocity? **S4P3**

CRCT Practice

6. A constant force of 5 N is applied to an object resting on a flat surface, causing it to accelerate to the right. A force of 10 N is then applied in the opposite direction. In which direction does the object now move?

A up   **C** right
B down   **D** left   **S4P3c**

7. The acceleration of an object depends on the size of the force used on it as well as the object's

A color   **C** temperature
B volume   **D** mass   **S4P3b**

8. A car is moving in a straight line at a constant 40 km/hr. What about the car changes?

 The Big Idea

A its speed   **C** its position
B its velocity   **D** its acceleration **S4P3**

Writing — ELA4W2

Narrative Writing

Write an action-packed adventure story that describes motion and uses the vocabulary from this lesson.

Math — M4N4b

Compare Accelerations

A car goes from 0 to 100 kilometers per hour in 10 seconds. Another car slows from 100 to 0 kilometers per hour in 10 seconds. Compare these accelerations.

Social Studies — IPS 11

History of Science

Use library resources to learn more about Isaac Newton. Explain what Newton's second law of motion is and how it relates to the ideas in this lesson.

For more links and activities, go to **www.hspscience.com**

FORCES IN FOOTBALL

at Georgia Tech

What does science have to do with first downs and field goals? Every football play involves force, speed, and motion—not only for the ball, but for the players, too. The Georgia Tech Yellow Jackets have won four national titles and 15 conference championships, all with the help of science.

The Yellow Jackets put science to work when they kick the ball. A kicker applies a force to the ball. The force is greater than the ball's inertia. The greater the force, the faster the ball travels. Direction makes a difference, too. A kick that sends the ball high into the air makes the ball travel a shorter distance than a long, low kick does. The kick is not the only force that affects the ball. Once the ball is in the air, gravity pulls it toward Earth. Contact between the ball and the air slows the ball's forward motion.

The Georgia Tech quarterback (in gold) is about to apply a force to the ball to set it in motion.

It's harder to move a big, heavy player than a small, light one. This is why teams line up their biggest players in front.

Players' Inertia

Before a play begins, players from opposing teams line up and face each other. The players in the front line of each team are called linemen. Have you ever wondered why the biggest football players are usually linemen? The answer has to do with inertia. The greater the mass of an object, the greater the force needed to overcome its inertia. This means that when linemen collide, the heavier one can push the lighter one back and out of the way. Making use of science can result in another big play for Georgia Tech!

Strong forces act on players during a game. Protective gear helps lessen these forces.

Safety on the Field

As play starts, the linemen crash into one another. One big lineman speeds toward a running player and brings him to the ground with a forceful thump. Force, speed, and motion are things players apply to win games. However, force, speed, and motion can also bring injury to the players. To absorb some of the forces and reduce the risk of injury, players wear safety equipment. Gear such as helmets, shoulder pads, and pads for the hips, knees, and thighs all use science to help players stay healthy.

✍️ Think and Write

① Picture a player throwing the football down the field and another player catching it. Describe the forces that act on the ball. **S4P3d**

② Suppose a 250-pound Georgia Tech player and a 200-pound player from the opposing team are running toward each other at the same speed. What will happen when the players hit head-on? **S4P3b**

Georgia Performance Standards in This Lesson

Content

S4P3d Demonstrate the effect of gravitational force on the motion of an object.

Characteristics of Science

S4CS8a

Essential Question

How Does Gravity Affect Motion?

Georgia Fast Fact

What Goes Up . . .

The same force that pulls sky divers to Earth keeps planets in their orbits around the sun. In the Investigate, you'll learn how an object can travel a circular path like the orbits of the planets.

230

gravity [GRAV•ih•tee] The force of attraction between Earth and other objects (p. 235)

gravitation [grav•ih•TAY•shuhn] A force that acts between any two objects and pulls them together (p. 235)

weight [WAYT] A measure of the gravitational force acting on an object (p. 236)

friction [FRIK•shuhn] A force that resists motion between objects that are touching (p. 237)

231

Making Circular Motion

Start with Questions

This girl has been whirling an object attached to a string over her head to model how planets and other objects orbit the sun.

- In what direction did the girl pull the string to make the object move in a circle?

- What happens when she lets go?

Investigate to find out. Then read to find out more.

Prepare to Investigate

Inquiry Skill Tip

When you experiment, you carry out a fair test of a hypothesis. In order to compare the results from repeated experiments, you should test and gather data in the same way each time.

Materials

- safety goggles
- rubber stopper
- string, 1-m length
- tape
- cardboard tube

Make an Observation Chart

How the String Is Pulled

Follow This Procedure

1 CAUTION: **Put on safety goggles.** Tie the stopper to the end of the string.

2 Put tape over the string on the stopper to hold the string in place. Be sure the stopper is securely fastened. Thread the string through the tube.

3 Go outdoors. Stand where you have a clear space 3 meters around you in all directions.

4 Holding the string, move the tube to whirl the stopper in a circular path over your head. Be sure to hold the string securely! The circular path of the stopper should be level with the ground.

5 **Observe** the direction in which you are pulling the string.

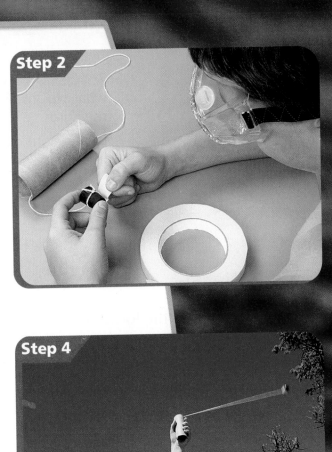
Step 2

Step 4

Draw Conclusions

1. In what direction did you pull the string to keep the stopper moving in a circle?

2. Standards Link What would have happened if the string had broken? `S4P3d`

3. Inquiry Skill What materials would you need for an **experiment** to test the hypothesis that spinning the stopper faster requires a stronger pull? `S4CS8a`

Independent Inquiry

Try whirling the stopper in an up-and-down circle in front of you. Observe the direction in which you pull. Compare it with the direction in Step 5. `S4CS8a`

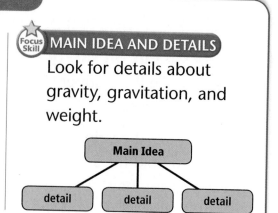

S4P3d

VOCABULARY
gravity p. 235
gravitation p. 235
weight p. 236
friction p. 237

SCIENCE CONCEPTS
▶ what weight measures
▶ how weight differs from mass

Focus Skill MAIN IDEA AND DETAILS
Look for details about gravity, gravitation, and weight.

Natural Forces

Every day, you use the force of your muscles to sit, stand, and walk. What other forces do you use every day? You know how magnets interact. You also know about electric charges. You use electric devices and machines with magnets all the time.

The force between electric charges is one of the most important in nature. It holds together tiny particles of matter.

These particles are so small that you don't see how electricity affects their motion.

You do see the result of electric force when it pulls and pushes charged objects. For example, you've probably seen a balloon stick to a wall after you rubbed it against fabric or your hair.

Focus Skill MAIN IDEA AND DETAILS

Give an example of how you used the force of your muscles today.

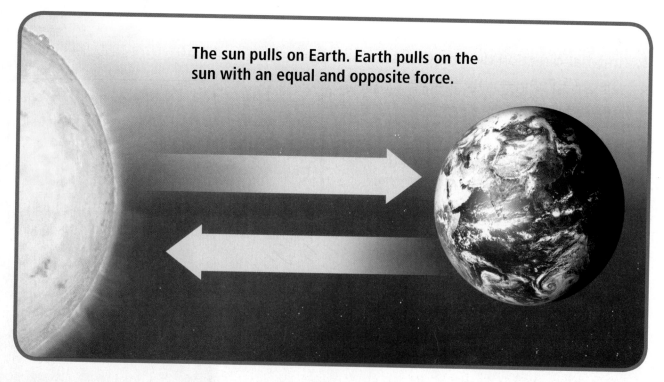

The sun pulls on Earth. Earth pulls on the sun with an equal and opposite force.

Gravity

Besides the force of your own muscles, gravity is probably the force you notice most. **Gravity** is the force that pulls things toward Earth. If you toss a ball upward, gravity pulls it back down to the ground.

Gravity is an effect of gravitation. **Gravitation** is a force that acts between all masses and causes them to attract one another. It acts everywhere, all the time. Gravitation helps hold the moon in its orbit around Earth. It pulls the moon and Earth toward each other. This pull prevents the moon from flying off in a straight line because of its inertia. It is similar to the pull that held the stopper in its path in the Investigate.

Gravitation also holds Earth in its orbit around the sun. The other planets, too, are held in their orbits by gravitation.

The larger and closer two masses are, the more gravitation affects them. Sometimes the force is very weak, but it's always there. Earth's gravitation affects you more than any other object's, because Earth is so large and so close to you.

 **MAIN IDEA AND DETAILS**

What keeps the moon in a circular path?

▼ Gravity is the force that pulls you toward Earth. Roller coasters use this force to provide thrills.

Weight

How can you measure the force of gravity on an object? Simple—just weigh the object on a scale.

An object's **weight** is the gravitational force acting on it. Because it is a force, weight is measured in newtons (N). One newton is about the weight of an apple, or just under a quarter of a pound.

Don't confuse weight with mass—they aren't the same thing. Mass is the amount of matter in an object. It's measured on a balance, not on a scale. The unit of mass is the gram.

Your weight is the gravitational force acting on you. So your weight would change if you were away from Earth's gravity. The moon's gravitational force is less than Earth's. On the moon, you would weigh only one-sixth of what you weigh on Earth. Your mass, however, is the same wherever you are.

Focus Skill MAIN IDEA AND DETAILS

Is the doctor measuring this girl's weight or mass? Explain your answer.

The child weighs 271 newtons (61 lb). She's being weighed on a doctor's scale. The bear cub is much lighter. A different kind of scale is being used to measure the force of gravity acting on the cub.

236

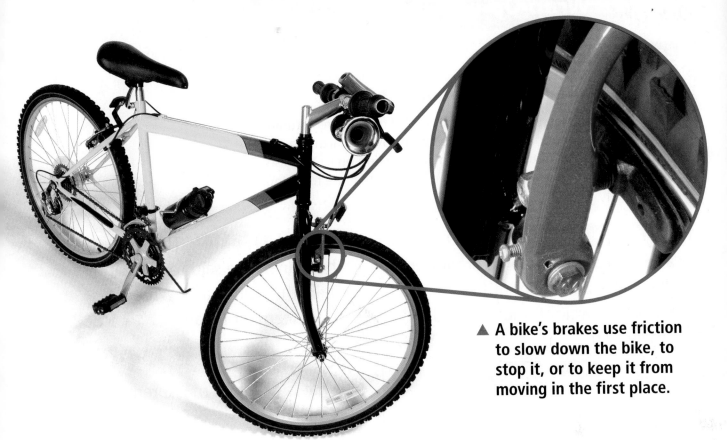

▲ A bike's brakes use friction to slow down the bike, to stop it, or to keep it from moving in the first place.

Friction

Have you ever heard tires squeal when a car stopped suddenly? That sound is caused by another familiar force—friction. **Friction** is a force that resists the motion of objects, relative to each other, when the objects are touching. Friction changes energy of motion to heat. Over time, friction slows down motion and stops it. Friction is measured in newtons, just like other forces.

The force of friction is always present when one surface touches another. Often, friction is useful. For example, your bike slows down when you apply the brakes. The brakes are rubber pads that create friction when they press against a wheel. The friction slows the wheel and finally stops it.

Sports shoes have rubber soles that increase friction. This helps keep you from slipping while you run and play.

MAIN IDEA AND DETAILS

If your friend pushes you to the right, in what direction does friction act?

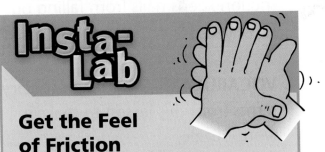

Get the Feel of Friction
Rub your hands together. Put a drop of baby oil or hand lotion on your hands, and rub them together again. Now put on some rubber gloves, and rub your hands together. How is the friction different each time?

How does gravity affect motion?

In this lesson, you learned that gravitation and friction are natural forces that affect motion. Gravity pulls things toward Earth. An object's weight is a measure of the gravitational force acting on it. You also learned that friction resists the motion of objects that are touching.

1. (Focus Skill) **MAIN IDEA AND DETAILS** Draw and complete a graphic organizer that gives details about the following: weight, friction, and gravitation. **S4P3d**

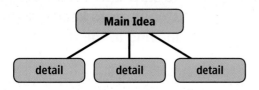

2. SUMMARIZE Use your completed graphic organizer to write a lesson summary. **S4P3d**

3. DRAW CONCLUSIONS Explain how friction keeps nails from falling out of walls. **S4P3**

4. VOCABULARY Use the vocabulary terms from this lesson to make a word puzzle. **S4P3**

5. Critical Thinking The moon and the planets are said to constantly "fall" through space. What does this statement mean? **S4P3d**

CRCT Practice

6. What is weight a measurement of?

  A electricity   **C** gravity

  B friction   **D** acceleration **S4P3d**

7. Which factor would increase the gravitational attraction between two objects?

  A more mass

  B faster speed

  C higher velocity

  D greater separation **S4P3d**

8. Suppose you are carrying out an investigation in which you hold a toy car at the top of a ramp and then let go. You are careful not to push the car. Why does the car roll down the ramp? What other force affects the car's motion? **S4P3d**

The Big Idea

Writing

ELA4W2

Informational Writing

This boy is putting oil on the chain and gears of his bike to make his ride easier. Research and then write about a product that either reduces or increases friction. Explain how the product works and why people need it.

Math

M4A1c

Solve a Problem

You push an eraser forward with a force of 2 newtons. The eraser doesn't move. How great is the frictional force acting on the eraser?

Music

Make a Glass Sing

The friction between a wet finger and the rim of a thin-walled glass can make a pleasing sound. See if you can make music this way. Be careful! Hold the glass with one hand while you run a finger around its rim.

For more links and activities, go to **www.hspscience.com**

SCIENCE SOARS
AT THE OLYMPICS

To train for the Winter Olympics, athlete Chris Soule stands at the top of a long hill holding a small sled. He springs forward, jumps on the sled, and races down the hill as fast as he can. Soule competes in a kind of Olympic sled race called *skeleton*. To compete in skeleton takes speed, strength, and science. That's right—science.

Chris Soule races down a hill on his sled to train for the Winter Olympics.

Shaving Time

The athlete who finishes with the fastest time wins the race and the gold medal. "Some of the sports events are won by one-hundredth or even one-thousandth of a second," Peter Davis told *Weekly Reader.* Davis is the head of coaching and sport sciences for the United States Olympic Committee.

Racing with Science

At the U.S. Olympic Training Facility in Lake Placid, New York, scientists called biomechanists (by•oh•MEH•kuhn•ists) use computers to help skeleton racers.

The scientists videotape the athletes during their push starts. The tapes are fed into a computer. The scientists can then study every movement and every angle of the athletes' bodies. They decide, for example, whether the athlete is leaning too far forward at the start.

MORE SPORTS SCIENCE

- Uniforms are being made with new kinds of slick fabrics that help speed skaters perform better and stay cooler.
- Blood tests can show how much lactic acid is in an athlete's blood. Too much lactic acid makes the muscles work harder than they should.
- Skiers practice in wind tunnels that show them how to go faster.

Virtual Training

Another training tool that's being used more and more is virtual reality. "We can set up an athletic event on a computer," Davis said. "An athlete uses video goggles to see the event and react to what is happening." By using virtual reality, athletes who compete in winter sports can train throughout the year.

✏️ Think and Write

1. Why are even small improvements important for some sports? **S4P3**

2. How is videotape used to help racers? **S4CS8c**

Find out more. Log on to **www.hspscience.com**

241

CHAPTER 5

Wrap-Up

▶ Visual Summary

Tell how each picture helps explain the **Big Idea**.

The Big Idea Forces act on and change the motion of objects in measurable ways.

Lesson 1 ▶ S4P3

Motion

Motion is the change in position of an object relative to a frame of reference. Speed tells you how quickly the position of an object changes.

Lesson 2 ▶ S4P3b, c

Velocity and Acceleration

Velocity includes both speed and direction. Forces cause objects to accelerate, or change their velocity. An object's mass affects how quickly it accelerates when a force acts on it.

Lesson 3 ▶ S4P3d

Natural Forces

Gravitation is a force that acts between all masses, causing them to attract one another. The combination of inertia and gravitation keeps the planets in their orbits. Gravity pulls objects toward Earth. Gravity affects the motion of objects. Weight is a measure of gravity.

Show What You Know

Chapter Writing Activity

Write a Script/Informational Writing

Take on the role of a sportscaster. Choose a sport, and write a script that describes the action during a game. Include the following concepts in your script: force, velocity, acceleration, inertia, and momentum.

ELA4W2

Georgia Performance Task

Experiment with Motion

Use a ramp and toy cars to investigate how gravity and mass affect motion. Use a stack of books and a board to make a ramp. Place a catch box at the bottom of the ramp. Release the car, and time how long it takes the car to travel to the bottom of the ramp. You may change the height of the ramp and use cars of different mass, but make sure you change only one variable at a time. Record your data in a table. Graph your data, and share your graphs with your classmates during a brief presentation.

S4P3b, d

Vocabulary Review

Use the terms below to complete the sentences. The page numbers tell you where to look in the chapter if you need help.

position p. 208   force p. 222
motion p. 208   inertia p. 224
speed p. 210   gravitation p. 235
velocity p. 220   weight p. 236
acceleration p. 221   friction p. 237

1. The force that slows or stops the motion of objects, relative to each other, when the objects are touching is _____.   **S4P3**

2. A push or pull measured in newtons is a _____.   **S4P3b**

3. The measurement of the gravity acting on an object is the object's _____.   **S4P3d**

4. A change in velocity is _____.   **S4P3**

5. A change in position is _____.   **S4P3**

6. The property that describes an object's resistance to changing its motion is _____.   **S4P3b**

7. The force of attraction that exists between any two masses anywhere in the universe is _____.   **S4P3d**

8. Speed and direction taken together are _____.   **S4P3**

9. The distance an object travels divided by the time it takes to travel is its _____.   **S4P3**

10. An object's location is its _____.   **S4P3**

Check Understanding

Write the letter of the best choice.

11. **MAIN IDEA AND DETAILS** What force holds the moon in its orbit around Earth? (p. 235)   **S4P3d**
    A friction   **C** position
    B gravitation   **D** weight

12. If an object has a large mass on Earth, what else does it have a lot of? (pp. 224, 236)   **S4P3b, d**
    A inertia and volume
    B weight and inertia
    C weight and speed
    D weight and volume

13. **CAUSE AND EFFECT** If you increase the force on an object, what else increases? (p. 222)   **S4P3c**
    A acceleration
    B gravity
    C inertia
    D mass

Use the picture to answer 14 and 15.

14. A dial in the picture tells you how many kilometers per hour the car is going. What does this measure? (p. 210) **S4P3**

   A acceleration   **C** velocity

   B speed   **D** weight

15. What information about the car can you find by using the dial and compass together? (p. 220) **S4P3**

   A its acceleration   **C** its speed

   B its motion   **D** its velocity

16. What force is shown by Arrow 2? (p. 235) **S4P3d**

   A electric force   **C** gravity

   B magnetic force **D** friction

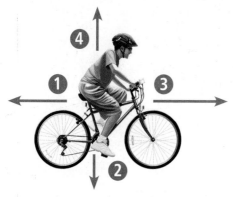

Inquiry Skills

17. How do you **observe** friction when you erase a pencil mark? **S4CS5**

18. A girl pulls a wagon by applying a force to it. What other force can you **infer** acts on the wagon in the opposite direction? **S4CS5**

Critical Thinking

19. Can an object that moves at a constant speed be accelerating? Explain your answer. **S4P3**

20. A truck, a car, and a bicycle are driving away from a stoplight. The truck uses a big engine for this acceleration. A car uses a smaller engine, and the bicycle rider uses his muscles. Why does each vehicle require a different amount of force to accelerate? Which vehicle will be moving the fastest after one minute if the same force is used to push each one? Why? **S4P3b, c**

The **Big** Idea

Georgia Performance Standards in This Chapter

Content

S4P3 Students will demonstrate the relationship between the application of a force and the resulting change in position and motion on an object.

S4P3a

This chapter also addresses these co-requisite standards:

Characteristics of Science

S4CS1 Students will be aware of the importance of curiosity, honesty, openness, and skepticism. . . .

S4CS1c

S4CS5 Students will communicate scientific ideas and activities clearly.

S4CS5c

S4CS6 Students will question scientific claims and arguments. . . .

S4CS6b

S4CS7 Students will be familiar with the character of scientific knowledge. . . .

S4CS7b

S4CS8 Students will understand important features of the process of scientific inquiry.

S4CS8a, d

What's the Big Idea?

The six main kinds of simple machines make work easier by changing the force needed to move objects.

Essential Questions

Go online for student eBook
www.hspscience.com

Chattahoochee River Park in Roswell

Dear Matt,

My folks and I spent the day fishing on the Chattahoochee.

Dad never misses a chance to talk about his favorite subject—science. He told me that my rod and reel are actually machines. I always thought that machines were big and complex, like cars. Since Dad's a teacher, I guess I had better listen to him!

Your best friend,
Micah

What kinds of machines did Micah learn about? How does this relate to the **Big Idea?**

Georgia Performance Standards in This Lesson

Content

S4P3a Identify simple machines and explain their uses (lever, pulley, wedge, inclined plane, screw, wheel and axle).

Characteristics of Science

S4CS8a

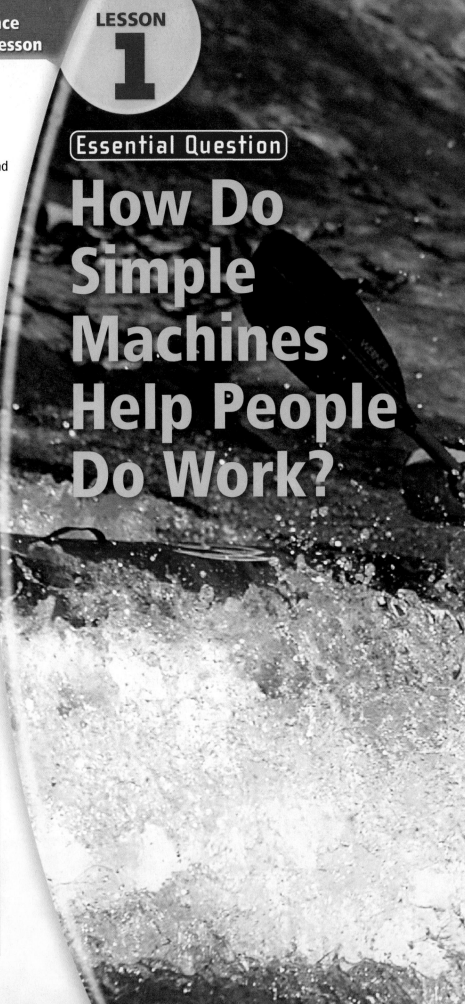

LESSON

1

Essential Question

How Do Simple Machines Help People Do Work?

▶ Georgia Fast Fact

Whitewater Paddling

This person is paddling a kayak, which is a light, narrow boat that is similar to a canoe. A kayaker uses a special paddle with a blade on either end to steer and propel the craft. The paddle is a simple machine. Although you may not go kayaking, you do use simple machines for many different tasks. In the Investigate, you'll explore the forces that act on one kind of simple machine.

The Chattooga River in northeast Georgia

work [WERK] The use of force to move an object over a distance (p. 252)

simple machine [SIM•puhl muh•SHEEN] A machine with few or no moving parts that you apply just one force to (p. 253)

lever [LEV•er] A simple machine made of a bar that pivots on a fixed point (p. 254)

fulcrum [FUHL•kruhm] The fixed point on a lever (p. 254)

249

Up and Down

Start with Questions

These circus acrobats are using a kind of seesaw called a teeterboard. Notice that one of the men is flying through the air.

- What will happen when the man lands on the raised side of the seesaw?

- How can we identify the forces that act on a seesaw?

Investigate to find out. Then read to find out more.

Prepare to Investigate

Inquiry Skill Tip

When you use space relationships, you look at how objects move and how they change positions in relation to one another. You also watch for changes in size. In this Investigate, you'll compare the changes in length that occur in two rubber bands.

Materials

- tape
- safety goggles
- 2 rubber bands
- 2 wooden rulers

Make a Data Table

Mark Where Force Is Applied	Length of Rubber Band Closest to 0 cm (cm)	Length of Rubber Band Closest to 30 cm (cm)
15-cm mark		
17-cm mark		
19-cm mark		
21-cm mark		

Follow This Procedure

1 **CAUTION: Put on safety goggles.** Work in groups of three. Tape a rubber band 2 cm from each end of one ruler.

2 One person should hook a finger through each rubber band and lift the ruler. This person should pull enough to keep the ruler level while a second person presses down on the 15-cm mark.

3 The third person should measure the length of each rubber band. Record your observations and measurements.

4 Repeat Steps 2 and 3, with the second person pressing on the 17-cm, 19-cm, and 21-cm marks.

Draw Conclusions

1. What happened as the second person pressed farther from the ruler's center?

2. **Standards Link** How do you account for the changes you observed? S4P3

3. **Inquiry Skill** Sometimes scientists can learn about what they can't see by watching how it affects other things. For example, the ruler affected the rubber bands. How did you use space relationships to observe what was happening to the ruler and rubber bands? S4CS8a

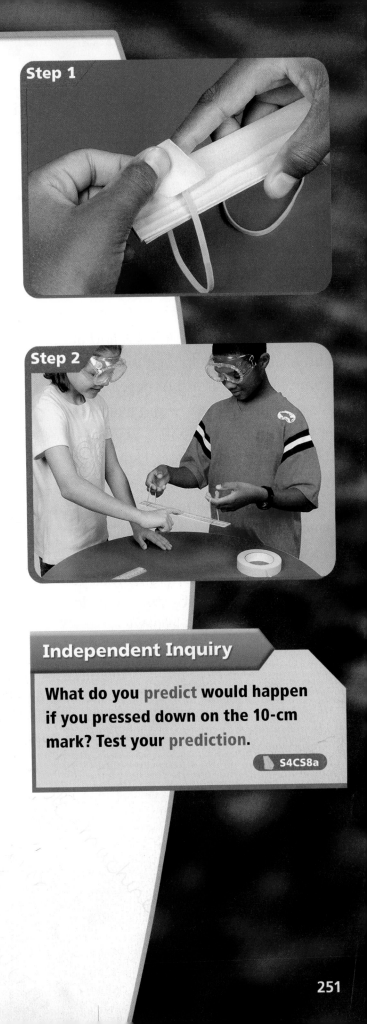

Step 1

Step 2

Independent Inquiry

What do you predict would happen if you pressed down on the 10-cm mark? Test your prediction.
S4CS8a

VOCABULARY
work p. 252
simple machine p. 253
lever p. 254
fulcrum p. 254

SCIENCE CONCEPTS
▶ what a scientist means by *work*
▶ what a simple machine is
▶ how a lever changes the way work is done

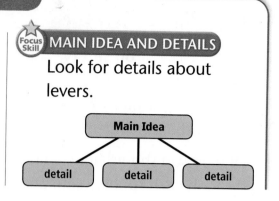

MAIN IDEA AND DETAILS
Look for details about levers.

Work and Simple Machines

You do schoolwork in class and at home. You may help with work at home by baby-sitting or mowing lawns. For most people, these are examples of work. But to a scientist, *work* has a different meaning. **Work** is the use of force to move an object over a distance.

When you do homework, you have to concentrate. But to a scientist, the only work you might do is lifting a pencil.

Imagine you're pushing with all your might on a door that's stuck. If it doesn't move, you're not doing work.

For work to be done, an object also has to move in the direction of the force applied to it. If you lift a box, you apply a force upward and the box moves up. That's work.

But what if you then carry the box across the room? Your arms are lifting up, but the box is moving sideways. So, your arms aren't doing any work on the box, no matter how tired they might get.

The girl uses an upward force on the dog, and the dog moves up. The girl is having fun but is doing work, too.

A lawn mower makes the work of mowing lawns easier. It's a complex machine with many parts.

This wheelbarrow is a simple machine— a lever. The boy lifts the handles, and the pile of leaves goes up. He does the same amount of work as carrying the leaves by hand. It takes less force, but he lifts further. ▶

Here's another scientific definition: A *machine* is anything that changes the way work is done. You just read that work is the use of force applied over a distance. A machine might change the direction of a force or the amount of force that is needed.

You probably use a lot of machines every day. Most machines have many moving parts. But some machines are very simple. In fact, they're called simple machines.

A **simple machine** is a machine with few or no moving parts to which you apply just one force. Some simple machines have very few moving parts.

Others have no moving parts.

Imagine that you want to pry up a board nailed to the floor. You slide one end of a pry bar under the board and press down on the other end. After a good push, the board comes up.

The pry bar is a simple machine. You applied a force when you pushed down. The bar changed the direction of the force, and the board moved up. The bar also changed the amount of force that was needed. After all, you couldn't pry up the board with just your hands!

 **MAIN IDEA AND DETAILS** How might a machine change the way work is done?

Levers

A **lever** is a bar that pivots on a fixed point. The fixed point is called the **fulcrum**. For example, a seesaw is a lever. The board of the seesaw is the bar, and the place in the middle, where the board pivots, is the fulcrum.

The pry bar you just read about is one kind of lever. The fulcrum was the point where the pry bar touched the floor. A force was applied at one end of the bar. The thing that moved—the board—was at the other end.

With the seesaw and the pry bar, the fulcrum is between the force and the thing that moves. But there are other kinds of levers. In a picture on the previous page, a boy lifts one end of a wheelbarrow. He applies force at that end, and the wheelbarrow pivots at the other end. The thing that is moved—the pile of leaves—is between the force and the fulcrum.

A broom is a third kind of lever. You hold the handle at one end—the fulcrum. The thing that is moved—the dirt—is at the other end. You apply force between the thing that is moved and the fulcrum.

Focus Skill MAIN IDEA AND DETAILS

Give three examples of a lever.

A hockey stick is one kind of lever. The girl holds one end of the stick. That's the fulcrum, where the stick pivots. The other end moves the puck. The girl applies force between the two ends. ▶

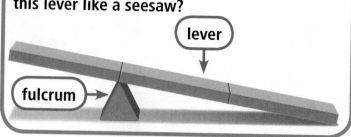

A lever is just a bar that pivots on a fulcrum. In this diagram, the fulcrum is between where you push and where the work is done. How is this lever like a seesaw?

lever

fulcrum →

fulcrum

lever

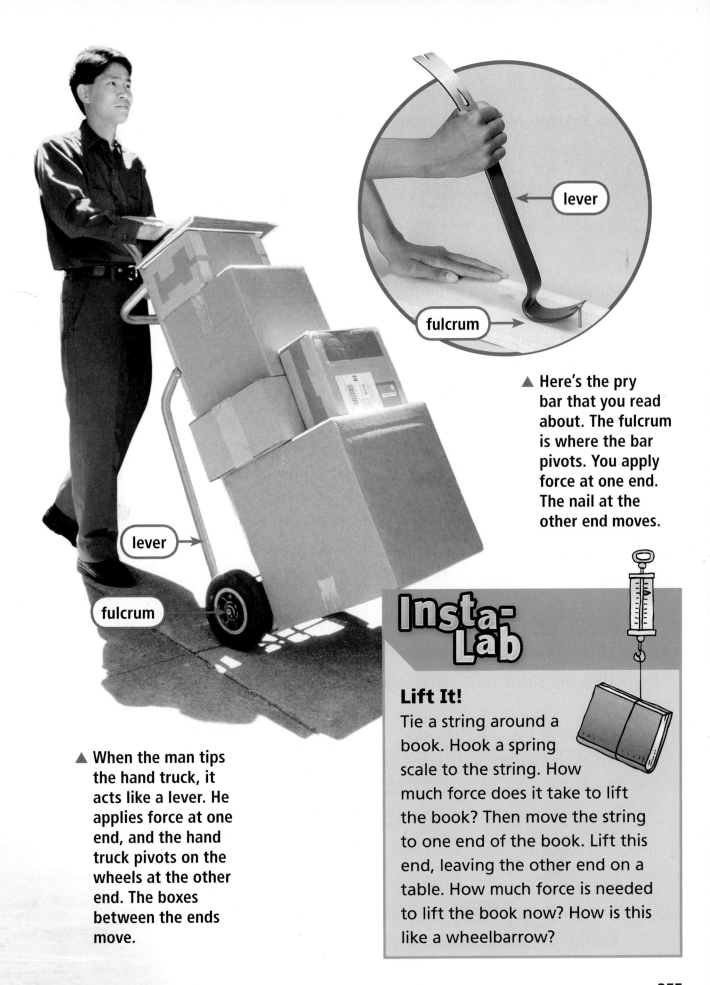

lever

fulcrum

▲ Here's the pry
bar that you read
about. The fulcrum
is where the bar
pivots. You apply
force at one end.
The nail at the
other end moves.

lever

fulcrum

▲ When the man tips
the hand truck, it
acts like a lever. He
applies force at one
end, and the hand
truck pivots on the
wheels at the other
end. The boxes
between the ends
move.

Insta-Lab

Lift It!
Tie a string around a
book. Hook a spring
scale to the string. How
much force does it take to lift
the book? Then move the string
to one end of the book. Lift this
end, leaving the other end on a
table. How much force is needed
to lift the book now? How is this
like a wheelbarrow?

255

Essential Question

How do simple machines help people do work?

In this lesson, you learned that work is done when an applied force moves an object over a distance. Machines—both simple and complex—make work easier. You also learned that there are different kinds of levers.

1. (Focus Skill) **MAIN IDEA AND DETAILS** Draw and complete a graphic organizer to give details about work, simple machines, and levers. Make sure you give an example of each.

S4P3a

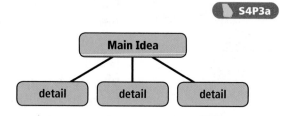

2. SUMMARIZE Use the graphic organizer to help you write a summary of this lesson. S4P3a

3. DRAW CONCLUSIONS There are three kinds of levers. How do you think they are classified? S4P3a

4. VOCABULARY Write a definition for each of the vocabulary terms in this lesson. S4P3a

5. Critical Thinking Annie is using a screwdriver to pry open a can of paint. To get the lid to pop up, she has to press down on the screwdriver's handle. Why?

S4P3a

CRCT Practice

6. Which of the following is a lever?
   A a bottle opener
   B a drinking straw
   C a match
   D a pencil S4P3a

7. Which of the following is an example of work?
   A packing a lunch box
   B thinking about homework
   C pushing against a wall
   D holding a baseball S4P3

8. Some athletes lift weights to make their arms stronger. Explain why the forearm acts as a lever during this process.

The Big Idea

S4P3a

Writing　ELA4W2

Informational Writing

Many everyday objects, such as pry bars and seesaws, are levers. Choose one such object, and write a how-to paragraph that tells how to set it up and how to use it.

9÷3 **Math**　M4A1a

Solve Problems

Mrs. Ikeda has three pry bars. The shortest is 50 centimeters long. The second is twice as long. The longest is three times as long. What is the length of each bar?

Health

Levers in the Human Body

Use library resources to research the levers in your body, such as your forearm. Ilustrate the parts of one "body lever" that you find. Present your findings to the class.

For more links and activities, go to **www.hspscience.com**

▶ **DEAN KAMEN**

▶ **Inventor of the Segway and IBOT**

▶ Believes inventions should make life easier

Dean Kamen

When Dean Kamen sees that people need something, he invents it. In college, he invented a portable medicine pump that patients could use at home. Then came the IBOT—a six-wheeled wheelchair that climbs curbs and stairs.

Kamen saw that cars in cities cause traffic and pollution, so he invented the Segway Human Transporter. This two-wheeled scooter moves easily over paved surfaces and can ride over small obstacles.

Now Kamen is working on a small, nonpolluting engine. It will provide power and clean water to people in remote villages around the world.

Besides inventing, Kamen spends a lot of time trying to get young people interested in science. He started FIRST, an organization that pairs high school students with engineers to create robots and invent other things. If Dean has his way, scientists and engineers will be the superheroes of the twenty-first century!

The IBOT has two sets of back wheels that can turn on top of each other.

 ## Think and Write

❶ What does Dean Kamen look for when he thinks about a new invention? **S4CS8d**

❷ How would Kamen's nonpolluting engine help people who live far from cities? **S4CS8d**

Segway riders control their speed and direction by shifting their weight and turning the handlebars.

Ayanna Howard

Can robots think? They soon will, if Ayanna Howard has anything to do with it. She designs robots that can do amazing things, in space and on Earth.

Howard hopes that within 10 years, her robots will be able to make decisions, much as people can. She designed her SmartNav robot to find the smoothest path across the surface of Mars by analyzing surface features. She has developed computer software that will enable a robotic spacecraft to choose the best place on a planet to land, just as a human pilot would do.

Howard has been interested in robots since she was 12 years old. After watching "The Bionic Woman" on television, she wanted to build a bionic person! In high school, Howard enjoyed math, but she did not like biology and chemistry. She decided to build robots instead of becoming a medical doctor. Now she encourages girls to go into math and science. After she tells them about her career, Howard likes to hear them say, "Maybe I could do that!"

▶ **AYANNA HOWARD**
▶ **Associate Professor, Georgia Institute of Technology**
▶ Builds "smart" robots

Think and Write

1 How will Howard's robots be the same as and different from robots in the past? `S4CS7b`

2 Which simple machines might be part of Howard's high-tech robots? Explain your answer. `S4P3a`

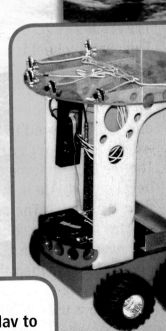

When Howard worked at NASA's Jet Propulsion Lab, she designed SmartNav to explore the surface of Mars independently.

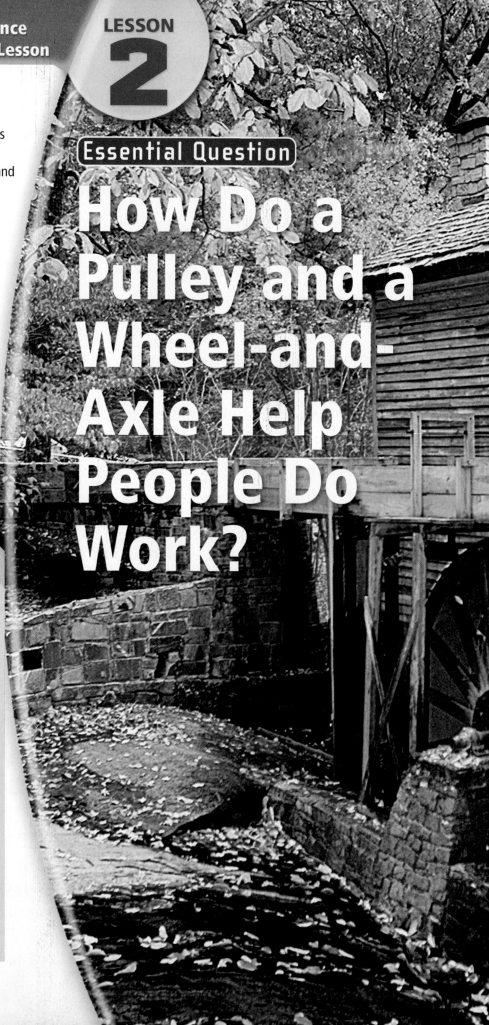

Content

S4P3a Identify simple machines and explain their uses (lever, pulley, wedge, inclined plane, screw, wheel and axle).

Characteristics of Science

S4CS6b   **S4CS8a**

LESSON 2

Essential Question

How Do a Pulley and a Wheel-and-Axle Help People Do Work?

Georgia Fast Fact

Grind Away!

This water wheel is a kind of simple machine. The force of the water falling on the wheel is increased as it is transferred to the axle at the wheel's center. The increase in force occurs because the axle is smaller than the wheel. The axle rotates through a smaller distance—but with a much greater force—than the wheel. Inside the mill, this force is used to crush grains of wheat or corn into flour.

Gristmill near
Stone Mountain

pulley [PUHL•ee] A simple
machine made of a wheel
with a line around it (p. 264)

wheel-and-axle
[WEEL•and•AK•suhl] A simple
machine made of a wheel
and an axle that turn
together (p. 266)

Investigate

Hoist Away

Guided Inquiry

Start with Questions

This girl is practicing her rock-climbing skills on an indoor wall using equipment like this pulley.

- What are the parts of a pulley?

- How do pulleys change forces to make it easier to lift objects?

Investigate to find out. Then read to find out more.

Prepare to Investigate

Inquiry Skill Tip

As you plan and carry out an experiment, you must identify the variable that you will test and the variable that you will measure or observe. You must also identify the variables that you will control, or keep the same.

Materials

- string
- ruler
- book
- scissors
- wire coat hanger
- spring scale

Make a Data Table

	Step 3 (Pull Down)	Step 4 (Pull Up)
Spring scale reading		
Distance spring scale moved (cm)		
Distance book moved (cm)		
Observations		

Follow This Procedure

1 Work with a partner. Tie a loop of string tightly around the book. Bend the hanger into a diamond shape. Hang it from a doorknob.

2 Cut a 1-m length of string. Tie one end to the loop of string around the book. Pass the other end through the hanger, and attach it to the spring scale.

3 One partner should lift the book by pulling down on the spring scale. Note the reading on the spring scale. The other partner should **measure** the distance the spring scale moved and the distance the book moved. **Record** your **observations** and measurements.

4 Hook the hanger to the loop of string on the book. Untie the long string. Pass it through the hanger, and tie it to the doorknob. Repeat Step 3, but pull up on the spring scale.

Draw Conclusions

1. How did Steps 3 and 4 differ?

2. **Standards Link** How did the force needed to lift the book change? **S4P3a**

3. **Inquiry Skill** What **variable** did you hold constant in Steps 3 and 4 so that you could make a fair comparison? **S4CS6b**

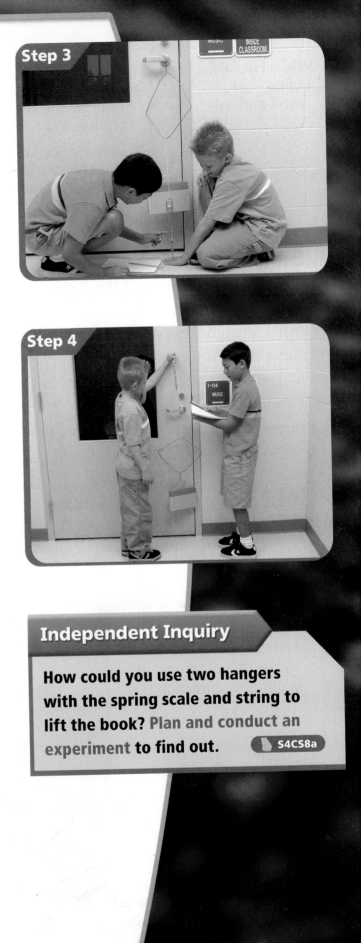

Step 3

Step 4

Independent Inquiry

How could you use two hangers with the spring scale and string to lift the book? **Plan and conduct an experiment** to find out. **S4CS8a**

Understand Science

VOCABULARY
pulley, p. 264
wheel-and-axle, p. 266

SCIENCE CONCEPTS
▶ how a pulley changes the way work is done
▶ how a wheel-and-axle changes the way work is done

Focus Skill **MAIN IDEA AND DETAILS**
Look for details about pulleys and wheel-and-axles.

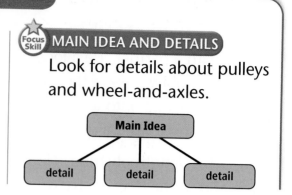

Pulleys

Changing the direction of the force can make a job much easier. For example, imagine you want to raise a flag up a pole. You could climb to the top of the pole and pull the rope up. But who would do that?

Instead, you can use a pulley that's at the top of the flagpole. A rope attaches to the flag, goes up around the wheel, and runs back down to the ground. You pull down on one end of the rope, and the other end goes up, taking the flag with it. That's easier, isn't it?

A **pulley** is a wheel with a line around it. The line might be a rope, a cord, or a chain. The wheel has a lip around its edge to keep the line from slipping off.

Most sailboats have pulleys attached to the sails. Pulleys enable the sails to move in different directions—up, down, and even sideways. ▼

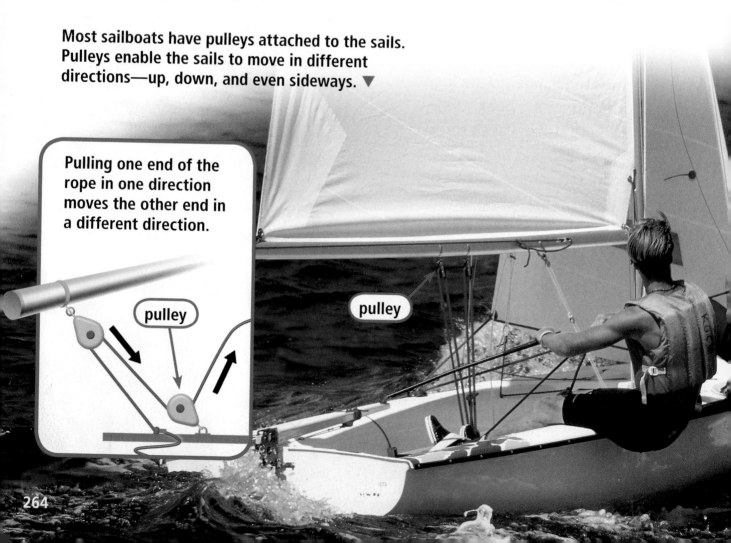

Pulling one end of the rope in one direction moves the other end in a different direction.

pulley

pulley

As you know, all simple machines change the way work is done. A pulley changes the direction of the force. If you pull down on one end of the line, the other end goes up.

A single, fixed pulley doesn't change the amount of force needed. For example, suppose you wanted to lift a 200-newton (45-lb) box. You'd still need to lift 200 newtons, even with a pulley. Pulleys come in all sizes. A child might use a tiny pulley to open a window blind. A mechanic might use a large group of pulleys with a chain to lift an engine out of a car.

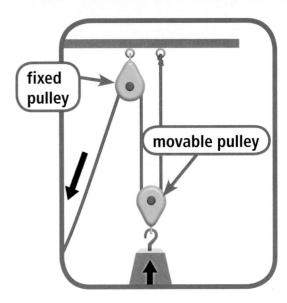

▲ Adding pulleys can lower the force needed to do work. But, you have to pull a greater distance.

 **MAIN IDEA AND DETAILS** How does a pulley change the way work is done?

This man is using a large group of pulleys to increase his lifting force.

Wheel-and-Axles

A wheel-and-axle is exactly what its name says—a wheel and an axle. An axle is a rod that goes into or through a wheel. You can see wheels as well as axles on wheelbarrows and on skateboards, but those wheels and those axles are not simple machines.

To be a simple machine, a **wheel-and-axle** must have a wheel and an axle that turn *together*. If you turn the axle, the wheel turns with it. If you turn the wheel, the axle turns, too.

A wheel-and-axle changes the way work is done. If you turn the wheel, the axle turns with more force. You have to move the wheel over a greater distance, but you use less force. If you move the axle, the wheel moves a greater distance. You have to use more force, but you don't have to move the axle as far.

Focus Skill MAIN IDEA AND DETAILS

What must a wheel and an axle do to be a simple machine?

▼ A wheel-and-axle can work in two ways. You can turn the wheel to make the axle move. Or you can turn the axle to make the wheel move.

wheel

axle

Science Up Close

The Faucet: A Wheel-and-Axle in Use

Did you ever wonder how a faucet works? The water flows through a small opening inside the faucet. When a washer blocks that opening, no water can get out. If you raise the washer a little, a little water does flow. When the opening is completely unblocked, lots of water flows.

water

Insta-Lab

A Model Wheel-and-Axle

Hold a 2-L bottle by the cap. Have a partner turn the bottle by the base so it tightens the cap. Can you stop the bottle from turning? Now roll the bottle along your desk by turning the cap. How far do your fingers move? How far does the bottle roll?

The moving part of the faucet is a wheel-and-axle. The handle is like one spoke of a wheel. The washer is on the end of an axle. The axle moves up and down because of a screw. Without the handle, you'd have to turn the axle by hand to adjust the water. That would be hard to do. But when you turn the handle, you turn the axle, too. You can use much less force, which makes it easier to open and close the faucet.

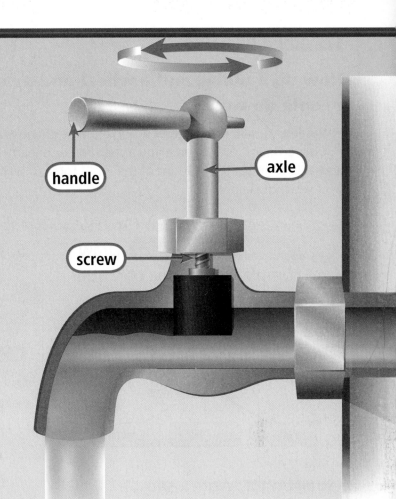

handle

axle

screw

 For more links and animations, go to **www.hspscience.com**

This salad spinner handle is a wheel-and-axle. The outside part is the wheel. The axle is inside. It is what moves the basket. ▶

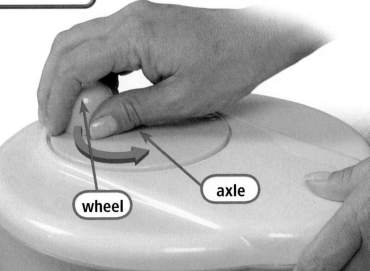

wheel

axle

How do a pulley and a wheel-and-axle help people do work?

In this lesson, you learned that a single pulley changes the direction, but not the amount, of the force you apply. You also learned that a wheel-and-axle changes the amount of the input force as well as the distance over which it is applied.

1. (Focus Skill) **MAIN IDEA AND DETAILS** Draw and complete a graphic organizer to give details about this main idea: *A pulley and a wheel-and-axle each have two parts.* S4P3a

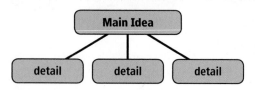

2. SUMMARIZE Write a short paragraph telling what this lesson is mainly about. S4P3a

3. DRAW CONCLUSIONS How does the pulley in a window blind change the way work is done? S4P3a

4. VOCABULARY Use each of the vocabulary terms in a sentence. S4P3a

axle

wheel

5. Critical Thinking How is a doorknob an example of a wheel-and-axle? S4P3a

CRCT Practice

6. Which kind of simple machine is the beater part of an electric mixer?
  A pulley
  B wheel-and-axle
  C pulley and lever
  D two pulleys   S4P3a

7. Which simple machine would you most likely use to move a basket of fruit from the ground into a treehouse?
  A lever
  B wheel-and-axle
  C pulley
  D a group of levers   S4P3a

8. Explain how a pulley and a wheel-and-axle both make work easier. S4P3a

The **Big** Idea

Writing
ELA4W2

Informational Writing

Write to a first-grader explaining how to raise a flag by using a pulley. Draw pictures to go with your writing.

Math
M4G2c

Define Geometric Relationships

A wheel is a short, wide cylinder, and an axle is a long, thin cylinder. What do the two cylinders of a wheel-and-axle have in common?

Social Studies
IPS 6

Ancient Simple Machines

Research how pulleys may have been used to help build the Egyptian pyramids. Write a paragraph or draw a picture to report your findings.

For more links and activities, go to **www.hspscience.com**

Content

S4P3a Identify simple machines and explain their uses (lever, pulley, wedge, inclined plane, screw, wheel and axle).

Characteristics of Science

S4CS1c **S4CS5c**

S4CS8a

LESSON

3

Essential Question

How Do Other Simple Machines Help People Do Work?

Georgia Fast Fact

Screws

Machines like those shown here can move large amounts of water uphill. These are screws that each move about 38,000 liters (10,000 gal) of water each minute. In the Investigate, you'll use another kind of simple machine—a ramp—that makes lifting things easier.

water ride

inclined plane [IN•klynd PLAYN] A simple machine that is a slanted surface (p. 274)

screw [SKROO] A simple machine made of a post with an inclined plane wrapped around it (p. 276)

wedge [WEJ] A simple machine made of two inclined planes placed back-to-back (p. 278)

271

Moving Up

Start with Questions

This man is doing work as he pushes a chair up a ramp into a moving van.

- Why doesn't the man simply lift the chair directly into the truck?

- Does the ramp affect the amount of force the man uses?

Investigate to find out. Then read to find out more.

Prepare to Investigate

Inquiry Skill Tip

When you interpret data, you make a statement that agrees with all of the data in an investigation. As you analyze the data, look for patterns or relationships.

Materials

- cardboard
- tape measure
- toy car
- scissors
- spring scale
- string

Make a Data Table

	Distance (cm)	Force Shown on Spring Scale (N)
Straight		
Short ramp		
Long ramp		

Follow This Procedure

1. Use some of the cardboard to make a ramp from the floor to a chair seat. Make a second ramp, twice as long as the first. Using the tape measure, find and **record** the distance from the floor to the seat, both straight up and along each ramp.

2. Tie a loop of string to the toy car. Attach the spring scale to the string.

3. Hold on to the spring scale, and lift the car from the floor directly to the chair seat. **Record** the force shown.

4. Hold on to the spring scale, and pull the car up the short ramp from the floor to the chair seat. **Record** the force shown. Do the same for the long ramp.

Draw Conclusions

1. According to your data, when did the spring scale measure the greatest force?

2. **Standards Link** How did using the ramps affect the amount of force needed to move the car to the chair seat? **S4P3a**

3. **Inquiry Skill** Scientists interpret data to draw conclusions. After examining your data, what conclusions can you draw? **S4CS1c** **S4CS5c**

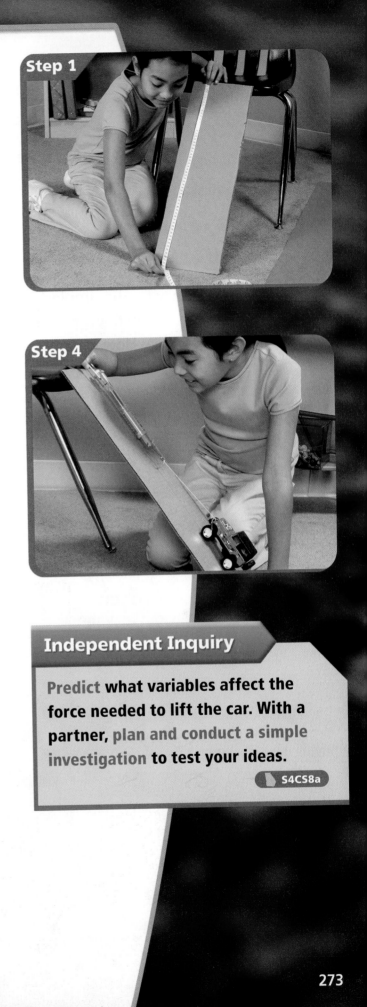

Step 1

Step 4

Independent Inquiry

Predict what variables affect the force needed to lift the car. With a partner, plan and conduct a simple investigation to test your ideas.
S4CS8a

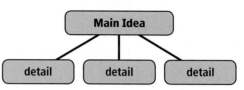
VOCABULARY
inclined plane, p. 274
screw, p. 276
wedge, p. 278

SCIENCE CONCEPTS
▶ how an inclined plane, a wedge, and a screw change the way work is done

Focus Skill | **MAIN IDEA AND DETAILS**

Look for details about inclined planes, wedges, and screws.

```
        Main Idea
     /      |      \
detail    detail    detail
```

Inclined Planes

An inclined plane may be the simplest simple machine of all. An **inclined plane** is simply a slanted surface. How can a surface be a machine? It changes the way work is done. An inclined plane changes the amount of force needed, and it changes the direction of the force.

Look at the sloping shore in the picture on this page. This sloping shore is an inclined plane.

Suppose that raising the boat out of the water involves lifting it up 2 meters (7 ft). You'd need a crane to lift the boat 2 meters straight up. It's much easier to use a truck to pull the boat up the slope.

There's something else, too. A truck's engine might not be able to lift the boat straight up. But with the slope, it doesn't have to. To lift the boat 2 meters (7 ft), the truck might actually move forward 15 meters (49 ft). But the truck will use a lot less force to move the boat.

There are two ways that the sloping shore changes how the work is done in lifting the boat.

1 The truck moves forward to move the boat up.

2 The truck moves 15 meters (49 ft) to lift the boat 2 meters (7 ft), and it uses less force.

An inclined plane enables you to lift an object by using less force. But you must move that object a greater distance.

The pictures on this page show other examples of inclined planes. It may seem odd to think of something in nature as being a simple machine, but a hill is an inclined plane. Remember, an inclined plane is simply a slanted surface.

Imagine that the bikers in the two pictures are riding to the top of the same hill. The biker in the red shirt is on a steep path. He has to pedal hard to reach the top. Even so, taking the path is easier than lifting the bike straight up would be.

The biker in the striped shirt is on a path that is less steep. He doesn't have to pedal as hard to reach the top. But because the path is less steep, it's longer. He has to pedal a greater distance to reach the top of the hill.

Focus Skill MAIN IDEA AND DETAILS

How does an inclined plane change the way work is done?

▲ How would the work of pushing the cart be different if the ramp were steeper?

▲ The road is less steep than the rocky hill. It's easier to pedal along the road. But you have to travel farther to reach the hilltop.

Screws

You've read that using an inclined plane enables you to use less force to move something, even though you must apply the force over a greater distance. A screw is another type of simple machine. It does exactly the same thing.

A **screw** is a post with threads wrapped around it. If you were to unwrap the threads, you would have an inclined plane. Or, to put it another way, the threads are an inclined plane that curls around a post.

Look at the neck of the bottle. Imagine an ant climbing from the bottom of the neck to the opening. It can climb straight up. Or it can walk along the threads. It will use less force if it follows the threads, but it will walk farther.

There are two screws here. The threads on the neck of the bottle slide along the threads on the inside of the cap. ▼

Focus Skill **MAIN IDEA AND DETAILS**

What is a screw?

An Inclined Plane and a Screw

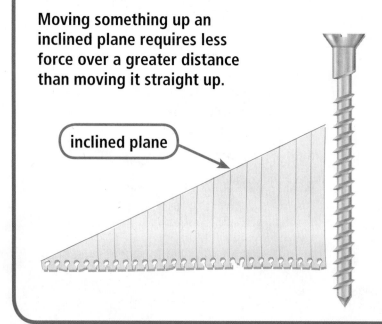

Moving something up an inclined plane requires less force over a greater distance than moving it straight up.

inclined plane

A screw is just an inclined plane wrapped around a post. When something moves along the threads of a screw, it is actually moving along an inclined plane.

threads

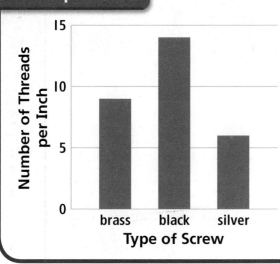

Number of Threads per Inch

15

10

5

0

brass   black   silver

Type of Screw

The graph describes the three kinds of screws in Beth's workshop. You know that the threads of a screw form an inclined plane. Which kind of screw has the steepest threads? Explain.

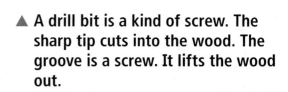

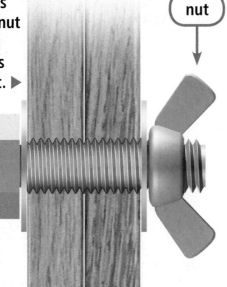

▲ A drill bit is a kind of screw. The sharp tip cuts into the wood. The groove is a screw. It lifts the wood out.

A nut and a bolt both have screw threads, like a cap and a bottle. The threads inside the nut slide along the threads on the bolt. ▶

nut

bolt

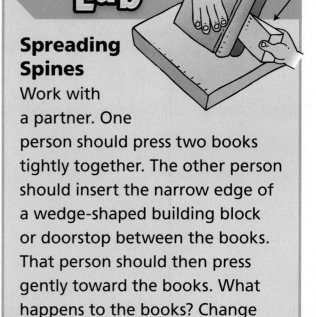

Insta-Lab

WEDGE

Spreading Spines

Work with a partner. One person should press two books tightly together. The other person should insert the narrow edge of a wedge-shaped building block or doorstop between the books. That person should then press gently toward the books. What happens to the books? Change roles and do this again.

Wedges

Another simple machine related to the inclined plane is the wedge. A **wedge** is two inclined planes placed back to back.

An inclined plane and a wedge both change the direction of a force. If you want to raise a heavy object, you can slide it along the slanted part of an inclined plane.

Imagine using a wedge to split a log. You stick the narrow edge into the wood. Then you use a big hammer to apply a downward force. The wedge makes the force greater and redirects it outward, away from the wedge's surfaces. The wedge pushes the parts of the log apart until the log splits.

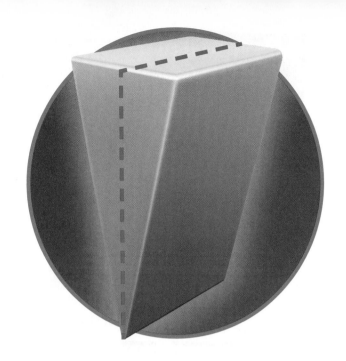

▲ A wedge is really just two inclined planes back to back.

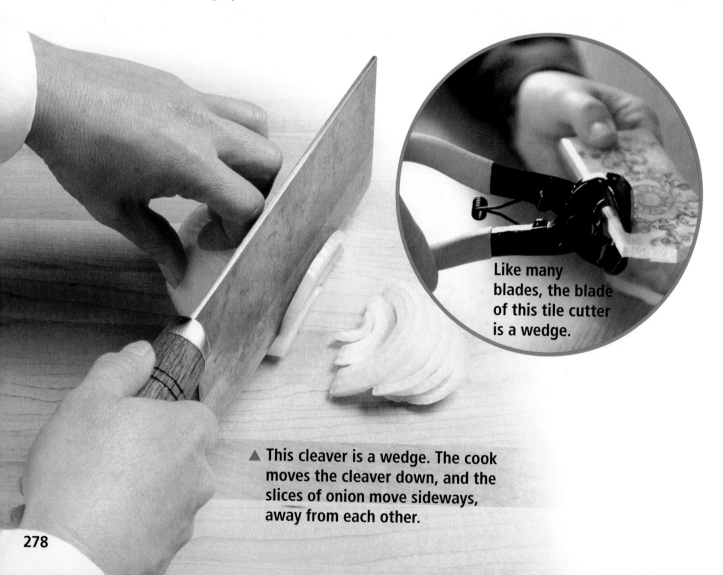

Like many blades, the blade of this tile cutter is a wedge.

▲ This cleaver is a wedge. The cook moves the cleaver down, and the slices of onion move sideways, away from each other.

As the plow cuts through the soil, it lifts the soil and turns it over. This action buries leaves and other decaying plant matter, which will nourish the soil.

As you drive the wedge downward, it pushes against the two halves of the log, causing the log to split.

Although a needle is round, its sharp end is like many inclined planes meeting at a point.

If you examine a knife with a hand lens, you'll see two inclined planes sloping away from the sharp edge. Once the edge breaks into a material, continued force pushes the material apart until it's cut all the way through.

Wedges are not only used to cut or split things, but also to lift and push objects. A doorstop is a wedge that pushes against a door to hold it open. How does it work? You put the sharp edge of the doorstop under the door. It pushes upward on the door with a force large enough to lift the door slightly. At the same time, the door applies an equal but opposite force to the doorstop. This force pushes the doorstop hard against the floor. Friction between the doorstop and the floor holds the doorstop in place.

Focus Skill MAIN IDEA AND DETAILS

How is a wedge like an inclined plane?

Essential Question

How do other simple machines help people do work?

In this lesson, you learned that an inclined plane makes work easier by allowing the user to apply less force over a longer distance. You also learned that a screw and a wedge contain inclined planes.

1. **MAIN IDEA AND DETAILS** Draw and complete a graphic organizer in which you define and give two examples of an inclined plane, a screw, and a wedge. `S4P3a`

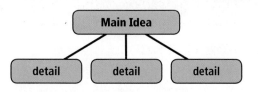

2. **SUMMARIZE** Write a summary of this lesson by using each lesson vocabulary term in a sentence. `S4P3a`

3. **DRAW CONCLUSIONS** How does the screw on a bottle cap change the direction of a force? `S4P3a`

4. **VOCABULARY** Make a flash card for each lesson vocabulary term. Include a definition and a labeled diagram on each flash card. `S4P3a`

5. **Critical Thinking** One screw has many threads close together. Another screw has few threads, and they're spread out. Which screw is like a steep inclined plane? Explain. `S4P3a`

CRCT Practice

6. An ax blade is which kind of simple machine?

  A ramp   **C** wedge

  B screw   **D** lever

`S4P3a`

7. Your friend lives at the top of a hill. Which simple machine would you most likely use to go to your friend's house?

  A pulley   **C** wedge

  B inclined plane   **D** lever

`S4P3a`

8. Imagine your teacher asks you to make two simple machines using a ruler and a rubber eraser. Draw diagrams to show what the machines would look like. `S4P3a`

The Big Idea

Writing

ELA4W2

Persuasive Writing

Suppose your city is planning to improve wheelchair access to public buildings. However, some officials want to put the project off for a year. Write a letter you might send to your local newspaper expressing your support for doing the project now.

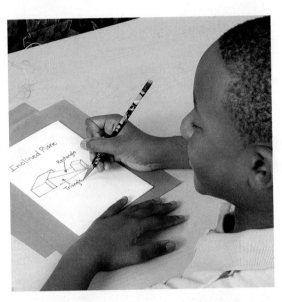

9÷3 Math

M4G2c

Classify Geometric Figures

Draw one diagram each that shows an inclined plane, a screw, and a wedge. Label the geometric figures on each diagram.

Social Studies

IPS 6

Ancient Invention

Use library resources to research the Greek scientist Archimedes, who lived about 2,200 years ago. Write a brief report about Archimedes and the ideas for which he is now famous.

For more links and activities, go to **www.hspscience.com**

The Georgia AGRIRAMA

At the Agrirama, farmers plow fields the old-fashioned way. A mule pulls a plow, which is a wedge, to break up the soil.

What was life in Georgia like in the late 1800s? You can find out at a special kind of museum that takes you back in time.

At the Georgia Agrirama, you can visit a traditional farm from the 1870s. You can also check out a "modern" farm from the 1890s. As you stroll down main street, stop at the sawmill and the blacksmith shop. Walk through the feed-and-seed store, the print shop, and the drugstore. Visit the one-room schoolhouse, and picture students of all ages solving arithmetic problems on their slates, or small, individual chalkboards. Would you like to learn how to make syrup? Just visit the sugar-cane mill.

Simple Machines at Work

In the late 1800s, people used many simple machines to make work easier. You can see this clearly at the Agrirama. At the sawmill, workers use ramps to move heavy loads higher and lower. A steam engine powers a large circular saw that cuts logs lengthwise. The steam engine makes a wheel spin. A circular belt connects this wheel to a wheel-and-axle. As the belt turns, the saw blade rotates.

At the farm, simple pulleys help lift bales of hay into barn lofts. Wedge-shaped hatchets and axes split wood. At the gristmill, a large, flat, circular stone—a kind of wheel-and-axle—turns against another huge stone. The stones crush the grains of wheat or corn into flour. The turning stone moves because it is attached to a water wheel, another kind of wheel-and-axle.

Moving water provides the force that turns the large grinding stone on this gristmill.

Get Your Hands Dirty!

The Agrirama covers 95 acres near Tifton, Georgia. It opened in 1976 as a living museum. This means that visitors get to experience life as it was. Staff members may invite visitors to help them tackle chores the old-fashioned way. You may get to plow behind a mule and sew a quilt. You might even ride the logging train. As hard as these tasks were, they would have been difficult—or impossible—without simple machines.

This person is using a spinning wheel to make cotton thread. This machine, which is powered by the worker's foot, uses wheel-and-axles.

Think and Write

1. How did people of the past figure out how to use simple machines? `S4CS7b`

2. Do people today use simple machines? Explain your answer. `S4P3a` `S4CS7b`

Wrap-Up

▶ Visual Summary

Tell how each picture helps explain the **Big Idea**.

The Big Idea The six main kinds of simple machines make work easier by changing the force needed to move objects.

Lesson 1 S4P3a

Levers

A lever is a bar that pivots around a fixed point. Some levers, such as a pry bar or a paint-can opener, change both the amount and direction of a force. Other levers do not, but all make work easier.

Lesson 2 S4P3a

Pulleys and Wheel-and-Axles

A single pulley changes only the direction of the applied force. Wheel-and-axles change the amount of the input force as well as the distance over which it is applied.

Lesson 3 S4P3a

Inclined Planes, Screws, and Wedges

An inclined plane is a slanted surface. An inclined plane changes the amount of force needed as well as the direction of that force. The threads of a screw are an inclined plane that wraps around a post. Two inclined planes placed back to back form a wedge.

► Show What You Know

Writing About Simple Machines/A Persuasive Letter

Suppose you have a friend who thinks simple machines are no longer useful today. Write a letter in which you try to persuade your friend that simple machines are important in everyday life. To help make your letter convincing, give examples of commonly used simple machines. Be sure to tell how these machines make work easier.

ELA4W2

Georgia Performance Task

Combinations of Simple Machines

You may already know that some common machines are made up of two or more simple machines. For example, a pair of scissors is made up of two levers and two wedges. Use library and trusted Internet sources to look for other examples. Make a poster on which you display labeled diagrams of these machines. Present your poster to the class.

S4P3a

Georgia Performance Standards

Vocabulary Review

Use the terms below to complete the sentences. The page numbers tell you where to look in the chapter if you need help.

work p. 252	simple machine p. 253
lever p. 254	fulcrum p. 254
pulley p. 264	inclined plane p. 274
screw p. 276	wedge p. 278

1. The moving part of a water faucet is an example of a _____.

> S4P3a

2. A hill is an example of an _____.

> S4P3a

3. A bar that pivots on a fulcrum is a _____.

> S4P3a

4. Two inclined planes that are back to back form a _____.

> S4P3a

5. A wheel with a rope or chain around it is a _____.

> S4P3a

6. A post with threads wrapped around it is a _____.

> S4P3a

7. The point where a lever pivots is the _____.

> S4P3a

8. Using force to move an object over a distance is _____.

> S4P3a

Check Understanding

Write the letter of the best choice.

9. Which of the following is an example of work, to a scientist? (p. 252)

> S4P3a

  A solving a mental math problem

  B carrying a book across the room

  C pushing against the floor

  D lifting a chair off the floor

10. Where can the fulcrum of a lever NOT be? (p. 254)

> S4P3a

  A the end of the bar

  B the middle of the bar

  C between the middle and the end

  D not touching the bar

11. How is the screwdriver being used in this picture? (p. 254)

> S4P3a

  A as a lever

  B as a screw

  C as a pulley

  D as a wheel-and-axle

12. MAIN IDEA AND DETAILS An inclined plane is a part of which other simple machine? (p. 276)

S4P3a

A lever   **C** screw
B pulley   **D** wheel-and-axle

13. Which of the following does NOT change the direction of a force? (p. 266) **S4P3a**
A inclined plane   **C** wedge
B pulley   **D** wheel-and-axle

14. MAIN IDEA AND DETAILS Which detail about an ax blade lets you know that it is a wedge? (p. 278) **S4P3a**
A It has just one inclined plane.
B It changes the way work is done.
C It has two inclined planes.
D It changes the direction of the applied force.

15. Which simple machine could you use to hold two objects together? (p. 276) **S4P3a**
A lever   **C** screw
B pulley   **D** wheel-and-axle

16. Which kind of simple machine is the wheelchair resting on? (p. 275) **S4P3a**
A inclined plane
B lever
C pulley
D screw

Inquiry Skills

17. Think about a spiral staircase. Which simple machine can you **compare** it to? Explain. **S4CS5**

18. This table shows the force needed to lift a heavy box 1 meter by using four different methods. What conclusions can you draw about the distance the box traveled by **interpreting the data**? **S4CS5a**

Method Used	Force Needed
Lever	200 newtons
Inclined plane	300 newtons
Pulley	500 newtons
Lifting straight up	500 newtons

Critical Thinking

19. Tamyra and Marv are loading boxes onto identical trucks. Tamyra slides the boxes up a ramp that is 1 meter long. Marv uses a ramp that is 2 meters long. Who uses more force? Explain. **S4P3a**

20. You have to put a 20-kilogram box on a shelf. You can lift it 1 meter, or you can push it up a ramp. The ramp is 2 meters long. If you use the ramp, you'll feel as if you're moving 10 kilograms. Which method might make you feel more tired? Explain. **S4P3a**

The **Big** Idea

1. Which pipe in a pipe organ makes the highest-pitched sound?

   A. the oldest one
   B. the heaviest one
   C. the shortest and thinnest one
   D. the newest and shiniest one

    S4P2b

2. If you were to investigate an object that produces sound, which would you definitely find?

   A. The object conducts electricity.
   B. The object is magnetic.
   C. The object is vibrating.
   D. The object reflects light.

    S4P2a

3. Tom strikes two pipes with a wooden mallet. The short brass pipe makes a high-pitched sound. The long iron pipe makes a low-pitched sound. Tom concludes that brass pipes make higher-pitched sounds than iron pipes. What's wrong with his conclusion?

   A. The length of the pipes could affect their pitch.
   B. He didn't use a rubber mallet.
   C. Different metals do not vibrate at the same rate.
   D. Pitch depends on air temperature.

    S4P2b S4CS6b

4. A musician plucks two guitar strings. One makes a higher-pitched sound. What is true of that string?

   A. It is longer than the other string.
   B. It produces less energy.
   C. It moves more slowly.
   D. It vibrates faster.

    S4P2b

Use the graph below to answer question 5.

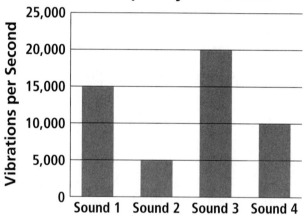

Frequency of Sounds

5. The graph shows the number of vibrations per second for four different sounds. Which has the lowest pitch?

   A. Sound 1
   B. Sound 2
   C. Sound 3
   D. Sound 4 S4P2b S4CS5c

6. All of these windows face the same pine tree. Which window contains a transparent material?

A.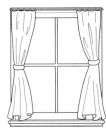

C.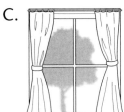

B.

D.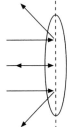

7. Which of these should you use to separate the colors in visible light?

A. prism

C. convex lens

B. concave lens

D. laser

8. Which two simple machines are MOST alike?

A. screw and lever

B. lever and wedge

C. pulley and wheel-and-axle

D. screw and inclined plane

9. Which simple machine would be the BEST to use to slice celery?

A. wedge

C. screw

B. pulley

D. inclined plane

10. You notice that an opaque object looks blue. Which is true?

A. The object reflects blue light and absorbs all other colors.

B. The object reflects all the colors of light except blue.

C. The object reflects all the colors of light equally, but your eye detects only the blue.

D. The object absorbs all the colors of light equally, but your eye detects only the blue.

11. Which correctly shows the path of light as it strikes a convex lens?

A.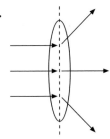

C.

B.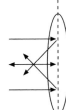

D.

12. You stand in front of your friend. Your friend hides behind you. Why can't people see your friend?

A. You are transparent.

B. You are translucent.

C. You are opaque.

D. You are concave. S4P1a

13. Why can you see colors in the sky on a rainy day?

A. Raindrops act like convex lenses.

B. Raindrops act like concave lenses.

C. Raindrops act like prisms.

D. Raindrops act like rainbows. S4P1c

14. Which kind of lens makes objects look bigger?

A. convex

B. concave

C. light-reflecting

D. corrective S4P1c

15. Which of these objects reflects nearly all of the light that strikes it?

A. flashlight   C. mirror

B. light bulb   D. window S4P1b

16. The spheres shown below are all made of pure iron. Which sphere requires the MOST force to set it in motion?  S4P3b

A.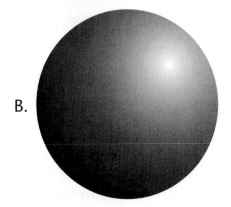

B.

C.

D.

Use the table below to answer question 17.

Object	Mass (kilograms)	Force Applied (Newtons)
1	10	40
2	20	100
3	30	100
4	40	105

17. The table shows the masses of four objects and the amount of force applied to each. Which object will move the fastest?

   A. Object 1

   B. Object 2

   C. Object 3

   D. Object 4   **S4P3b**   **S4CS5c**

18. Which of the following is NOT a lever?

   A. a pry bar

   B. a wheelbarrow

   C. a broom

   D. a ramp   **S4P3a**

19. Which of the following changes the direction of a force but not the amount of force needed to do work?

   A. wedge

   B. wheel-and-axle

   C. inclined plane

   D. single pulley   **S4P3a**

Use the diagram below to answer question 20.

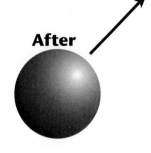

Before   **After**

20. An object is moving at a constant speed in the direction shown in the *"before"* picture. A force causes the object to change direction, as shown in the *"after"* picture. A force from which direction would cause this change?   **S4P3c**   **S4CS4b**

A. ←

B. ↓

C.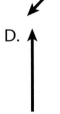

D. ↑

UNIT C LIFE SCIENCE

What do YOU wonder?

This osprey is catching a fish to eat. What would happen to the osprey if the water were polluted and all the fish died?

Chapter 7 Food Energy in Ecosystems
Chapter 8 Adaptations for Survival

 for student eBook
www.hspscience.com

Water Quality and Plant Growth   Living things respond to factors in their environments. For example, most organisms need water to grow and stay heathy. But does water quality affect living things? Plan and conduct an experiment to find out.

Osprey captures fish

Georgia Performance Standards in This Chapter

Content

S4L1 Students will describe the roles of organisms and the flow of energy within an ecosystem.

S4L1a–d

This chapter also addresses these co-requisite standards:

Characteristics of Science

S4CS1 Students will be aware of the importance of curiosity, honesty, openness, and skepticism . . . and will exhibit these traits. . . .

S4CS1b, c

S4CS4 Students will use ideas of system, model, change, and scale. . . .

S4CS4c

S4CS5 Students will communicate scientific ideas. . . .

S4CS5b

S4CS6 Students will question scientific claims . . . effectively.

S4CS6b

S4CS8 Students will understand important features of the process of scientific inquiry.

S4CS8a, b, d

What's the Big Idea?

All living things need energy and matter to live and grow.

Essential Questions

GO online for student eBook
www.hspscience.com

Science in Georgia

Grand Bay Wetland Education Center

Dear Quincy,

After we left Valdosta, Mom and I took your advice and visited the Grand Bay wetland.

It reminded me so much of the Okefenokee Swamp. We even saw pitcher plants. You know that these plants are carnivorous, right? That means they eat insects. How cool is that! Thanks for telling us about this place.

Your cousin,
Tynan

USA

What did Tynan say about the pitcher plants? How do you think this relates to the **Big Idea?**

Content

 S4L1 Students will describe the roles of organisms and the flow of energy within an ecosystem.

Characteristics of Science

S4CS4c   **S4CS8a**

Essential Question

What Is an Ecosystem?

Georgia Fast Fact

Land of Trembling Earth

The Okefenokee Swamp is the largest swamp in North America. It covers about 1800 square kilometers (700 square miles) in the southeastern corner of Georgia. The Okefenokee has a variety of habitats. The abundant wildlife includes more than 200 varieties of birds and more than 60 kinds of reptiles. The Okefenokee is truly a natural wonder!

The Okefenokee Swamp

environment
[en•VY•ruhn•muhnt] All of the living and nonliving things surrounding an organism (p. 300)

ecosystem [EE•koh•sis•tuhm] A community and its physical environment together (p. 300)

population
[pahp•yuh•LAY•shuhn] All the individuals of the same kind living in the same ecosystem (p. 302)

community
[kuh•MYOO•nuh•tee] All the populations of organisms living together in an environment (p. 304)

297

Modeling an Ecosystem

Guided Inquiry

Start with Questions

Look under a rock. You might find a whole ecosystem there!

- Do you live in an ecosystem?
- Is everything in your ecosystem living?

Investigate to find out. Then read to find out more.

Prepare to Investigate

Inquiry Skill Tip
Making a model can make it easier to understand how things work. When you make a model, it should be as much like the real thing as possible.

Materials

- gravel
- sand
- soil
- 6 small plants
- clear plastic wrap
- 2 rubber bands
- water in a spray bottle
- 2 empty 2-L soda bottles with tops cut off

Make an Observation Chart

	Day 1	Day 2	Day 3
Sunny Terrarium			
Dark Terrarium			

Follow This Procedure

❶ Pour a layer of gravel, a layer of sand, and then a layer of soil into the bottom of each bottle.

❷ Plant three plants in each bottle.

❸ Spray the plants and the soil with water. Cover the top of each bottle with plastic wrap. If necessary, hold the wrap in place with a rubber band.

❹ Put one of the terrariums you just made in a sunny spot. Put the other one in a dark closet or cabinet.

❺ After three days, **observe** each terrarium and **record** what you see.

Step 2

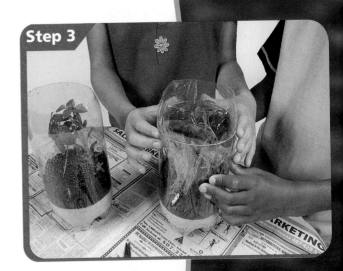
Step 3

Draw Conclusions

1. What did you observe about each of your ecosystems after three days?

2. **Standards Link** Which parts of the ecosystems were alive? What can you infer about what every ecosystem needs? **S4L1**

3. **Inquiry Skill** Scientists often learn more about how things affect one another by **making a model**. What did you learn by making a model and observing how its parts interact? **S4CS4c**

Independent Inquiry

What effect does sunlight have on seeds that have just been planted? First, write your hypothesis. Then plan an experiment to see if your hypothesis is supported. **S4CS8a**

VOCABULARY
environment p. 300
ecosystem p. 300
population p. 302
community p. 304

SCIENCE CONCEPTS
▶ how living and nonliving parts of an ecosystem interact
▶ what populations and communities are

Focus Skill **MAIN IDEA AND DETAILS**
Look for the parts that make up an ecosystem.

Main Idea

detail | detail | detail

Ecosystems

Where do you live? You might name your street and town. You also live in an environment. An **environment** is all the living and nonliving things that surround you. The living things in your environment are people, other animals, and plants. The nonliving things around you include water, air, soil, and weather.

The parts of an environment affect one another in many ways. For example, animals eat plants. The soil affects which plants can live in a place. Clean air and clean water help keep both plants and animals healthy. All the living and nonliving things in an area form an **ecosystem** (EE•koh•sis•tuhm).

An ecosystem can be very small. It might be the space under a rock. That space might be home to insects and tiny plants. You might need a microscope to see some of the things living there.

This prairie smoke plant grows well in the hot, dry climate of prairies and grasslands. ▼

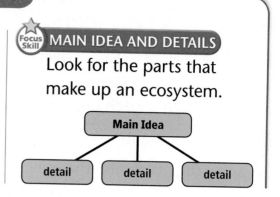

Prairie dogs also live on the prairies and grasslands. ▼

Moose thrive in a coniferous, or evergreen, forest ecosystem.

The small ecosystem found under a rock has nonliving parts, too. They include pockets of air and the soil under the rock. You might find a few drops of water or maybe just damp soil. All ecosystems must have at least a little water.

The ecosystem under this rock has a climate. The climate in an area is the average weather over many years. Climate includes temperature and rainfall. The climate of an ecosystem depends on where the ecosystem is. If this rock is in Florida, its climate is warm and wet. If the rock is in Maine, its winters are icy.

An ecosystem can also be as large as a forest. A forest can provide many kinds of food and shelter. This ecosystem may include hundreds of kinds of plants and animals. Each organism finds what it needs in the forest.

Like all ecosystems, a forest has nonliving parts. They include water, air, soil, and climate. Later, you will read more about ways living and nonliving parts of an ecosystem affect one another.

Focus Skill **MAIN IDEA AND DETAILS**

Name the two parts of an ecosystem, and give two examples of each part.

301

This individual waterlily is part of a large population of waterlilies.

Individuals and Populations

One plant or animal is an *individual.* For example, one blueberry bush is an individual. One honeybee is an individual. One blue jay is an individual. You are an individual.

A group made up of the same kind of individuals living in the same ecosystem is a **population**. A group of blueberry bushes is a population. So is a hive of bees. So are all the blue jays living in one forest. So are all the people living in one city.

Robins might live in the same forest as the blue jays. Robins are a different kind of bird. That makes them a different population.

The members of a population might not live in a group. For example, frogs don't live in families. Still, a number of green tree frogs may live near the same pond. They belong to the same population. Bullfrogs might also live near that pond. They are a different population.

Many animals live in groups. People live in families. How many people are in your family? Wolves live in packs. A pack can have from 3 to 20 wolves. A wolf population may have several packs. The wolf population in Yellowstone National Park includes 19 packs.

Some populations can live in more than one kind of ecosystem. For instance, red-winged blackbirds often live in wetlands, but they are also found in other areas. Red-winged blackbirds can live in different ecosystems. If one ecosystem no longer meets the needs of these birds, they fly to another one.

Some populations can live in only one kind of ecosystem. One such animal is the Hine's emerald dragonfly. This insect can live only in certain wetlands. It can't survive in other places. Because this dragonfly can live only in specific places, its total number is very small.

Ecosystems are often named for the main population that lives there. For example, one kind of ecosystem forms where a river flows into the ocean. There, fresh water mixes with salt water. Many trees can't live in salty water. But mangrove trees have roots that allow

them to get rid of the salt in the water. When many mangrove trees live in a salty ecosystem, the area is called a *mangrove swamp.*

Focus Skill MAIN IDEA AND DETAILS

Name an individual and a population that are not mentioned on these pages.

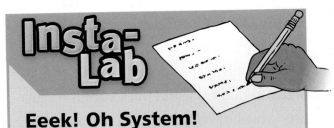

Eeek! Oh System!

Work with a partner to list some of the populations in your school ecosystem. Think about the building and the land around it. Then compare lists with other students. Did you list the same populations?

This individual male red-winged blackbird is part of a large population of blackbirds.

A population of red-winged blackbirds can include several million birds. Some of the birds fly 80 kilometers (50 mi) to find food.

Communities

You live in a community. Other animals and plants do, too. A **community** is all the populations that live in the same place.

Have you visited the Okefenokee Swamp? It has a number of distinctive habitats, including swamp forests, marshes, and areas of open water.

The swamp forests are dominated by cypress, black gum, and bay trees. Grasses, rushes, and ferns live in the drier areas, while waterlilies and golden club are found in wetter sites. Several kinds of carnivorous plants, such as pitcher plants, sundews, and bladderworts, live in the swamp. These plants attract, capture, and digest insects.

Animals found in the Okefenokee include alligators, snakes, and many kinds of freshwater fish, including gars and eels. Bird-watchers like to visit the swamp to see the great variety of birds that can be found there. These include blue herons and sandhill cranes, as well as seasonal birds, such as the blue-winged teal. The swamp also supports about 30 kinds of mammals, ranging in size from rabbits to raccoons, to gray foxes, to bobcats and black bears.

This forest community on Cumberland Island includes live oaks draped with Spanish moss and saw palmettos.

These sand dunes on Cumberland Island are part of a coastal community. Sea oats and other grasses grow on the dunes. Loggerhead sea turtles nest on the beach.

The populations of living things in coastal communities are different from those found in the Okefenokee Swamp. Many of the plants and animals in these communities, for example, must be able to survive in salt water.

The populations of living things in a forest community are different, too. Picture the Blue Ridge mountains. The Blue Ridge is the coldest and wettest part of Georgia. It has the highest elevations in the state. Many of the plants and animals that thrive in the Okefenokee Swamp could not survive in the Blue Ridge.

Instead of cypress trees, forests contain oak and other broadleaf trees. Canada warblers and winter wrens nest at the highest elevations. Although black bears live in the Blue Ridge as well as the Okefenokee Swamp, small mammals that live in the Blue Ridge, such as the deer mouse and the smoky shrew, are found nowhere else in Georgia.

All communities, no matter where they are located, have at least one thing in common. The plants and animals in them depend on one another.

MAIN IDEA AND DETAILS Name three populations in a swamp community.

▼ The climate in the Blue Ridge is similar to that of southern New England. Many of the animals that live in this community are commonly found in more northern regions of the United States.

Essential Question

What is an ecosystem?

In this lesson, you learned that different types of ecosystems have different living and nonliving parts. Within ecosystems, populations combine to form communities of living things.

1. (Focus Skill) **MAIN IDEA AND DETAILS** Draw and complete a graphic organizer to give examples that support this main idea: *A pond ecosystem is made up of living and nonliving things.* **S4L1**

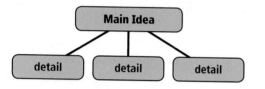

Main Idea

detail   detail   detail

2. **SUMMARIZE** Write a summary of this lesson by using the lesson vocabulary words in a paragraph. **S4L1**

3. **DRAW CONCLUSIONS** Why do some ecosystems include more living things than other ecosystems? **S4L1**

4. **VOCABULARY** Use the lesson vocabulary words to create a matching quiz. **S4L1**

5. **Critical Thinking** How is a population different from a community? **S4L1**

CRCT Practice

6. Which word describes a group of cows standing together?
   A community
   B ecosystem
   C individual
   D population **S4L1**

7. Which of the following could NOT be true about waterlilies and frogs?
   A They are members of the same population.
   B They are part of the same ecosystem.
   C They live in the same community.
   D They are living. **S4L1**

8. You are traveling from one ecosystem to another. What can you expect to change? **S4L1**

The **Big** Idea

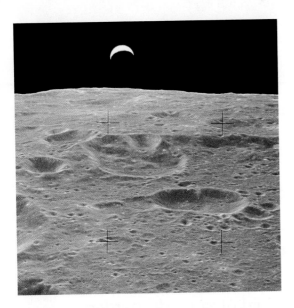

Writing ELA4W2

Expository Writing

You are a scientist planning an ecosystem for people to set up on the moon. Write several paragraphs explaining what this ecosystem should include.

Math M4N5e

Solve a Problem

A certain community is made up of 650 populations of living things. It has as many plant populations as animal populations. How many plant populations does the community have?

Social Studies SS4H1b

Adapting to Nature

These Inuit know how to survive in a cold environment. Choose a Native American group. Write a report about its early people to explain how their environment affected their food, clothing, and shelter.

For more links and activities, go to **www.hspscience.com**

▶ **JARGAL JAMSRANJAV**

▶ **Conservationist**

▶ Chevening Scholar and Whitney Award recipient, training nomadic herders to monitor wildlife in the Gobi.

Jargal Jamsranjav

The Gobi, a desert area in Asia, gets less rainfall than it used to. This means there is less natural vegetation for camels, goats, and horses. These are the animals on which Mongolian herders depend for survival. Jargal Jamsranjav grew up in Mongolia and has witnessed the shrinking of the Gobi's natural resources. Jamsranjav is the grandchild of nomadic herders. She understands the relationship between the nomads' lifestyle and the environment. She recognizes that the resources must support the nomads and wildlife at the same time.

Jamsranjav works with the Mongolian herders of the desert steppe, which is like a plain. They have planted trees to help keep water and soil from washing away. Wells that had been abandoned are being repaired for the herders to use as a water source. The wells allow natural stream and river water to be conserved for wild mammals like gazelle and wild donkeys. This helps prevent overgrazing. Jamsranjav is also teaching the herders to record the numbers and types of wild animals they see. Monitoring wildlife will help ensure that the Gobi has the resources to support herders and animals alike.

Think and Write

❶ What is Jargal Jamsranjav trying to accomplish in her work with the Mongolian herders?

S4L1c, d

❷ How has Jamsranjav helped the nomadic people of the Gobi?

S4CS8d

Eugene Odum

Eugene Odum wrote a book called *Fundamentals of Ecology* in 1953. Before then, ecologists studied only small ecosystems—like ponds and marshes. In his book, Odum taught that the parts of small ecosystems are connected to larger ecosystems. He showed how all living and nonliving things in one ecosystem affect those in other ecosystems.

Odum founded the University of Georgia's Institute of Ecology. He also helped establish the university's Savannah River Ecology Laboratory and the Marine Institute on Sapelo Island. In the late 1960s, when development threatened Georgia's coastal wetlands, Odum took part in an effort that helped persuade the Georgia legislature to pass the Coastal Marshlands Protection Act of 1970.

During the decades that followed, his writings helped people understand how the actions of humans affect all living things. "The work of Dr. Odum changed the way we look at the natural world and our place in it," said former President Jimmy Carter. Dr. Odum helped us understand how important it is to protect our environment.

▶ **EUGENE ODUM**
▶ **1913–2002**
▶ "Father of modern ecosystem ecology"

Odum (right) studied under Victor Shelford, a leading American ecologist, at the University of Illinois.

✎ Think and Write

❶ How did Odum's ideas change the science of ecology? `S4CS8a`

❷ Would Odum have said that the whole world is an ecosystem? Explain your answer. `S4L1c`

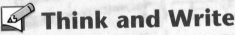

Georgia Performance Standards in This Lesson

Content

S4L1a Identify the roles of producers, consumers, and decomposers in a community.

Characteristics of Science

S4CS1b, c   **S4CS4c**

Essential Question

What Are the Roles of Producers, Consumers, and Decomposers?

Georgia Fast Fact

Natural Enemies

This brown-and-black ladybug is gobbling up tiny insect pests known as aphids. Eating aphids gives the ladybug the energy it needs to live. Aphids get energy by sucking the sap from plants. When ladybugs and aphids die, their bodies decay. In the Investigate, you'll find out how decomposers (dee•kuhm•POHZ•erz) help once-living matter decay.

Ladybug eating aphids

producer [pruh•DOOS•er] A living thing, such as a plant, that can make its own food (p. 314)

consumer [kuhn•SOOM•er] A living thing that can't make its own food and must eat other living things (p. 314)

herbivore [HER•buh•vawr] An animal that eats only plants, or producers (p. 316)

carnivore [KAHR•nuh•vawr] An animal that eats only other animals (p. 316)

omnivore [AHM•nih•vawr] An animal that eats both plants and other animals (p. 316)

decomposer [dee•kuhm•POHZ•er] A living thing that feeds on the wastes of plants and animals (p. 318)

311

Decomposing Bananas

Start with Questions

You were looking forward to a banana with your lunch, but this one doesn't look good to eat!

- What changes do you observe?

- What is causing these changes?

Investigate to find out. Then read to find out more.

Prepare to Investigate

Inquiry Skill Tip

Scientists use time relationships to measure and compare how things change. In the Investigate, think about the amount of time it takes for the change you're observing to take place.

Materials

- spoon
- marker
- 2 slices of banana
- 2 zip-top plastic bags
- package of dry yeast

Make an Observation Chart

Bag	Day 1	Day 2	Day 3	Day 4	Day 5
P					
D					

Follow This Procedure

1. Put a banana slice in each bag. Label one bag *P* for *Plain.*

2. Sprinkle $\frac{2}{3}$ spoonful of dry yeast on the other banana slice. Yeast is a decomposer, so label this bag *D.*

3. Seal both bags. Put the bags in the same place.

4. Check both bags every day for a week. Observe and record the changes you see in each bag.

Draw Conclusions

1. Which banana slice shows more changes?

2. **Standards Link** Why does the banana change? Is it becoming food for organisms other than you? Explain. **S4L1a**

3. **Inquiry Skill** Scientists use time relationships to measure progress. How long did it take for your banana slices to start decomposing? How long do you think it would take for your banana slices to completely decompose? **S4CS4c**

Step 2

Step 4

Independent Inquiry

What will happen if you put flour, instead of yeast, on one banana slice? Write down your prediction, and then try it. **S4CS1b, c**

VOCABULARY
producer p. 314
consumer p. 314
herbivore p. 316
carnivore p. 316
omnivore p. 316
decomposer p. 318

SCIENCE CONCEPTS
▶ how living things use the energy from sunlight
▶ how living things get energy from other living things

MAIN IDEA AND DETAILS
Look for details about the movement of energy among living things.

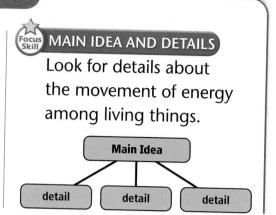

Producers and Consumers

Most living things on Earth get the energy to live from sunlight. Green plants and algae (AL•jee) use energy in sunlight, plus water and carbon dioxide, to make their own food. Any living thing that can make its own food is called a **producer**. Producers can be as small as a tiny moss or as large as a huge redwood tree.

Some animals, such as deer and cattle, get the energy they need to live by eating plants. When these animals eat, the energy stored in the plants moves into the animals' bodies.

Not all animals eat plants. Lions and hawks, for example, get the energy they need by eating other animals.

An animal that eats plants or other animals is called a **consumer**. Consumers can't make their own food, so they must eat other living things.

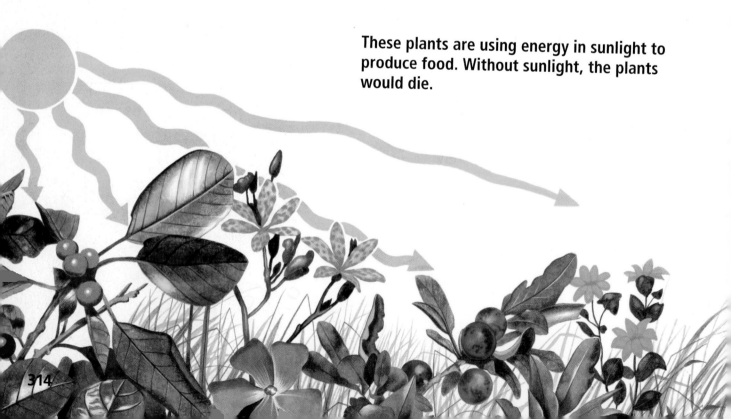

These plants are using energy in sunlight to produce food. Without sunlight, the plants would die.

Horses on
Cumberland Island

Which animal gets its energy directly from producers? Which one gets its energy from other consumers? Which one gets its energy from both?

Bobcat

Black bear

Some consumers eat the same kind of food all year. Horses, for example, eat grass during warm weather. During winter, they eat hay, a kind of dried grass.

Other consumers eat different things in different seasons. For example, black bears eat grass in spring. Later on, they might eat birds' eggs. Bears might also dig up tasty roots or eat fish from streams. In fall, bears eat ripe berries.

Bobcats eat other consumers, but their diet varies. Rabbits make up about half of a bobcat's diet. Other favorite meals include rodents and birds. Bobcats also eat young deer, which are easier to catch than adult deer.

Focus Skill MAIN IDEA AND DETAILS

What is a producer? What is a consumer? Give two examples of each.

Kinds of Consumers

Consumers are not all the same. In fact, there are three kinds—herbivores, carnivores, and omnivores.

A **herbivore** is an animal that eats only plants, or producers. Horses are herbivores. So are giraffes, squirrels, and rabbits.

A **carnivore** is an animal that eats only other animals. Bobcats, Florida panthers, and lions are carnivores. A carnivore can be as large as a whale or as small as a frog.

An **omnivore** is an animal that eats both plants and other animals. That is, omnivores eat both producers and other consumers. Bears and hyenas are omnivores. Do any omnivores live in your home?

Producers and all three kinds of consumers can be found living in water. Algae are producers that live in water. They use sunlight to make their own food. Tadpoles, small fish, and other small herbivores eat algae. Larger fish that are carnivores eat the tadpoles. Some animals, including green sea turtles, are omnivores. Green sea turtles eat seaweed, algae, and fish. In fact, algae make the flesh of the green sea turtle green!

(Focus Skill) MAIN IDEA AND DETAILS

Name the three kinds of consumers. Give two examples of each.

This diagram shows how kinds of consumers in a community get energy to live. The arrows show the direction of energy flow.

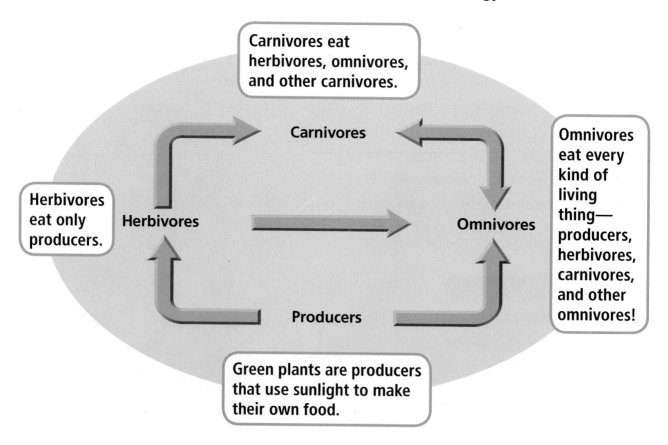

Carnivores eat herbivores, omnivores, and other carnivores.

Omnivores eat every kind of living thing—producers, herbivores, carnivores, and other omnivores!

Herbivores eat only producers.

Green plants are producers that use sunlight to make their own food.

Carnivores

Herbivores

Omnivores

Producers

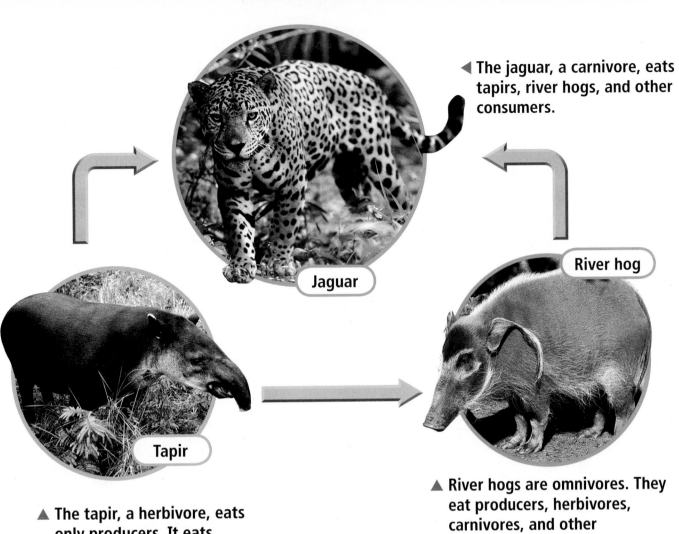

Jaguar

◀ The jaguar, a carnivore, eats tapirs, river hogs, and other consumers.

River hog

Tapir

▲ River hogs are omnivores. They eat producers, herbivores, carnivores, and other omnivores.

▲ The tapir, a herbivore, eats only producers. It eats tender buds and twigs.

Jungle bush

▲ This plant is a producer. It makes its own food and provides stored energy for consumers.

Insta-Lab

Who's an Omnivore?

Read the nutrition labels on several food containers. Think about the source of each kind of food. What does the food's source tell about consumers who eat it?

Decomposers

A **decomposer** is a living thing that feeds on wastes and on the remains of dead plants and animals. Decomposers break down wastes into nutrients. Nutrients are substances that are taken in by living things to help them grow.

Soil contains many nutrients. Plants take them in through their roots. By eating the plants, animals get the nutrients. When plants and animals die, decomposers break down their bodies and return the nutrients to the soil. The cycle is repeated again and again.

Decomposers come in many shapes and sizes. Some of the biggest decomposers are earthworms and mushrooms. Mushrooms are fungi (FUHN•jy), living things that absorb nutrients from living plants and dead plant materials.

In many forests, fungi are the main decomposers of wood. These fungi have special ways of digging into wood and releasing a chemical that breaks down the cells of the wood. Other types of fungi feed on plant leaves and plant matter in soil.

Sow bugs

Sow bugs are related to lobsters. They help plant matter decay faster than it would without them.

Millipede

In the forest, millipedes chew up dead plant material. Like sow bugs, millipedes aren't insects.

Bracket fungi often grow on dead tree trunks. They help the wood decay quickly.

Bacteria are tiny organisms that can be seen only with a microscope. Many of them are decomposers. The bacteria in soil break down tiny pieces of animal and plant matter. By doing this, they fill the soil with the nutrients that plants need to grow.

Bacteria found in water are similar to soil bacteria. They break down plant and animal matter and return nutrients to the water. Other living things use these nutrients for food. These living things are in turn eaten by larger organisms. When these living things die, bacteria break down their bodies into nutrients, completing the cycle.

Without decomposers, Earth would be covered with dead plants and animals. Instead, decomposers turn waste and dead matter into useful nutrients. They allow living things to use recycled nutrients.

Focus Skill MAIN IDEA AND DETAILS

Name two kinds of decomposers, and describe their role in nature.

Although many bacteria are helpful, some, such as the rod-shaped bacteria shown in this picture, can infect people and harm them.

These bacteria are found in the ground.

Essential Question

What are the roles of producers, consumers, and decomposers?

In this lesson, you learned that plants produce food for themselves using the sun's energy. Other organisms consume the plants or organisms that have eaten the plants to get energy for themselves. You also learned that there are many kinds of decomposers.

1. (**Focus Skill**) **MAIN IDEA AND DETAILS** Draw and complete a graphic organizer to give details about producers, consumers, and decomposers.   **S4L1a**

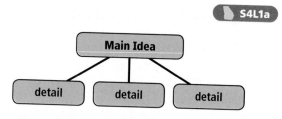

2. **SUMMARIZE** Write four sentences that tell what this lesson is mainly about.   **S4L1a**

3. **DRAW CONCLUSIONS** How are decomposers consumers?   **S4L1a**

4. **VOCABULARY** Using your own words, write a definition for each vocabulary term. Then give one example for each.   **S4L1a**

5. **Critical Thinking** How do eagles depend on sunlight for their energy?   **S4L1a**

CRCT Practice

6. Which term describes a hyena?
   A carnivore
   B herbivore
   C omnivore
   D producer   **S4L1a**

7. Which is NOT a consumer?
   A carnivore
   B herbivore
   C omnivore
   D producer   **S4L1a**

8. How are decomposers part of a cycle?   **S4L1a**

The
Big
Idea

 Writing ELA4W2

Informational Writing

Some types of bacteria have been used to clean up oil spills in oceans or in lakes. Gather information about how the bacteria were used, and prepare a report. Share your findings with your classmates.

 Math M4M1b

Solve a Problem

A shrew eats about $\frac{2}{3}$ of its body weight daily. Suppose a child who weighed 30 kilograms (66 lb) could eat $\frac{2}{3}$ of his or her body weight. How many kilograms of food is that?

Tidal Pool Community

sea urchin

crab

starfish

 Art

Producers and Decomposers

Choose a community like a tide pool or a forest. Research the types of producers and consumers in that community. Use pictures to make a display to show what you learned.

 For more links and activities, go to **www.hspscience.com**

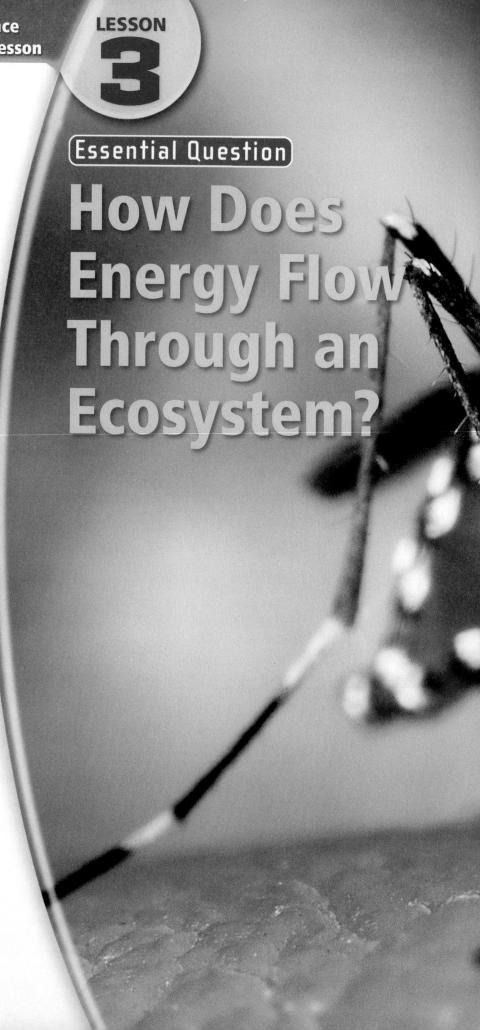

Content

S4L1b Demonstrate the flow of energy through a food web/food chain beginning with sunlight and including producers, consumers, and decomposers.

Characteristics of Science

S4CS5b **S4CS8b**

LESSON
3

Essential Question

How Does Energy Flow Through an Ecosystem?

Georgia
Fast Fact

Ouch!

More than 50 kinds of mosquitoes live in Georgia. They can be found in every county in the state. Only female mosquitoes bite people and other animals. They need the blood to produce eggs. You may think mosquitoes are nothing but pests, but they are an important food source for some animals.

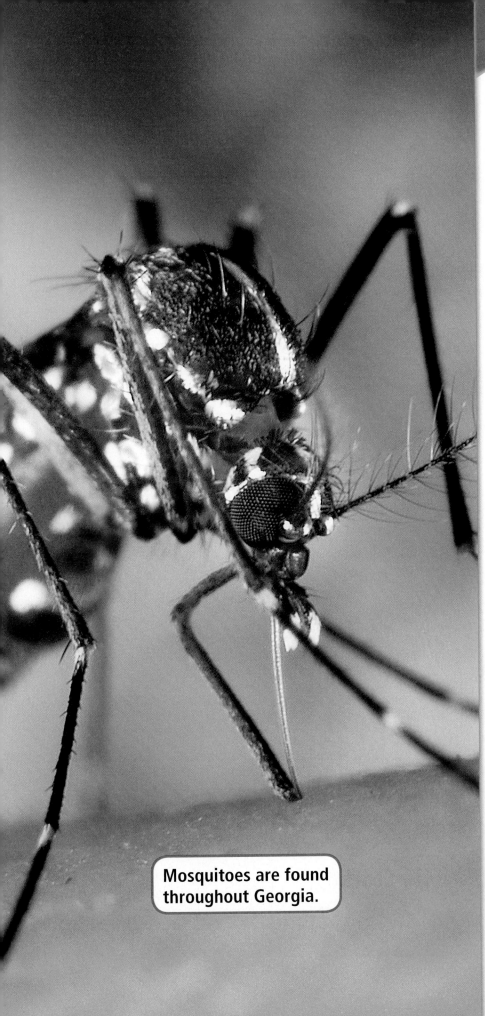

Mosquitoes are found throughout Georgia.

habitat [HAB•ih•tat] An environment that meets the needs of an organism (p. 326)

niche [NICH] The role of an organism in its habitat (p. 327)

food chain [FOOD CHAYN] A series of organisms that depend on one another for food (p. 328)

prey [PRAY] Consumers that are eaten by predators (p. 328)

predator [PRED•uh•ter] A consumer that eats prey (p. 328)

food web [FOOD WEB] A group of food chains that overlap (p. 330)

energy pyramid [EN•er•jee PIR•uh•mid] A diagram showing how much energy is passed from one organism to the next in a food chain (p. 333)

Make a Food Chain

Start with Questions

This snake has just swallowed food in order to get the energy it needs to live.

- What kinds of animals do snakes eat? What do these animals eat?

- How can we show the feeding relationships in ecosystems?

Investigate to find out. Then read to find out more.

Prepare to Investigate

Inquiry Skill Tip

Scientists communicate their ideas in many ways. Before you communicate, think about ways to present your ideas, such as the order in which to put things or whether you should include diagrams or pictures.

Materials

- 8 to 10 blank index cards
- reference books about animals
- colored pencils or markers

Make an Observation Chart

Kind of Organism	What It Eats

Follow This Procedure

1. Choose a place where animals live. Some examples are pine forest, rain forest, desert, wetland, and ocean.

2. On an index card, draw a living thing that lives in the place you have chosen. Draw more living things, one kind on each card. Include large animals, small animals, and producers. Look up information about plants and animals if you need help.

3. Put your cards in an order that shows what eats what. You might have more than one set of cards. If one of your animals doesn't fit anywhere, trade cards with someone. You can also draw another animal to link two of your cards. For example, you could draw a rabbit to link a grass card and a hawk card.

Draw Conclusions

1. Could the same animal fit into more than one set of cards? Why?

2. **Standards Link** Why do frogs eat flies? What kind of animal eats other animals? **S4L1b**

3. **Inquiry Skill** What do your cards communicate about the relationships of these living things to one another? **S4CS8b**

Step 2

Step 3

Independent Inquiry

Draw a series of cards in order, with yourself as the last consumer. Compare your role with the roles of other consumers. **S4CS5b**

325

VOCABULARY
habitat p. 326
niche p. 327
food chain p. 328
prey p. 328
predator p. 328
food web p. 330
energy pyramid p. 333

SCIENCE CONCEPTS
▶ how consumers depend on other living things
▶ how energy moves through food chains and food webs

Focus Skill SEQUENCE
Look for the order in which things happen.

☐ → ☐ → ☐

Habitats

You probably wouldn't see a heron in a desert or a penguin in a swamp. Animals must live in places that meet their needs. A **habitat** is an environment that meets the needs of a living thing. An insect's habitat can be as small as the space under a rock. A migrating bird's habitat can cross a continent.

Many habitats can overlap. For example, the three living things pictured on this page all live in a desert habitat. This desert habitat meets all their needs. Sagebrush grows well here. Sidewinders and tarantulas find many small consumers to eat.

These living things thrive in the desert habitat, even though it's hot and has little water.

The venomous sidewinder eats mice, rats, lizards, and birds. ▶

Sidewinder

◀ Tarantulas are venomous, too. They eat insects, other spiders, and small lizards.

Tarantula

Sagebrush can grow where other plants can't. Sheep and cattle often eat sagebrush in the winter. ▶

Sagebrush

Each living thing in a habitat has a role, or **niche** (NICH). The term *niche* describes how a living thing interacts with its habitat. Part of a living thing's niche is how it gets food and shelter. Its niche also includes how it reproduces, cares for its young, and avoids danger. Each animal has body parts that help it carry out its role. For example, a cat's pointed claws and sharp eyes help it catch its food.

Part of the sidewinder's niche is to eat small animals in its habitat. If all these snakes died, the desert would have too many mice, birds, and lizards. These small animals would eat all the available food and would soon starve. The sidewinder's niche helps keep the number of small desert animals in balance.

Focus Skill SEQUENCE

What would happen next if all the sagebrush disappeared from a desert?

Crab

Lion-fish

Anemone

This coral reef habitat has a balance of producers and consumers. Everything in this picture is a consumer.

Food Chains

Living things depend on one another to live. A **food chain** is the movement of food energy in a sequence of living things. Every food chain starts with producers. Some consumers, such as deer, eat these producers. Then the deer are eaten by other consumers, such as mountain lions. Consumers that are eaten are called **prey**. A consumer that eats prey is a **predator**. Prey are what is hunted. Predators are the hunters.

Some animals in a habitat are prey, while other animals are predators. Predators limit the number of prey animals in a habitat. Wolves are predators of antelope. They keep the population of antelope from increasing too much, so the antelope don't eat all of the producers. Predators often compete for the same prey. This limits the number of predators in a habitat.

Focus Skill SEQUENCE What would happen next if the number of predators in a habitat increased too much?

A swamp is a forested, freshwater wetland. Swamps are often classified by the types of trees that grow in them. The most common tree in the Okefenokee Swamp is the cypress.

Cypress trees have wide bases and large, deep roots that help to give them stability.

American eels are one of 39 kinds of fish in the Okefenokee. Their varied diet includes insects, worms, crayfish, frogs, and other fish.

Without hawks, the chipmunk population would get very large. The chipmunks would eat all the acorns and then starve.

Acorns provide energy for the chipmunk, which in turn provides energy for the hawk.

Snakes are common in swamps. The Okefenokee Swamp has 36 kinds. One of the most beautiful and rare of these is the rainbow snake. Its preferred meal is the American eel.

Although the alligator is just one of the predators in a swamp habitat, it is the dominant reptile.

Food Webs

A food chain shows how an animal gets energy from one food source. But food chains can overlap. One kind of producer may be food for different kinds of consumers. Some consumers may eat different kinds of food. For example, hawks eat sparrows, mice, and snakes.

Several food chains that overlap form a **food web**. There are food webs in water habitats, too. For example, herons eat snails, fish, and other birds.

On the next page, you can see an ocean food web. It shows that energy moves from plankton, small producers in the ocean, to small shrimp. These shrimp are called *first-level consumers*.

These shrimp then become prey for fish and other *second-level consumers*. They, in turn, are eaten by the biggest fish and mammals in the ocean, called *top-level consumers*.

Focus Skill **SEQUENCE** What happens after a first-level consumer eats a producer?

Follow several paths in this food web. Begin at the bottom, with a producer, and trace the movement of energy through the web.

Antarctic Ocean Food Web

This food web begins with energy from the sun. The producers are tiny plantlike organisms called phytoplankton (FYT•oh•plangk•tuhn). They float near the water's surface because sunlight can't reach deep underwater. No plants grow at the bottom of the ocean. Where would decomposers fit in this food web?

For more links and animations, go to **www.hspscience.com**

Energy Pyramids

Not all the food energy of plants is passed on to the herbivores that eat them. Producers use about 90 percent of the food energy they produce for their own life processes. They store the other 10 percent in their leaves, stems, roots, fruits, and seeds.

Animals that eat producers get only 10 percent of the energy the producers made. These herbivores then use 90 percent of the energy they got from the producers. They store the other 10 percent in their bodies.

Math in Science
Interpret Data

Only 10 percent of the food energy, measured in Calories, passes up to the next level in an energy pyramid. Suppose the bottom level contains 10,000,000 Calories. How many would be passed up to each level?

The fox and the owl must eat many smaller animals to get enough energy to live. ▶

Birds, mice, and other small animals must eat many producers to get the energy they need to live. ▶

The bottom of an energy pyramid can include thousands of producers. ▶

An **energy pyramid** shows that each level of a food chain passes on less food energy than the level before it. Most of the energy in each level is used at that level. Only a little energy is passed on to the next level.

Because each level passes so little energy to the next, the first-level consumers need many producers to support them. In the same way, the second-level consumers need many first-level consumers to support them. This pattern continues up to the top of the food chain.

That's why the base of an energy pyramid is so wide. That's also why only one or two animals are at the top of the pyramid. Most food chains have only three or four levels. If there were more, a huge number of producers would be needed at the base of the pyramid!

Sometimes, things in the environment may cause the number of organisms at one level of the pyramid to change. Then the whole food chain is affected. Suppose a drought kills most of the grasses in an area. Then some of the first-level consumers will starve. Many of the second- and higher-level consumers will go hungry, too.

◀ A wolf must eat many smaller animals, such as foxes and owls, to get the energy it needs to live.

Focus Skill **SEQUENCE** What can happen to a food chain if the number of second-level consumers increases?

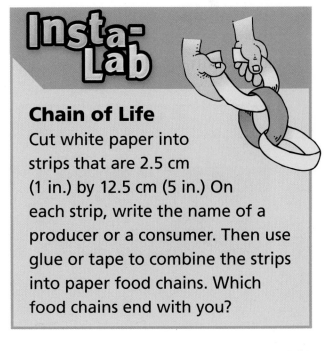

Insta-Lab

Chain of Life
Cut white paper into strips that are 2.5 cm (1 in.) by 12.5 cm (5 in.) On each strip, write the name of a producer or a consumer. Then use glue or tape to combine the strips into paper food chains. Which food chains end with you?

Essential Question

How does energy flow through an ecosystem?

In this lesson, you learned that each living thing in a habitat has its role, or niche. You also learned that producers and consumers are all connected in food chains and food webs.

1. (Focus Skill) **SEQUENCE** Draw and complete a graphic organizer in which you order the following organisms to make a food chain: *woodpecker, hawk, leaves, and insects.* S4L1b

2. **SUMMARIZE** Write a summary of this lesson. Begin with this sentence: *Living things depend on one another.* S4L1b

3. **DRAW CONCLUSIONS** How are predators good for prey? S4L1b

4. **VOCABULARY** Use the vocabulary terms to make a quiz. Then trade quizzes with a partner. S4L1b

5. **Critical Thinking** How would the deaths of all of one kind of consumer affect a food web? S4L1b

CRCT Practice

6. Which of these BEST shows why deer must eat grass all day long?
   A diagram
   B energy pyramid
   C food chain
   D food web   S4L1b

7. Which term describes animals that eat producers?
   A first-level consumers
   B second-level consumers
   C third-level consumers
   D top-level consumers   S4L1b

8. What might happen to the rabbits in a certain area if all the wolves in this area died?

The **Big** Idea

S4L1b

 Writing | ELA4W2

Informational Writing

Write about ways that people might affect a food web. For example, people might cut down trees to have a place for building houses, or they might feed the deer in a park. Think about the sequences of living things in the food web, and then tell what might change.

 Math | M4N5e

Solve a Problem

Producers in a field have stored 20,000 Calories. The first-level consumers that eat all the producers store 2000 Calories. If the pattern continues, how much energy could the next level of consumers store?

 Art

Food Chains

Choose any art medium, such as watercolor, charcoal, collage, or torn paper, and show the living things in a food web. (You don't have to show them eating one another!)

 For more links and activities, go to **www.hspscience.com**

LESSON 4

Content

S4L1c Predict how changes in the environment would affect a community (ecosystem) of organisms.

S4L1d Predict effects on a population if some of the plants or animals in the community are scarce or if there are too many.

Characteristics of Science

S4CS6b **S4CS8a**

Essential Question

What Factors Influence Ecosystems?

Georgia Fast Fact

Prescribed Burn
Frequent fires are needed to keep this ecosystem healthy. Fire clears the ground, leaving bare, nutrient-rich soil, which longleaf-pine seeds need to germinate. Fire also causes many other plants to flower. Without fire, other kinds of trees would eventually replace the longleaf pine, changing the nature of this important ecosystem.

Burned longleaf-pine forest

biotic [by•AHT•ik] Describes a living part of an ecosystem (p. 340)

abiotic [ay•by•AHT•ik] Describes a nonliving part of an ecosystem (p. 342)

Observing the Effects of Water

Guided Inquiry

Start with Questions

The Atacama Desert in Chile, shown below, is the driest place on Earth. It hasn't rained in some parts of this desert for 400 years!

- Can living things survive without water?

- How are ecosystems affected by lack of rain?

Investigate to find out. Then read to find out more.

Prepare to Investigate

Inquiry Skill Tip

When you compare things, you tell how they are alike and how they are different. Observe the things carefully, and make a short list that describes each one.

Materials

- water
- large labels
- 4 small identical plants in clay pots

Make an Observation Chart

	Day 1	Day 4	Day 7	Day 10
Plant 1 (watered)				
Plant 2 (watered)				
Plant 3 (not watered)				
Plant 4 (not watered)				

Follow This Procedure

1 Use the labels to number the pots 1, 2, 3, and 4. Label pots 1 and 2 *watered.* Label pots 3 and 4 *not watered.*

2 Make a chart like the one shown on page 338. Draw a picture of each plant under Day 1.

3 Place all four pots in a sunny window.

4 Water all four pots until the soil is a little moist. Keep the soil of pots 1 and 2 moist during the whole experiment. Don't water pots 3 and 4 again.

5 Wait three days. Then observe and record how each plant looks. Draw a picture of each one under Day 4.

6 Repeat Step 5 twice. Draw pictures of the plants on Days 7 and 10.

Draw Conclusions

1. What changes did you observe?

2. **Standards Link** Based on your observations, what can you conclude? **S4L1c**

3. **Inquiry Skill** How could you compare how fast the soil dries out in a clay pot with how fast it dries out in a plastic pot? **S4CS6b**

Step 1

Step 4

watered

not watered

Independent Inquiry

How does covering a plant with plastic wrap affect the plant's need for water? Write your hypothesis. Then design and carry out an experiment to check your hypothesis. **S4CS8a**

S4L1c, d

SCIENCE CONCEPTS
▶ how biotic and abiotic factors affect ecosystems
▶ how climate influences an ecosystem

CAUSE AND EFFECT
Look for ways in which factors affect ecosystems.

cause ⟶ effect

Living Things Affect Ecosystems

Do plants and animals need each other? Yes, they do! Plants and animals are living parts of an ecosystem. These living parts are **biotic** factors. *Bio* means "life." Biotic factors affect the ecosystem and one another in many ways.

For example, plants provide food for caterpillars, birds, sheep, and other animals. People eat plants every day— at least they should.

Plants also provide shelter for animals. For instance, many insects live in grasses. Squirrels make dens in trees. Your home likely contains wood from trees.

Animals help plants, too. When animals eat one kind of plant, it can't spread and take over all the available space. This gives other kinds of plants room to grow.

A gypsy moth can lay 1000 eggs or more. Most of the eggs hatch into hungry caterpillars like this one. ▶

A healthy tree isn't hurt when a few insects nibble on it.

Gypsy moth caterpillars can eat all the leaves on a tree. Bad weather or an attack by other insects may kill trees.

Animals help plants in other ways. Animal droppings make the soil richer. Earthworms help loosen the soil. Rich, loose soil helps plants grow.

At the same time, too many plant eaters can be harmful. A herd of hungry deer can eat enough leaves to kill a tree. A huge swarm of locusts can leave a field bare of plants.

You know that animals affect one another. For example, wolves eat rabbits. If the wolf population becomes too large, wolves can wipe out the rabbits. Then the wolves go hungry. Without the rabbits to eat them, the grasses spread.

In this case, an increase in wolves causes a decrease in rabbits. Fewer rabbits causes an increase in plants.

A change in plants can also cause a change in animals. If dry weather or disease kills the grasses, the rabbits starve. Then the wolves go hungry, too. Disease can also kill animals in an ecosystem.

Sometimes, a new kind of plant or animal changes an ecosystem. For example, people brought the skunk vine to the United States from Asia in 1897. For a time, they planted it as a crop. Now it grows wild. This smelly vine can grow 9 meters (30 ft) long! It crowds out other plants, and it can even grow underwater.

Focus Skill CAUSE AND EFFECT

Explain how an increase in plants could affect an ecosystem.

Math in Science
Interpret Data

food supply

number of deer

0 5 years 10 years 15 years 20 years 25 years

What happened to the population of deer as the food supply got smaller?

Tree leaves are a main source of food for deer. It takes 15 to 30 acres of land to provide enough food for one deer.

341

Nonliving Things Affect Ecosystems

Plants and animals are the living parts of an ecosystem. The nonliving parts include sunlight, air, water, and soil. The nonliving parts are **abiotic** factors. They are just as important as the biotic factors.

For example, a change in the water supply can affect all the living things in an ecosystem. Too little rain causes many plants to wilt and die. Animals must find other homes. Some may die.

An ecosystem with rich soil has many plants. Where the soil is poor, few plants grow. Few plants mean few animals in the ecosystem.

Air, water, and soil can contain harmful substances. They can affect all living things in an ecosystem.

 **CAUSE AND EFFECT**

How might a change in the water supply affect a rabbit population?

Insta-Lab

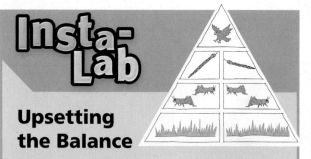

Upsetting the Balance

Make an energy pyramid. In the bottom row, draw grass. In the next row, draw four grasshoppers. In the next row, draw two snakes. At the top, draw one hawk. How would the hawk be affected if you took away half of the grass?

Science Up Close

Nonliving Factors

Without the nonliving parts of an ecosystem, there would be no living parts.

Sunlight
Plants need sunlight to produce food. Where trees shade the ground, not many other plants can grow.

Water
Almost all living things need water. Plant roots absorb water, and animals drink it.

Soil
Most plants need soil to grow. The kind of soil in an ecosystem is one of the factors that determines which plants grow there.

For more links and animations, go to **www.hspscience.com**

Climate Affects Ecosystems

What is the climate like where you live? Is it warm and sunny, or is it cool and rainy? Maybe it's something in between.

Climate is an abiotic factor. It's a combination of other abiotic factors. Climate includes the amount of rainfall and sunlight in a region. It also includes the repeating patterns of the temperature of the air during the year.

Climate affects the soil. Some climates allow many plants to grow and help dead plants decay. Animals that eat the plants leave behind their droppings. The decaying plants and droppings make the soil richer.

Climate affects the kinds of plants and animals in an ecosystem. For example, warm, wet climates support tropical rain forests. Hot summers and cold winters result in temperate forests.

The frozen tundra suits the hardy caribou. The mosses they eat thrive there. Zebras could not survive in the tundra. They need the mild climate and tender grasses of the savanna.

Focus Skill CAUSE AND EFFECT

What would happen to an ecosystem if its climate changed?

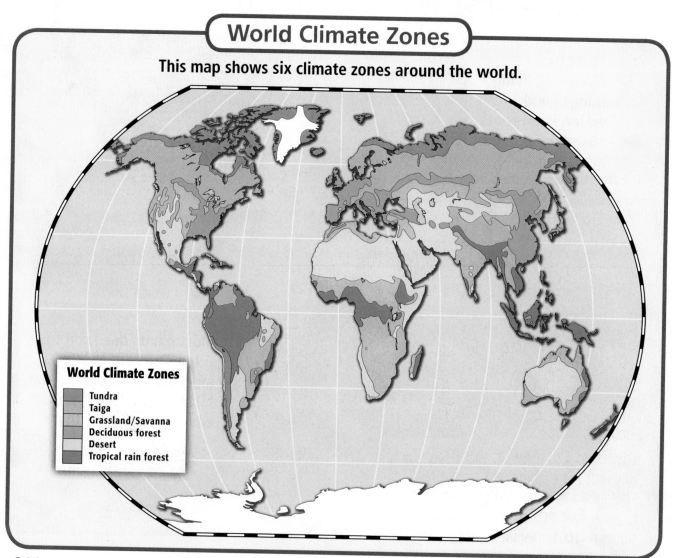

World Climate Zones

This map shows six climate zones around the world.

World Climate Zones
- Tundra
- Taiga
- Grassland/Savanna
- Deciduous forest
- Desert
- Tropical rain forest

Deciduous forests have four seasons. The trees, such as oaks and maples, lose their leaves in the fall. This helps them survive the cold winters.

Rain forests receive 2000 to 10,000 millimeters (7 to 33 ft) of rain each year! Tropical rain forests are near the equator.

The climate in the grassy savanna is nearly the same all year. The temperature stays between 18°C and 22°C (64°F and 72°F).

Deserts get only about 250 millimeters (10 in.) of rain a year. Plants there grow very quickly after a rain. Their seeds can survive for years as they wait for more rain.

The taiga covers more of Earth than any other kind of plant community. The taiga is mostly just south of the tundra and is very cold in winter. Most of its trees are evergreens.

The tundra has the coldest climate: −40°C to 18°C (−40°F to 64°F). *Tundra* means "treeless plain."

Essential Question

What factors influence ecosystems?

In this lesson, you learned how biotic and abiotic factors affect ecosystems. Climate, which is mostly determined by rainfall and temperature, affects the kinds of plants and animals that can live in a particular region.

1. (Focus Skill) **CAUSE AND EFFECT** Draw and complete a graphic organizer to tell how an ecosystem would be affected by each of the following changes: an increase in the hawk population; washing away of soil; and an increase in the average temperature. **S4L1c, d**

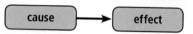

cause → effect

2. SUMMARIZE Write a summary of this lesson by using the vocabulary terms in a paragraph. **S4L1c, d**

3. DRAW CONCLUSIONS Which can exist without the other—biotic factors or abiotic factors? Explain your answer. **S4L1c, d**

4. VOCABULARY Write a quiz-show-type question for each of the vocabulary words. **S4L1c, d**

5. Critical Thinking The lynx and rabbit populations in an area decreased after a drought caused many of the plants to die. How do you account for these changes? **S4L1c, d**

CRCT Practice

6. Which is an abiotic factor?

 A earthworm **C** ant

 B decaying plant **D** sand

S4L1c

7. Bittersweet vines grow quickly up trees, where they block light and cause the trees to die. What is this an example of?

 A trees meeting a basic need

 B climate changing a community

 C pollution harming an ecosystem

 D a biotic factor changing an ecosystem **S4L1d**

8. How do the nonliving parts of an ecosystem affect the survival of the living parts? **S4L1c**

The **Big** Idea

Informational Writing

Cogongrass has been in the southeastern United States since the early 1900s but has only recently spread to Georgia. It forms thick mats that crowd out other plants. Use library resources to research other nonnative plants or animals. Write a report to summarize your findings.

9÷3 Math | M4N2d

Estimate

A sea otter that weighs 25 kilograms needs to eat at least 6.25 kilograms of food a day. What is the total amount of food the habitat must provide the sea otter during 100 days?

Social Studies | IPS 3, 9, 11

Water Resources

People use fresh water for many things. Do research to find out about freshwater resources in your county or region. Be sure to look for information about water quality and availability. Share your findings in an oral or written report.

For more links and activities, go to **www.hspscience.com**

Blairsville

The Georgia MOUNTAIN RESEARCH and EDUCATION CENTER

Nestled in the Blue Ridge Mountains near Blairsville is the Georgia Mountain Research and Education Center. It was set up in 1930. On its 415 acres, scientists test the health of cattle, field crops, fruit trees, vegetable plants, and grasses. In all, the staff oversees about 50 projects. There's even one that may save hemlock trees.

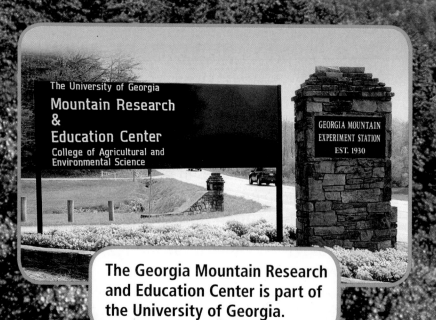

The University of Georgia
Mountain Research & Education Center
College of Agricultural and Environmental Science

GEORGIA MOUNTAIN EXPERIMENT STATION EST. 1930

The Georgia Mountain Research and Education Center is part of the University of Georgia.

Notice how gray the center hemlock has become. Infested with woolly adelgids, it may die soon.

In spring, adelgids hatch from white, cotton-like egg sacs. One sac can contain as many as 300 eggs.

This adult beetle eats woolly adelgid young.

Beetles or Poison?

An insect called the woolly adelgid is killing the hemlocks. Like an aphid, the adelgid sucks nutrients from the trees. The trees begin to drop needles and turn gray. Within four to ten years, they are dead.

Scientists at the research center are testing two ways to save the hemlocks. The first method uses a certain kind of beetle. This beetle eats the adelgid eggs and their young. In the second method, scientists put insecticide into the soil around the hemlocks. The trees absorb the insecticide through their roots. When the adelgids suck on the trees' needle-like leaves, the insecticide kills them.

The scientists are keeping careful records of these two investigations. In time, they will know which method kills more adelgids and is safer for the environment.

A Spreading Problem

The adelgid was accidentally brought to North America from Asia in about 1922. Since then, it has spread from northern Georgia to Maine and from northern California to Alaska. Wind, birds, animals, and people cause it to spread 15 to 20 miles a year.

After adelgids weaken a tree, other insects and diseases may attack it, too. If hemlocks disappear from the mountains, many ecosystems will be affected. If the researchers are able to find a safe way to get rid of the adelgids, thousands of trees can be saved.

✍ Think and Write

❶ How can predators help save the hemlocks?

S4L1a

❷ Scientists at the research center need to know what else these beetles may eat, besides adelgids. Why?

S4L1d

Wrap-Up

▶ Visual Summary

Tell how each picture helps explain the **Big Idea**.

The Big Idea

All living things need energy and matter to live and grow.

Lesson 1 S4L1

Ecosystems

Within ecosystems are communities made up of populations of different types of living things. Climate largely determines the kinds of plants and animals that live in an ecosystem.

Lesson 2  S4L1a

Roles of Organisms

Producers use the sun's energy to make their own food. Animals obtain some of this energy when they eat producers or other animals. Decomposers return nutrients to the environment.

Lesson 3 S4L1b

Energy Flow

Animals and plants live in specific habitats that meet their needs. Food webs consist of overlapping food chains, which show the movement of food energy among living things.

Lesson 4 S4L1c, d

food supply

number of deer

0   5 years 10 years 15 years 20 years 25 years

Ecosystems and Change

Various factors affect how an ecosystem functions. Biotic factors include the number and kinds of plants and animals. Abiotic factors are nonliving. Climate is a combination of abiotic factors.

Show What You Know

Writing About Ecosystems/Informational Writing

Producers, such as plants, are the first source of food in food webs. As cities and towns grow, more and more land is being used. There are fewer resources available for producers. Some cities and towns are trying to establish parks to give producers the resources they need. Research how parks are being used. Find out if the parks really help maintain healthy food webs. Explain your idea for the "perfect park." **ELA4W2**

Georgia Performance Task

Make a Food Web

Draw a scene that shows a food web in an ecosystem. Label each member of this food web with its role or roles. Then show the same food web in trouble in some way. Perhaps there are few or none of one kind of producer. Perhaps there are too many of one kind of consumer. Under your drawing, explain what is wrong and predict what is likely to happen. **S4L1b, d**

Vocabulary Review

Use the terms below to complete the sentences. The page numbers tell you where to look in the chapter if you need help.

producer p. 314   **niche** p. 327

consumer p. 314   **predator** p. 328

omnivore p. 316   **food chain** p. 328

decomposer p. 318   **energy pyramid** p. 333

1. An animal that eats other living things is a _____. `S4L1a, b`

2. Nutrients would be lost without _____. `S4L1a, b`

3. The animals at the top of a food chain are always _____. `S4L1b`

4. The kind of food that an animal eats is part of its _____. `S4L1b, c`

5. Animals that eat both producers and other consumers are _____. `S4L1a, b`

6. Herbivores and omnivores both eat _____. `S4L1a, b`

7. A food web shows relationships among living things more accurately than a _____. `S4L1b`

8. The loss of energy along a food chain is shown in an _____. `S4L1b`

Check Understanding

Write the letter of the best choice.

9. Which of these must a pond food chain have? (p. 314) `S4L1a, b`
   A algae   C tiny fish
   B sunlight   D whales

10. **MAIN IDEA AND DETAILS**
    Which term includes herbivores, carnivores, and omnivores? (pp. 314, 316) `S4L1a`
    A prey   C consumers
    B predators   D producers

11. Purple loosestrife is a pretty flower that grows in wetlands. It originally came from Europe. Wherever it grows, the population of native plants, such as cattails, shrinks. What is this an example of? (p. 341) `S4L1c, d`
    A pollution
    B climate change
    C humans destroying a habitat
    D a biotic factor affecting an ecosystem

12. Which of the following do herbivores eat? (p. 316) `S4L1a`
    A consumers
    B omnivores
    C predators
    D producers

13. What is shown below? (p. 328)

S4L1b

A niche   C food chain

B habitat   D food web

14. Which of the following has the greatest effect on an ecosystem? (p. 344)

S4L1c

A communities

B biotic factors

C population

D climate

15. Which of these is an abiotic factor? (p. 342)

S4L1c

A disease

B lack of food

C cold temperatures

D introduction of a new animal

16. SEQUENCE What is the first organism in a food chain? (p. 328)

S4L1b

A a consumer

B a decomposer

C a producer

D a predator

Inquiry Skills

17. Compare a carnivore and a predator. How are these living things the same? How are they different?

S4CS6a

18. While hiking with your family, you follow a trail that leads past many dead plants. Even the trees seem to be dying. The soil is very dry. What can you **infer** is happening to the consumers in this area?

S4CS8a

Critical Thinking

19. Biologists noticed that the wolf and rabbit populations in one area decreased after a drought. A year later, the biologists noticed an increase in the rabbit population. How do you account for these changes?

S4L1d

20. Different types of diagrams are used to show the relationships among living things. Study this diagram.

The **Big** Idea

How is this diagram different from a food chain? Would this diagram be correct if there were two snakes at the top? Tell why or why not.

S4L1b

Georgia Performance Standards in This Chapter

Content

S4L2 Students will identify factors that affect the survival or extinction of organisms such as adaptation, variation of behaviors (hibernation), and external features (camouflage and protection).

S4L2a, b

This chapter also addresses these co-requisite standards:

Characteristics of Science

S4CS4 Students will use ideas of system, model, change, and scale in exploring scientific and technological matters.

S4CS4c

S4CS8 Students will understand important features of the process of scientific inquiry.

S4CS8a, c

What's the Big Idea?

Certain body parts and behaviors can help living things survive, grow, and reproduce.

Essential Questions

GO online for student eBook www.hspscience.com

Calhoun County

Dear Jada,

We've been searching the sandhills of Calhoun County in hopes of seeing a gopher tortoise.

I had never seen our state reptile—until now. This is one BIG turtle! It uses its shovel-like front legs to dig in the sand. Dad told me that it shares its burrow with lots of other animals—even snakes. This turtle is BRAVE!

Your cousin,
Clarissa

USA

What did Clarissa say about the tortoise's body and behavior? How does this relate to the **Big Idea?**

Content

> **S4L2a** Identify external features of organisms that allow them to survive or reproduce better than organisms that do not have these features (for example: camouflage, use of hibernation, protection, etc.).

Characteristics of Science

> **S4CS8a**

LESSON

1

Essential Question

What Are Physical Adaptations?

▶ **Georgia Fast Fact**

Prey Beware!
The alligator snapping turtle, found in rivers in southwestern Georgia, is the largest freshwater turtle in North America. As the turtle lies quietly with its mouth open, the lure wiggles in the current, attracting prey. When the prey comes too close, the turtle snaps its powerful jaws shut. Clearly, this turtle has special body parts that help it meet its needs.

Alligator snapping turtle in the Flint River

356

basic needs [BAY•sik NEEDZ]
Food, water, air, and shelter that an organism needs to survive (p. 360)

adaptation
[ad•uhp•TAY•shuhn] A body part or behavior that helps an organism survive (p. 362)

camouflage [KAM•uh•flahzh]
A color or shape that helps an animal hide (p. 362)

Eating Like a Bird

Guided Inquiry

Start with Questions

The shape and size of your mouth makes it easy for you to eat many types of food. The shape and size of a bird's beak determines the kinds of food it can eat.

- Have you noticed that the beaks of a sparrow, a cardinal, and a duck are different?

- Why do you think their beaks are so different?

Investigate to find out. Then read to find out more.

Prepare to Investigate

Inquiry Skill Tip

To draw a conclusion, combine your observations or collected data with what you already know. Then decide what seems to be logical.

Materials

tools—
- 2 chopsticks or unsharpened pencils
- clothespin
- pliers
- spoon
- forceps

food—
- plastic worms
- raisins
- cooked spaghetti
- peanuts in shells
- water in a cup
- small paper plates
- cooked rice
- birdseed

Make an Observation Chart

Food	Best Tool (Beak)	Observations

Follow the Procedure

1. Make a chart like the one shown on page 358.

2. Put the tools on one side of your desk, and think of them as bird beaks. Put each kind of food on a paper plate.

3. Place one type of food in the middle of your desk. Try picking up the food with each tool (beak), and decide which kind of beak works best.

4. Test all the beaks with all the foods and with the water. Use the chart to **record** your observations and conclusions.

Draw Conclusions

1. Which kind of beak is best for picking up small seeds? Which kind is best for crushing large seeds?

2. **Standards Link** Why do different kinds of birds have different kinds of beaks?

   S4L2a

3. **Inquiry Skill** Scientists experiment and then **draw conclusions** about what they have learned. What **conclusions** can you draw about which beak works best with water?

   S4CS8a

Step 2

Step 3

Independent Inquiry

Use a reference book about birds. Match the tools you used with real bird beaks. Make a **hypothesis** about how beak shape relates to food. Then read your book to find out if you are correct.

S4CS8a

VOCABULARY
basic needs p. 360
adaptation p. 362
camouflage p. 362

SCIENCE CONCEPTS
▶ what basic needs are shared by all living things
▶ how adaptations allow living things to meet their needs

Focus Skill **MAIN IDEA AND DETAILS**
Look for different kinds of basic needs.

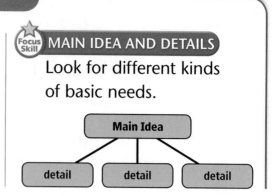

Basic Needs

What do you need to survive? You might want jeans in the latest style. You might want pizza for dinner every night. But you do not really need these things to survive. All living things have the same **basic needs**: food, water, air, and shelter.

Living things meet their needs in a variety of ways. Plants can make their own food, but they must have sunlight to do it. Most other living things depend on plants— or on animals that eat plants— for food.

Many animals, such as frogs and wolves, get their food by catching it. Some animals, such as vultures, wait until another animal has killed something. Then they eat the leftovers. Humans get most of their food by growing and raising plants and animals.

Plants get water from rain and from moist soil. Many animals drink water from streams and puddles, but some desert animals obtain enough water to survive from the foods they eat.

Like every other living thing, a tiger needs water.

All animals must take in oxygen. Animals that live on land and some animals that live in water get oxygen from air. Other animals that live in water get oxygen from the water.

Shelter can take many forms. Some insects live under rocks, while foxes make dens in hollow logs. Prairie dogs dig burrows in the ground, and eels hide in coral reefs. Delicate plants grow in protected places. People build homes of many sizes and shapes.

Hunger and thirst signal the need to eat and drink. Rain and cold tell many animals to find shelter. Meeting basic needs isn't always easy, but living things must do it to survive.

Focus Skill **MAIN IDEA AND DETAILS**

How do you meet your basic needs?

After beavers cut sticks and twigs from trees, they eat the leaves and bark. Then they use the sticks to build shelters. ▶

▼ The heron's long beak helps it catch frogs and fish in shallow water.

▲ Like other living things, this alligator needs air. It keeps its nostrils above water while it watches for food.

Adaptations

Plants and animals have adaptations that help them meet their needs. An **adaptation** is a body part or a behavior that a living thing gets from its parents and that helps it survive.

You have explored differences in bird beaks. Different kinds of feet also help birds meet their needs. A robin can perch on a branch because of the shape of its feet. An eagle uses its talons to snatch up food, while a duck swims by using its webbed feet.

Many frogs and lizards have long tongues that help them catch insects.

Lions use their speed, strength, long claws, and sharp teeth to catch food.

Fish and reptiles are covered with scales that help protect them from injury and from drying out. A snake's scales also help it slide along the ground.

Rattlesnakes locate prey by using their sense of smell and special organs that sense the heat given off by another animal's body. These heat-sensitive organs enable a rattlesnake to aim its strike with great accuracy, even in the dark. The rattlesnake disables its prey with a strong poison known as venom that moves into the prey's body through hollow teeth called fangs.

Another animal adaptation is called camouflage. **Camouflage** (KAM•uh•flahzh) is a color or shape that helps an animal blend with its environment. For example, during the summer, the snowshoe hare is rusty brown. The brown color matches the ground. In the winter, the rabbit's fur turns white, making it hard for predators to see it against the snow. The color change helps the rabbit hide.

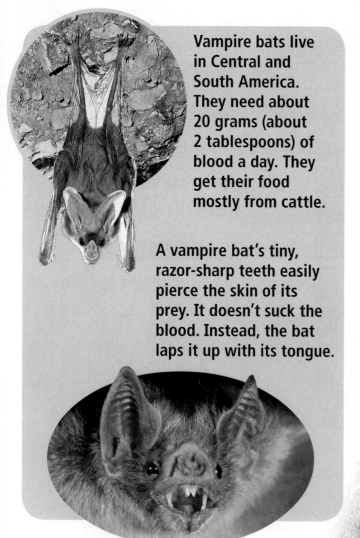

Vampire bats live in Central and South America. They need about 20 grams (about 2 tablespoons) of blood a day. They get their food mostly from cattle.

A vampire bat's tiny, razor-sharp teeth easily pierce the skin of its prey. It doesn't suck the blood. Instead, the bat laps it up with its tongue.

▼ A goat's teeth are adapted for the food it eats. Large and flat, these teeth are just right for grinding up grasses.

362

eastern coral snake

Many birds do not notice this leaf moth because it is camouflaged. The shape and color of its wings hide it from predators.

Both the coral snake and the scarlet king snake have yellow, red, and black bands. Looking like the deadly coral snake keeps the scarlet king snake safe.

scarlet king snake

Animals that are poisonous may advertise their poison with bright colors to warn predators to stay away. Animals that eat snakes know that the colorful stripes of the coral snake signal danger. The scarlet king snake has similar stripes. Even though the scarlet king snake is harmless, predators see its bright colors and leave it alone.

Plants also have adaptations that help them meet their needs. You know about the carnivorous plants that grow in the Okefenokee Swamp and in other Georgia wetlands. These plants get some of the nutrients they need by eating insects. For example, pitcher plants hold small pools of liquid inside their long stalks, or pitchers. The insect falls into the liquid and is digested.

The leaves of this sundew have long, stringy hairs that are covered with a sticky substance. When an insect becomes stuck, the leaf slowly closes and the insect is digested.

MAIN IDEA AND DETAILS

How does camouflage help animals?

Insta-Lab

All Thumbs
Use masking tape to tape your partner's thumb to his or her hand. Then ask your partner to write, pick up a pencil, eat, and so on. How is a thumb an adaptation?

363

What are physical adaptations?

In this lesson, you learned that animals and plants possess special body parts, or physical adaptations, that help them meet their basic needs within their particular habitats.

1. (Focus Skill) **MAIN IDEA AND DETAILS** Draw and complete a graphic organizer to give examples of adaptations that help animals obtain food, water, and shelter. **S4L2a**

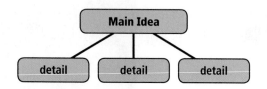

2. SUMMARIZE Write a summary of this lesson. Begin with the sentence *All living things have basic needs.* **S4L2a**

3. DRAW CONCLUSIONS In what ways is an animal's body covering important to its survival? **S4L2a**

4. VOCABULARY Write a paragraph that includes a blank for each vocabulary term. Have a partner fill in the terms. **S4L2a**

5. Critical Thinking An animal is dark brown, with a long, shaggy coat. It moves slowly and can't climb trees. How well do you think this animal would survive in a desert ecosystem? A rainforest? Explain your answer. **S4L2a**

CRCT Practice

6. Which adaptation helps a robin catch a worm?
  A sharp eyesight
  B feather coloring
  C perching feet
  D nest building **S4L2a**

7. Which of these is an example of camouflage?
  A sharp teeth
  B a long, pointed beak
  C the ability to climb trees
  D a body shape that resembles a twig **S4L2a**

8. Choose one animal or plant and tell how its adaptations help it to survive. **S4L2a**

The **Big** Idea

 Writing ELA4W2

Narrative Writing

Write a story about how a real animal in a tropical rain forest uses an adaptation to meet its needs in some way. Your story should have a beginning, a middle, and an end. Use vivid sensory details to describe the setting and the events. Don't forget to make your story exciting!

 Math M4N4d

Solve a Problem

A deer must have about 20 acres of land to meet its need for food, water, and shelter. One square mile has 640 acres. How many deer could live on 2 square miles of land?

 Art

Basic Needs

This barn owl meets one of its needs by finding shelter in a tree. Cut out magazine pictures, or use your own drawings, to make a collage of the basic needs of a specific animal or of a person. Then display your work.

 For more links and activities, go to **www.hspscience.com**

Science Spin

On the Prowl

Cameras are helping scientists count jaguars.

A sleek, spotted jaguar sneaks along the thick forest floor. As it passes a fig tree, there is a whirring noise. A flashing light and click follow. A camera has just snapped the cat's photograph.

No person was behind the camera's lens. The camera was triggered by motion and heat from the passing cat.

A Narrowing Range

Scientists from the Wildlife Conservation Society in New York have placed about 30 such cameras in trees throughout the tropical forest of Belize (beh•LEEZ). That is a country in Central America.

This forest is also the site of the world's first jaguar reserve. A reserve is an area set apart for a special purpose. At the reserve in Belize, jaguars are protected and can safely roam.

Belize has a healthy number of jaguars. The wildlife group estimates that about 14 jaguars live within a 143-square-km (55-square-mile) area there. The cameras are helping researchers count the jaguars within certain areas of Belize and in other places where jaguars roam.

"Camera trapping" will help scientists because jaguars are hard to study. Despite the cats' hefty size, their mysterious nature and the thick jungle where they live make them difficult to spot.

A camera snaps a photograph of a passing jaguar.

UNITED STATES
ATLANTIC OCEAN
MEXICO
PACIFIC OCEAN
CENTRAL AMERICA
SOUTH AMERICA

KEY
Where jaguars live now
Where jaguars used to live

The map shows how the range of jaguars has changed.

"The cameras help researchers determine how many cats are out there and where they make their homes," jaguar expert Kathleen Conforti told WR.

The researchers will use that information to help protect the endangered animals. They want to conserve, or save, the jaguars' habitat. A habitat is the area where the animal naturally lives.

The actions of people have caused a decline in the animal's range. The cutting down of trees has destroyed some of the jaguars' habitat.

Think and Write

1. How might the loss of trees affect how jaguars live? **S4L2b**

2. How might equipment such as cameras help protect endangered animals around the world? **S4CS8c**

What a Roar

- Jaguars, which are carnivorous, can grow up to 1.8 meters (6 ft) long and weigh up to 136 kilograms (300 pounds).
- Jaguars are the third-largest cats, after tigers and lions.
- The cats usually live alone and are very territorial. That means they protect their habitat from other jaguars.
- In Spanish, this cat's name is *el tigre,* which means "the tiger."

Find out more. Log on to **www.hspscience.com**

367

Content

S4L2a Identify external features of organisms that allow them to survive or reproduce better than organisms that do not have these features (for example: camouflage, use of hibernation, protection, etc.).

S4L2b Identify factors that may have led to the extinction of some organisms.

Characteristics of Science

S4CS4c   **S4CS8a**

Georgia Fast Fact

Fighting for Survival

The North Atlantic right whale is Georgia's official state marine mammal—as well as the world's most endangered large whale. Although this whale species spends much of the year in northern waters, pregnant females and others migrate during late fall to the waters off the coast of Georgia and northeastern Florida, where the calves are born. During April, the whales return to northern waters. Currently, fewer than 350 of these whales are thought to exist.

LESSON

2

Essential Question

What Are Behavioral Adaptations?

North Atlantic right whale off the coast of Georgia

instinct [IN•stingkt] A behavior that an animal begins life with and that helps it meet its needs (p. 372)

hibernation [hy•ber•NAY•shuhn] A dormant, inactive state in which normal body activities slow (p. 373)

migration [my•GRAY•shuhn] The movement of animals from one region to another and back (p. 374)

extinction [ek•STINGK•shuhn] The death of all the members of a certain group of organisms (p. 376)

Vanishing Habitats

Guided Inquiry

Start with Questions

Florida panthers were once found throughout the Southeast, including the Okefenokee Swamp and the Blue Ridge. The few remaining panthers live only in southern Florida.

- What is "habitat loss"?
- How does habitat loss affect animal populations?

Investigate to find out. Then read to find out more.

Prepare to Investigate

<table>
<tr><td>Inquiry Skill Tip</td></tr>
<tr><td>When you infer, you draw a conclusion based on your observations. Analyze your inferences to make certain that they agree with all of your observations and collected data.</td></tr>
</table>

Materials

- globe or world map
- graph paper
- graphic calculator or computer (optional)

Make an Observation Chart

Changes Over Time		
Time Period	Rain Forest Area	Population
1990–2000		
2000–2005		

Follow This Procedure

1 Locate Ecuador, a country in South America, on the globe or a world map.

2 Study the data table. It shows the area of Ecuador's rain forests and the size of its human population in 1990, 2000, and 2005.

Rain Forest Area and Human Population in Ecuador			
Year	1990	2000	2005
Rain Forest (square km)	138,000	118,000	108,000
Population (in millions)	10.5	12.6	13.4

3 Using graph paper and a pencil, a graphing calculator, or a computer, **display** the rain-forest data in a graph that shows the changes in forest area over time. Make another graph to **display** the changes in population size.

Step 3

4 **Compare** the two graphs. Look for patterns in the data. **Record** your observations in the chart.

Draw Conclusions

1. What relationship, if any, exists between the change in human population and the amount of rain forest?

2. **Standards Link** Based on the data, what do you think the size of the rain forests in Ecuador will be in 2010 if the human population continues to increase in the same way? **S4L2b**

3. **Inquiry Skill** If rain-forest habitats keep getting smaller, what can you **infer** about the populations of animals that live in them? **S4CS4c**

Independent Inquiry

Research the changes in the size of the human population over several decades in your area. Then make a graph to display the changes.

Hypothesize how these changes in the human population might have affected plant and animal populations in your area. Plan and conduct a simple investigation to test your hypothesis. **S4CS8a**

SCIENCE CONCEPTS
▶ how instinctive behaviors help animals meet their needs
▶ how extinction can occur

 **MAIN IDEA AND DETAILS**

Look for ways animals fill their basic needs.

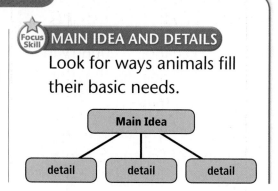

Instincts

When you were born, you already knew how to suck to get milk. You knew how to cry. Animals already know things, too. A spider knows how to spin a web to catch food. Some animals, like zebras, know that living together in herds helps protect them from predators. Some animals know how to protect themselves from the weather. All of these behaviors are **instincts**—behaviors that animals begin life with that help them meet their needs.

MAIN IDEA AND DETAILS

What are some instinctive behaviors?

▼ Orb-weaver spiders spin new webs every night. Each kind of spider begins life knowing the pattern for its own kind of web.

▲ Weaverbirds build complex nests from grasses and other materials. They hatch knowing how to weave their nests.

Hibernation

Some animals live where winters are very cold. Many of them know by instinct how to get ready for winter. First, they eat more food than normal, so they can gain fat. Then, they find dens or build shelters. When the days become short and cold, the animals move to shelters. They enter a dormant, inactive state called **hibernation** (hy•ber•NAY•shuhn). Normal body activities slow. The heart barely beats, and breathing almost stops. The body temperature drops to just above freezing.

Since the body is barely working, a hibernating animal doesn't use much energy and doesn't need to eat. There is enough fat stored in the animal's body to keep it alive through the winter. By springtime, hibernating animals are thin. They are very hungry!

MAIN IDEA AND DETAILS

Why do some animals hibernate?

▲ A bat's normal heartbeat rate is 400 beats per minute. When the bat hibernates, its heart beats 11 to 25 times per minute.

Some male frogs hibernate at the bottom of ponds. The female frogs and their young stay in holes or dens on land. ▼

▼ A woodchuck digs a winter burrow. Its body temperature drops from 36°C (97°F) to less than 8°C (46°F).

Migration

Every year, people gather to watch whales. People also like to watch caribou travel. It's possible to predict when to watch whales and caribou. These animals travel every year at about the same time.

Migrate means "to move from one region to another." When animals regularly move as a group from one region to another and back, it's a **migration**. Animal migrations can depend on seasons or on other factors.

Migration is an instinctive behavior. Generally, animals migrate to a place that has more food and a better climate. Some migrations are puzzling. For example, young salmon go out to sea. They return to lay eggs in the mountain stream where they were hatched.

Focus Skill MAIN IDEA AND DETAILS

How do animals know when to migrate?

Math in Science
Interpret Data

Which Animal Migrates the Farthest?

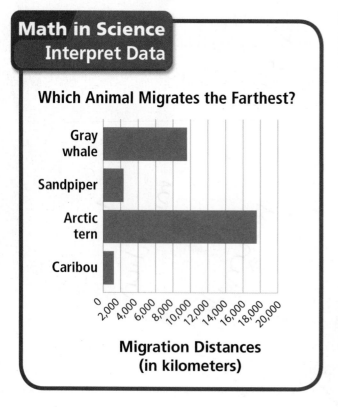

Migration Distances
(in kilometers)

Animal Migration Routes

Gray whales feed in cold northern waters in winter and travel south in summer to look for mates and to give birth.

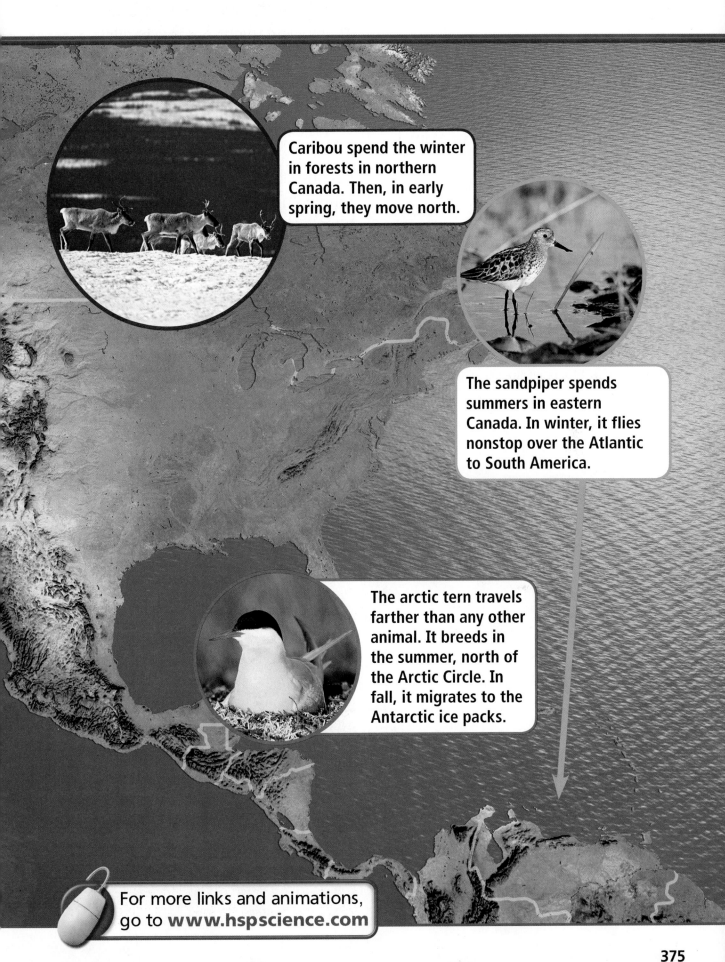

Caribou spend the winter in forests in northern Canada. Then, in early spring, they move north.

The sandpiper spends summers in eastern Canada. In winter, it flies nonstop over the Atlantic to South America.

The arctic tern travels farther than any other animal. It breeds in the summer, north of the Arctic Circle. In fall, it migrates to the Antarctic ice packs.

For more links and animations, go to www.hspscience.com

Extinction

You have learned that plants and animals have adaptations that enable them to survive in a particular habitat. If the habitat changes, these adaptations may no longer help the plant or animal meet its needs.

For example, suppose the habitat becomes drier or colder. Plants may die. Animals must move or they will die, too. Animals may also die if there is not enough food.

An environmental change can be so great that it affects many living things. About 65 million years ago, more than half of all the kinds of living things on Earth died out, including the dinosaurs. These living things became extinct (ek•STINGKT). **Extinction** of a certain group of living things means that all of its members have died.

This extinction was caused by a major change in Earth's climate. Some scientists think that an asteroid hit Earth, sending up a dust cloud so big that it blocked out the sun. Without sunlight, plants died, followed by many herbivores and most carnivores.

 MAIN IDEA AND DETAILS When a habitat changes, what may happen to the plants and animals that live there?

The last woolly mammoth died about 30,000 years ago. ▼

Bachman's warbler was found throughout the Southeast. It was last seen in the early 1960s and is now thought to be extinct. Loss of habitat is the primary cause. ▼

Fossils of saber-toothed cats have been found in California's La Brea (BRAY•uh) tar pits. The last saber-toothed cat died about 10,000 years ago.

Hairy rattleweed lives only in Georgia, in the pine woods of Wayne and Brantley Counties. Because of logging, this plant is endangered.

The gray bat is listed as endangered. It was known to live in northwest Georgia. The main reason for the drop in its numbers is that people have disturbed and damaged the caves in which it roosts.

Human Activity

Human activities can contribute to extinction. People destroy habitats when they cut down forests for timber or fill wetlands to make space for homes and shopping malls.

When people clear land to build homes and businesses, they break the land into small patches. Animals cannot travel from patch to patch in order to find food or mates.

Sometimes people introduce plants or animals from other regions. These organisms crowd out native plants and animals. Examples are the kudzu vine and Chinese privet, which have covered millions of acres in Georgia.

Humans also make positive changes. In 1973, the United States Congress passed the Endangered Species Act. The act lists plants and animals according to how small their populations are.

Things listed as *endangered* have populations so small that they are likely to become extinct if steps to save them aren't taken right away. Places such as state and national wildlife refuges protect endangered birds, mammals, reptiles, coral reefs, and plants.

Things listed as *threatened* are likely to become endangered if they aren't protected. Threatened animals are protected by strict hunting laws.

Focus Skill MAIN IDEA AND DETAILS

Give several reasons for habitat loss.

Observing Change

Look for photographs that show how your community looked 50 or 100 years ago. Then sketch or photograph areas that have since changed. Write about the changes. Tell whether they have been helpful or harmful.

Essential Question

What are behavioral adaptations?

In this lesson, you learned that animals are born with instinctive behaviors that help them to survive. You also learned about some of the reasons why living things become extinct.

1. (**Focus Skill**) **MAIN IDEA AND DETAILS** Draw and complete a graphic organizer to give details about three categories of instinctive behaviors: everyday behaviors, hibernation, and migration. **S4L2a**

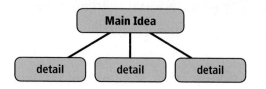

2. **SUMMARIZE** Use the graphic organizer to write a paragraph in which you summarize how animals meet their basic needs. **S4L2a**

3. **DRAW CONCLUSIONS** Think of an animal or plant in your state. What changes in the environment could cause it to become threatened or endangered? **S4L2b**

4. **VOCABULARY** Write a paragraph, using all the vocabulary terms from this lesson. **S4L2a, b**

5. **Critical Thinking** Which animal is most at risk of becoming extinct: an omnivore that is adapted to live in many habitats, or a herbivore that eats only one kind of plant? Explain. **S4L2b**

CRCT Practice

6. Why does a hibernating animal's temperature drop?

   A to gain energy

   B to provide food

   C to protect its young

   D to conserve energy **S4L2a**

7. Which of these would NOT cause extinction?

   A climate change

   B conservation

   C habitat loss

   D competition from nonnative species **S4L2b**

8. Summarize ways in which human activities can lead to the extinction of plants and animals.

   S4L2b

Writing

ELA4W2

Narrative Writing

Choose an animal that hibernates, such as a bat, chipmunk, hedgehog, woodchuck, or ground squirrel. Write a story about how that animal gets ready for hibernation.

Math

M4N2a

Round Whole Numbers

A bird called the Clark's nutcracker buries seeds to eat later. Last year, a flock of these birds buried 33,034 seeds and later dug up 21,987 of them. How many seeds were left in the ground? Round your answer to the nearest thousand.

Social Studies

IPS 1, 11, 13

Then and Now

Research what your region may have looked like 65 million years ago. What kinds of plants and animals lived in your neighborhood then? Write a brief report, with illustrations, to present your findings.

For more links and activities, go to **www.hspscience.com**

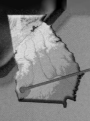
Joseph W. Jones
ECOLOGICAL RESEARCH CENTER
at Ichauway

Forest fires seem to destroy everything in their path, leaving nothing but burned trees and ash. However, fire is a natural part of many forest ecosystems. Animals depend on small fires to clear out brush. This gives them a place to live and also allows other small plants to thrive.

At the Joseph W. Jones Ecological Research Center, a private research facility not open to the public, scientists understand that fires help keep some ecosystems healthy. The forest in Ichauway is made up mostly of longleaf pine trees. The trees are adapted to handle fire. Their seeds are even fireproof.

The gopher frog spends much of its life near the temporary ponds where it breeds.

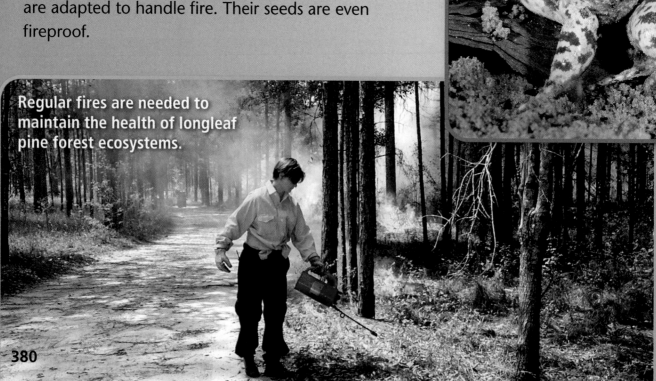

Regular fires are needed to maintain the health of longleaf pine forest ecosystems.

Habitat Protection

The longleaf pine ecosystem used to cover much of the southern United States. Now, these forests are much smaller. Years of cutting down trees and not planting new ones has caused this. Animals that live here depend on the longleaf pine forest to survive. Many are adapted to finding food and shelter in this type of forest. As the forest disappears, so do the animals.

The scientists at Joseph W. Jones Ecological Research Center have an opportunity to protect these animals. The land there contains some of the largest longleaf pine forests left in the country. Scientists use this area as an "outdoor laboratory." By learning more about the forest habitat, they can help protect the animals that live there.

Wildlife Research

Temporary ponds are a natural part of the longleaf pine ecosystem. They appear after a rainy period. This is where amphibians, such as frogs and newts, lay their eggs. The eggs are safe from being eaten by predators because there are no fish in the ponds. As the longleaf pine forest is destroyed or changed, these temporary ponds no longer form. As a result, the amphibians do not have a safe place to lay their eggs. Scientists at the Center are locating and protecting the ponds where these animals breed so that their populations will increase.

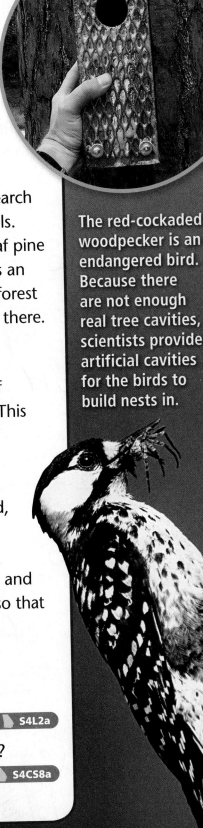

The red-cockaded woodpecker is an endangered bird. Because there are not enough real tree cavities, scientists provide artificial cavities for the birds to build nests in.

Think and Write

❶ How do animals depend on the longleaf pine ecosystem?

S4L2a

❷ How are scientists protecting rare amphibians?

S4CS8a

Visual Summary

Tell how each picture helps explain the **Big Idea**.

The Big Idea Certain body parts and behaviors can help living things survive, grow, and reproduce.

Lesson 1 — S4L2a

Physical Features
Living things need food, air, water, and shelter. Animals and plants have physical adaptations for specific habitats that enable them to meet these needs.

Lesson 2 — S4L2a, b

Survival and Extinction
Animals begin life with instinctive behaviors that help them to survive in their habitats. Loss of habitat is one of the main causes of population decline and of extinction.

Show What You Know

Chapter Writing Activity

Writing About the Environment/Persuasive Writing

Think of ways that your community could protect its plants and animals. One example might be using less weed killer on lawns. Then write a letter to the members of your city council. Convince them to adopt these changes so that living things in your community will not have to move or die. **ELA4W2, 3**

Georgia Performance Task

Environmental Education

Georgia is home to several endangered plant and animal species. Use library resources to identify one species that interests you. Find out how its population has changed over the past 30 years. Record your findings. Then make a poster that displays the data in a way that enables others to see a pattern. **S4L2a, b**

Vocabulary Review

Use the terms below to complete the sentences. The page numbers tell you where to look in the chapter if you need help.

basic needs p. 360   **hibernation** p. 373

adaptation p. 362   **migration** p. 374

camouflage p. 362   **extinction** p. 376

instincts p. 372

1. Both breathing rate and body temperature change during _____. **S4L2a**

2. The development of a thick beak for grinding seeds is an _____. **S4L2a**

3. Behaviors that you begin life with are _____. **S4L2a**

4. Air and water are _____. **S4L2**

5. When all the members of a species have died out completely, the result is _____. **S4L2b**

6. A color or body shape that helps an animal blend with its environment is called _____. **S4L2a**

7. When you see a flock of geese fly south in the fall, you are watching a _____. **S4L2a**

Check Understanding

Write the letter of the best choice.

8. Whales are mammals. Why does a whale surface? (p. 361) **S4L2a**
   A for fun   C for air
   B for food   D to see

9. **MAIN IDEA AND DETAILS** Which detail is NOT about instinctive behavior? (p. 372) **S4L2a**
   A You yawn.
   B Zebras live in herds.
   C A weaverbird builds its nest.
   D A kitten learns to hunt by watching its mother.

10. Which animal on this bar graph has the shortest migration route? (p. 374) **S4L2a**

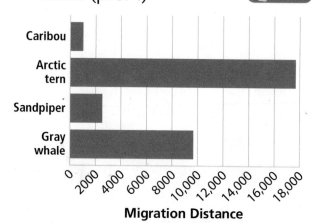

Migration Distance (km)

   A arctic tern
   B caribou
   C sandpiper
   D gray whale

11. MAIN IDEA AND DETAILS Which of the following is NOT a cause of extinction? (p. 377) **S4L2b**

A habitat loss

B climate change

C creation of a wildlife refuge

D competition from nonnative plants or animals

12. Notice the beak pictured here. What is it an adaptation for? (p. 361) **S4L2a**

A eating fruit   C grinding seeds

B eating leaves   D spearing fish

13. Why don't you see any ground squirrels in winter? (p. 373) **S4L2a**

A They are migrating.

B They don't like the cold.

C They are hiding.

D They are hibernating.

14. A rare fish lives in only one stream. A dam is built, and all the rare fish die. What is this an example of? (p. 376) **S4L2b**

A adaptation   C competition

B extinction   D migration

15. What are cows' teeth adapted for? (p. 362) **S4L2a**

A eating meat   C chewing grass

B eating fruit   D cracking seeds

16. Which is an example of camouflage? (p. 362) **S4L2a**

A a spider building a web

B a lion's sharp claws and teeth

C a lizard changing color to hide

D a woodchuck's dormant state during winter

Inquiry Skills

17. Woolly mammoth fossils have been found with human-made arrowheads embedded in them. Based on this evidence, **infer** what could have helped cause their extinction. **S4CS8**

18. What tool would you use as a **model** of the beak of a bird that eats seeds? **S4CS4**

Critical Thinking

19. Why do you think caribou grow hair on the bottom of each foot in winter and lose it in summer? **S4L2a**

20. Suppose you want to help save a bird that is threatened with extinction. What things should you study about its habitat? Why would it be a good idea to find out if the birds are laying eggs and how many chicks are hatching? **S4L2b**

The **Big** Idea

1. If resources are scarce in a community, populations may be affected. Which of the following describes a population?

A. a family living together in a house

B. a blue jay living alone in a tree

C. all the trout living in a lake

D. all the plants and animals in a forest

S4L1d

Use the picture below to answer question 2.

2. A scientist observed these sea turtles. The scientist MOST LIKELY said that the legs were adapted for

A. swimming.

B. catching fish.

C. eating plants.

D. walking on sand.

S4L2a

3. Bears are omnivores. Which meal would they eat?

A. grass only

B. berries and fish

C. fish only

D. herbivores only

S4L1b

4. Study the data in the table below.

	Number of Rabbits	Number of Wolves
Ecosystem #1	3,500	30
Ecosystem #2	1,550	62

What can you infer about these ecosystems?

A. Ecosystem #1 would be the first to be affected by a drought.

B. Ecosystem #2 would be the first to be affected by a drought.

C. Ecosystem #1 does not have enough carnivores.

D. Ecosystem #2 does not have enough plants.

S4L1c   S4CS5c

5. Where do producers get the energy they need to make their own food?

A. by eating

B. from the sun

C. from other producers

D. from the soil

S4L1b

Use the diagram below to answer question 6.

6. The energy pyramid above describes the flow of energy within a certain ecosystem. Which would BEST take the place of the question mark?

A. grass

B. fish

C. a beetle

D. a lion

7. Which type of organism breaks down wastes into nutrients that can be used by living things?

A. producer

B. consumer

C. decomposer

D. carnivore

S4L1a

8. Which list contains the basic needs of all living things?

A. plants, shelter, food, air

B. water, air, shelter, food

C. water, air, sunlight

D. water, shelter, salt

S4L2a

9. What type of animal is LEAST likely to become extinct?

A. an animal that eats many different things

B. an animal that is found only on a small island

C. an animal that can survive in only one climate

D. an animal that lives in only one river

S4L2b

Use the picture below to answer question 10.

10. Which is an adaptation that helps eagles catch food?

A. brown feathers

B. sharp talons

C. webbed feet

D. large, flat teeth

S4L2a

11. The rocks, soil, water, plants, and animals in an area make up

A. an ecosystem.

B. a population.

C. a niche.

D. climate.

S4L1c

Use the diagram below to answer question 12.

12. What would happen if rabbits were removed from this food chain?

A. The number of foxes would increase.

B. More grass would grow.

C. Less grass would grow.

D. There would be no change.

`S4L1d` `S4CS4b`

13. Which animal has the BEST camouflage for surviving life on or in a tree?

A. a blue beetle

B. a yellow bird

C. a brown caterpillar

D. an orange frog `S4L2a`

14. Canada geese survive harsh winters by flying south during the coldest months. This behavior is an example of

A. hibernation.

B. migration.

C. decomposing.

D. a food chain. `S4L2a`

Use the map below to answer question 15.

15. In which area on this map of South America would the living things in an ecosystem be MOST affected by a sudden and severe reduction in the amount of rain?

A. area 1: tropical rain forest

B. area 2: grassland

C. area 3: desert

D. area 4: tundra `S4L1c`

16. Which behavior is NOT an instinct?

A. a bird building a nest

B. whales migrating

C. tigers learning to hunt

D. spiders spinning webs `S4L2a`

17. Which of these organisms would occur first in a food chain?

A. bear

B. mushroom

C. grass

D. shark

18. What happens to an animal during hibernation?

A. Its heart rate increases.

B. Its body temperature increases.

C. Its rate of breathing slows.

D. All its body functions stop.

19. What would happen to an ecosystem if all its decomposers disappeared?

A. Wastes would be turned into nutrients.

B. The number of producers would increase.

C. The number of consumers would decrease.

D. Dead plant and animal matter would cover the ecosystem.

Use the graph below to answer question 20.

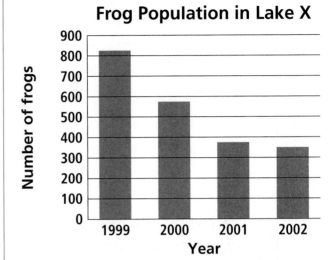

Frog Population in Lake X

20. What could have caused the change in the frog population that the graph shows?

A. The number of frog predators decreased.

B. Birds ate most of the insects the frogs usually eat.

C. The number of producers increased.

D. The frogs were hibernating.

1. Which statement about stars is true?

   A. The hottest stars are yellow.

   B. The newest stars are white.

   C. The hottest stars are red.

   D. The hottest stars are blue.

 S4E1a

2. Tony is pushing a box across the floor. Marta decides to help him. What is the effect of Marta's help?

   A. It increases the box's acceleration.

   B. It decreases the box's mass and acceleration.

   C. It reduces the box's momentum.

   D. It reduces friction between the box and the floor. S4P3c

Use the diagram below to answer question 3.

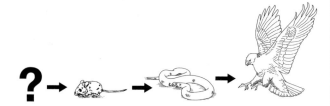

3. Which kind of organism is missing from this food chain?

   A. animal

   B. consumer

   C. decomposer

   D. producer

 S4L1a

4. Predict what might happen to plant life if all the decomposers in an ecosystem died.

   A. All the plants in the ecosystem would grow less because there would be fewer nutrients in the soil.

   B. All the plants in the ecosystem would grow more because there would be more nutrients in the soil.

   C. Plants would begin to take on the role of decomposer.

   D. Plants would live longer because there would be nothing in the ecosystem to break them down.

 S4L1a

5. You throw four balls of different masses with equal force. Which is the mass of the ball that will accelerate MOST (if air resistance has no effect)?

   A. 100 grams   C. 750 grams

   B. 500 grams   D. 950 grams

 S4P3b

6. A group of different populations that depend on each other for survival is

   A. an ecosystem.   C. a community.

   B. a niche.   D. a habitat.

 S4L1a

Use the diagram below to answer question 7.

7. What does this diagram BEST illustrate?

A. why the moon has phases

B. why the planets appear in different places in the sky

C. why we have night and day

D. why the sun is at the center of our solar system `S4E2a`

8. Which of the following describes the tundra?

A. very little precipitation; cactus and reptiles are the main living things

B. stable climate; living things include grasses and zebras

C. heavy rainfall; located near the equator

D. coldest climate, frozen soil; few trees can survive `S4L1c`

Use the graph below to answer question 9.

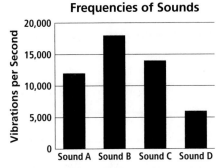

Frequencies of Sounds

9. The graph shows the number of vibrations per second for four different sounds. Which has the highest pitch?

A. Sound A

B. Sound B

C. Sound C

D. Sound D `S4P2b` `S4CS5c`

10. Damon plays a guitar. He pushes on a fret to shorten a thick string. Its sound has the same pitch as a longer, thinner string. He concludes that the thickness of a string has no effect on pitch. Why did Damon arrive at an incorrect conclusion?

A. Shortening a string has no effect on pitch.

B. The results would have been different if he had pushed on a different fret.

C. Strings of different thicknesses do not vibrate at the same rate.

D. A string's length also affects its pitch. `S4P2b` `S4CS6b`

Use the table below to answer question 11.

Type of Organism	Number of Individuals
W	27
X	3
Y	584
Z	112

11. Sophia investigated the living things in her neighborhood. She identified four kinds of organisms. She counted the number of each. Which is the BEST description of the living thing labeled Y?

A. producer

B. carnivore

C. consumer

D. herbivore

 S4L1a   S4CS5c

12. Which of the following does NOT change the amount of force needed to do work?

A. wedge

B. wheel-and-axle

C. inclined plane

D. single pulley S4P3a

13. A change in the amount of which abiotic factor would have an effect on organisms within that ecosystem?

A. worms

B. water

C. trees

D. consumers

S4L1c

14. What would happen if Earth's axis were tilted more than it is?

A. The Northern Hemisphere and the Southern Hemisphere would have the same seasons at the same time.

B. Winter at the North Pole and the South Pole would be even colder.

C. Earth would no longer have seasons.

D. Earth would rotate faster.

S4E2c

Use the diagram to answer question 15.

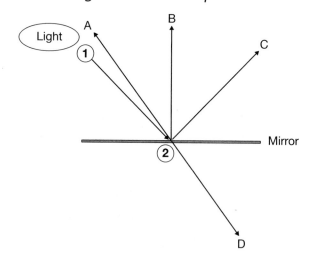

15. Light travels from point 1. It strikes a mirror at point 2. Which line indicates the direction in which the light is reflected?

A. line A

B. line B

C. line C

D. line D S4P1b   S4CS4b

392

16. Which kind of air is MOST likely to produce clouds?

A. cold, humid   C. warm, humid

B. cold, dry   D. warm, dry

 S4E3c

17. Patrick visited a desert ecosystem. While there, he observed the sun, jackrabbits, some wildflowers, and a coyote. Which of the following would appear on the top level of an energy pyramid?

A. coyote   C. sun

B. jackrabbits   D. wildflowers

 S4L1b

18. Suppose you view Ursa Major during winter. How will this constellation look if you view it from the same place in summer?

A. It will look the same because stars do not change their position in the sky.

B. It will look different because stars wander across the sky.

C. It will look different because Earth will have orbited halfway around the sun.

D. It will look different because Earth will have rotated on its axis.

S4E1c

19. Warm and wet conditions help plants and animals survive in

A. the tundra.

B. the taiga.

C. a desert.

D. a tropical rain forest.   S4L1a

Use this picture of a mountain road to answer question 20.

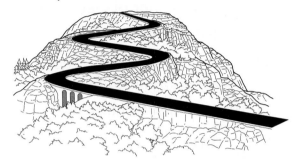

20. It is easier for vehicles to ascend a mountain using a winding road than by traveling straight up the mountain. A winding mountain road is actually a series of

A. wedges.

B. inclined planes.

C. wheel-and-axles.

D. levers.   S4P3a

21. Which is the BEST description of a bat's niche?

   A. lives in caves and old buildings

   B. has fur and wings

   C. is active only at night

   D. eats insects and helps keep the insect populations in balance

 S4L1a

22. How do the inner planets compare with the outer planets?

   A. The inner planets have more moons than the outer planets.

   B. The inner planets have longer years than the outer planets.

   C. The inner planets are windier than the outer planets.

   D. The inner planets are solid, but the outer planets consist of gases.

 S4E2d

23. You put your hand on a bell to stop its ringing. What have you done?

   A. stopped its vibrations

   B. increased the pitch of the sound

   C. increased the decibel level

   D. decreased the pitch of the sound

 S4P2a

24. Which statement is true?

   A. Planets shine with a steady light, while stars appear to twinkle.

   B. It is easier to see the planets in our solar system than stars because the planets glow with heat.

   C. Each planet keeps its position in the night sky, unlike the stars, which move across the sky.

   D. Stars are the brightest objects in the night sky. S4E1b

Use the picture to answer question 25.

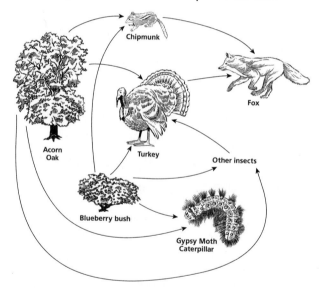

25. The diagram above shows a food web in a forest ecosystem. From which living thing does the chipmunk get some of its energy?

   A. fox

   B. turkey

   C. acorn oak

   D. gypsy moth caterpillar S4L1b

26. Doing which of the following will NOT raise the pitch of a sound made by a guitar?

A. tightening a string

B. shortening a string

C. loosening a string

D. replacing a thick string with a thin one

27. Which sequence correctly shows how energy flows among these four living things?

A. seeds → snake → mouse → hawk

B. seeds → mouse → snake → hawk

C. hawk → seeds → mouse → snake

D. snake → hawk → seeds → mouse

28. Which change in state is MOST likely to happen as ice warms up?

A. gas to solid

B. solid to gas

C. liquid to gas

D. solid to liquid **S4E3a**

29. You fill an empty glass with ice cubes from the refrigerator. What do you know about the ice cubes?

A. Their temperature is below 0°C.

B. Their temperature is above 0°C.

C. Their temperature is above 100°C.

D. Their temperature is just below 100°C. **S4E3b**

30. What happens to the sound made by a vibrating object when its rate of vibration increases?

A. Its loudness increases.

B. Its pitch increases.

C. Its pitch decreases.

D. Its frequency decreases.

31. If a winter wind is blowing from the south, the weather is likely to warm up. Which instrument below could help you decide which coat to wear to school?

A. anemometer

B. weather vane

C. rain gauge

D. barometer **S4E4a**

32. Which of the following BEST describes a decomposer?

A. changes energy in sunlight into food energy

B. breaks down remains of dead plants and animals

C. eats other living plants and animals

D. is a nonliving part of an ecosystem

33. Which of the following signals a change in the climate?

　A. a two-degree increase in air temperature over 30 years

　B. an unusually rainy spring

　C. an early, heavy winter snowfall

　D. record rainfall for October

34. Alexandria, Virginia, has warm summers and cold winters. Which living thing is BEST adapted to this environment?

　A. wolf

　B. polar bear

　C. cactus

　D. howler monkey

35. If a tree falls in the woods and no one is there to hear it, does it make a sound? A scientist would say "Yes." Why?

　A. The impact can be heard if a listener is close enough to the forest.

　B. Trees bend and sway and make noises in the wind even when they don't fall.

　C. The sound continues long after the tree has fallen.

　D. The impact of the tree with the ground produces vibrations.

36. Read the descriptions of diets in the table below.

Animal	Diet
Shark	Other fish, some mammals
Deer	Shrubs and flowers
Bear	Fish, roots and stems, berries
Eagle	Fish, mice, and other small mammals

Which of these animals is an omnivore?

　A. Shark

　B. Deer

　C. Bear

　D. Eagle

37. Why is wind speed important in predicting weather patterns?

　A. High winds mean that cool, dense air is surrounded by warmer, less dense air.

　B. High winds bring cirrus clouds.

　C. A polar air mass has high winds.

　D. High winds often mean that the air mass over an area is changing.

38. Which lenses may be used in one pair of eyeglasses or contact lenses?

A. convex only

B. concave only

C. either convex or concave

D. both convex and concave

 S4P1c

39. What happens to most of the light that strikes a transparent object?

A. It bounces backward.

B. It passes through.

C. It is absorbed.

D. It is separated.

 S4P1a

40. The fur of an arctic fox is white in winter and brown in summer. This color change is an example of

A. extinction.

B. migration.

C. camouflage.

D. hibernation.

 S4L2a

Use the weather map below to answer question 41.

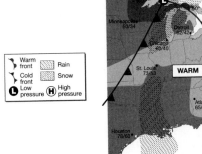

41. What has just happened and what is the weather likely to be in Atlanta tomorrow?

A. A warm front has just passed over, so it will be cooler and drier.

B. A warm front has just passed over, so it will be warmer and more humid.

C. A cold front has just passed over, so it will be cooler and drier.

D. A cold front has just passed over, so it will be warmer and more humid. S4E4b S4CS4b

42. Which part of the water cycle explains how dew forms on grass?

A. Heat turns water into water vapor.

B. Water vapor loses heat and condenses.

C. Water vapor condenses and freezes.

D. Water droplets become heavy and fall as precipitation.

 S4E3d

43. Which object bends light waves inward, so that they are closer together?

A.

C.

B.

D.

Use the table below to answer question 45.

Plant	Characteristics
A	Can live only in very salty water
B	Must live in very dry soil
C	Tolerates soggy soil but not salt
D	Able to live in both salt water and fresh water

45. Marcus lives near wetlands that used to contain mostly fresh water from a river. After the river was dammed, the area was often flooded with salt water from the ocean. Which plant from the list above would be able to survive this kind of change?

A. Plant A   C. Plant C

B. Plant B   D. Plant D

44. A person building a house wants light in a bathroom, but he does not want his neighbors to see into the room. Which kind of glass should he put in the bathroom windows?

A. transparent

B. opaque

C. translucent

D. mirrored

46. You look out your window and see hail. What caused this type of precipitation?

A. Water vapor condensed on the ground.

B. Water vapor condensed and froze at ground level.

C. Water vapor turned directly into ice crystals.

D. Water droplets passed through very cold air.

47. Sam uses a light meter to measure the amount of light that passes through different materials. He first measures clear glass. He calls the amount of light that passes through it 1.00. The table shows his results for glass and the other four materials.

Material	Amount of Light That Passes Through
Glass	1.00
1	0.10
2	0.25
3	0.60
4	0.03

Which material is the MOST opaque?

A. 1
B. 2
C. 3
D. 4

48. What is the original source of energy for most living things?

A. grass
B. sun
C. river
D. trees   S4L1b

Use the illustration below to answer question 49.

49. Which phase comes next, and why?

A. third quarter, because the amount of the moon's lit surface that we can see will decrease

B. first quarter, because the amount of the moon's lit surface that we can see will increase

C. new moon, because the moon will move within Earth's shadow

D. full moon, because we will see the side of the moon that faces the sun   S4E2b

50. Which word helps explain why "space junk" remains in orbit around Earth instead of flying off into deep space?

A. force   C. motion
B. mass   D. gravity

References

Contents

Health Handbook

Reading in Science Handbook

Math in Science Handbook   R28

Your Skin

Your skin is your body's largest organ. It provides your body with a protective covering. It protects you from disease. It provides your sense of touch, which allows you to feel pressure, texture, temperature, and pain. Your skin also produces sweat to help control your body temperature. When you play hard or exercise, your body produces sweat, which cools you as it evaporates. The sweat from your skin also helps your body get rid of extra salt and other wastes.

Epidermis
Many layers of dead skin cells form the top of the epidermis. Cells in the lower part of the epidermis are always making new cells.

▼ The skin is the body's largest organ.

Pore
These tiny holes on the surface of your skin lead to your dermis.

Dermis
The dermis is much thicker than the epidermis. It is made up of tough, flexible fibers.

Oil Gland
Oil glands produce oil that keeps your skin soft and smooth.

Hair Follicle
Each hair follicle has a muscle that can contract and make the hair "stand on end."

Fatty Tissue
This tissue layer beneath the dermis stores food, provides warmth, and attaches your skin to the bone and muscle below.

Caring for Your Skin

- To protect your skin and to keep it healthy, you should wash your body, including your hair and your nails, every day. This helps remove germs, excess oils and sweat, and dead cells from the epidermis, the outer layer of your skin. Because you touch many things during the day, you should wash your hands with soap and water frequently.

- If you get a cut or scratch, you should wash it right away and cover it with a sterile bandage to prevent infection and promote healing.

- Protect your skin from cuts and scrapes by wearing proper safety equipment when you play sports or skate, or when you're riding your bike or scooter.

Your Digestive System

Your digestive system is made up of connected organs. It breaks down the food you eat and disposes of the leftover wastes your body does not need.

Mouth to Stomach

Digestion begins when you chew your food. Chewing your food breaks it up and mixes it with saliva. When you swallow, the softened food travels down your esophagus to your stomach, where it is mixed with digestive juices. A strong acid continues the process of breaking your food down into the nutrients your body needs to stay healthy. Your stomach squeezes your food and turns it into a thick liquid.

Small Intestine and Liver

Your food leaves your stomach and goes into your small intestine. This organ is a long tube just below your stomach. Your liver is an organ that sends bile into your small intestine to help it digest fats in the food. The walls of the small intestine are lined with millions of small, finger-shaped bumps called villi. Tiny blood vessels in these bumps absorb nutrients from the food as it moves through the small intestine.

Large Intestine

When the food has traveled all the way through your small intestine, it passes into your large intestine. This last organ of your digestive system absorbs water from the food. The remaining wastes are held there until you go to the bathroom.

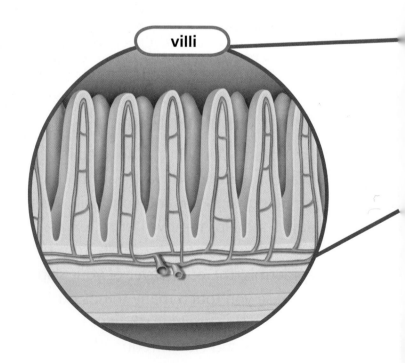

villi

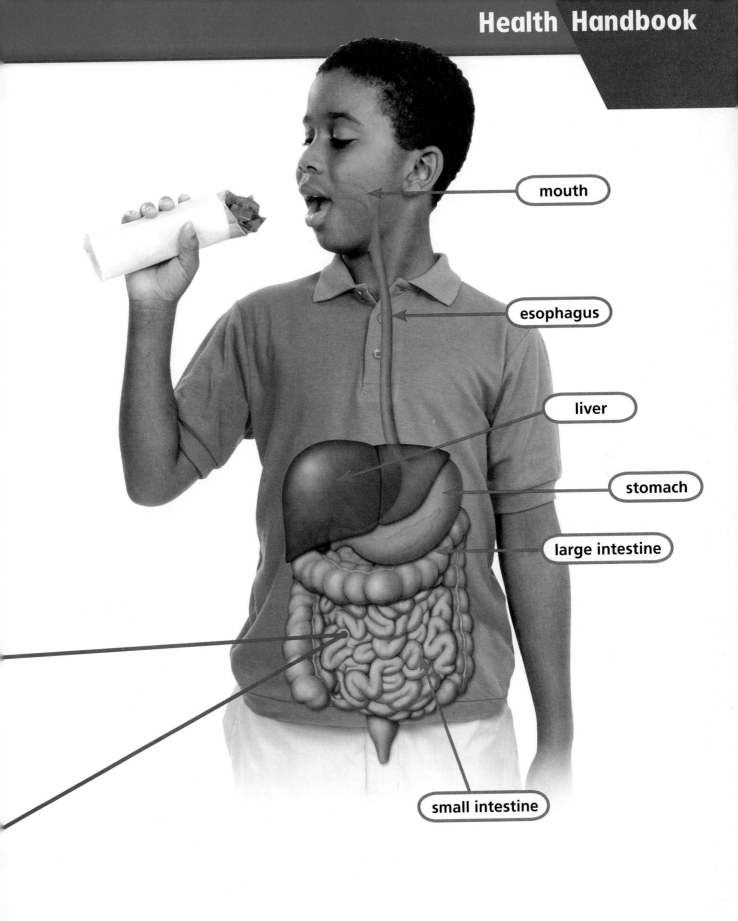

mouth

esophagus

liver

stomach

large intestine

small intestine

Your Circulatory System

Your circulatory system carries nutrients from the food you eat and oxygen from the air you breathe to every cell in your body. As your blood moves through your body, it helps your body fight infections, control your temperature, and remove wastes from your cells.

vein

heart

Your Heart and Blood Vessels

Your heart is the organ that pumps your blood through your circulatory system. It is a strong muscle that beats all the time. As you exercise, it adjusts itself to beat faster to deliver the nutrients and oxygen your muscles need to work harder.

artery

Blood from your heart is pumped first to your lungs, where it releases carbon dioxide and picks up oxygen. Your blood then travels back to your heart to be pumped through your arteries to every part of your body. The blood then returns to your heart through your veins, ready to be pumped out again.

Your Blood

The blood in your circulatory system is a mixture of fluids and specialized cells. The liquid part of your blood is called plasma. Plasma allows the cells in your blood to move through your blood vessels to every part of your body. It is also important in helping your body control your temperature.

Blood Cells

There are three main types of cells in your blood. Each type of cell in your circulatory system plays a special part in keeping your body healthy and fit.

Red blood cells are the most numerous cells in your blood. They carry oxygen from your lungs throughout your body. They also carry carbon dioxide from your cells back to your lungs so that you can breathe it out.

White blood cells help your body fight infections when you become ill.

Platelets help your body stop bleeding when you get a cut or other wound. Platelets clump together as soon as you start to bleed. The sticky clump of platelets traps red blood cells and forms a blood clot. The blood clot hardens to make a scab that seals the cut. Beneath the scab, your body begins healing the wound.

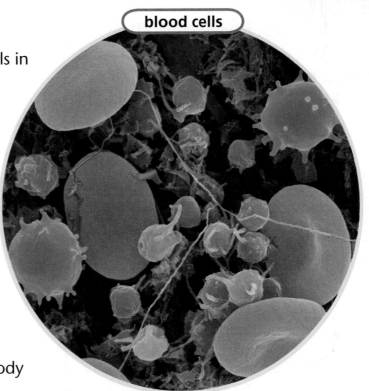

blood cells

Caring for Your Circulatory System

- Eat foods that are low in fat and high in fiber. Fiber helps take away substances that can cause fat to block your blood vessels.

- Eat foods high in iron to help your red blood cells carry oxygen.

- Drink plenty of water to help your body make enough blood.

- Avoid contact with another person's blood.

- Exercise regularly to keep your heart strong.

- Never smoke or chew tobacco.

Your Skeletal System

Your skeletal system includes all of the bones in your body. These strong, hard parts of your body protect your internal organs, enable you to move, and allow you to sit and to stand up straight.

Your skeletal system works with your muscular system to hold your body up and give it shape. It includes more than 200 bones of different shapes and sizes.

Your Skull

The wide, flat bones of your skull fit tightly together to protect your brain. The bones in the front of your skull give your face its shape.

Your Spine

Your spine, or backbone, is made up of nearly two dozen small, round bones. These bones fit together and connect your head to your pelvis. Each of these bones, or vertebrae (VER•tuh•bree), is shaped like a doughnut, with a small round hole in the center. There are soft, flexible disks of cartilage between your vertebrae. This allows you to bend and twist your spine. Your spine, pelvis, and leg bones work together to allow you to stand, sit, and move.

Your spinal cord is a bundle of nerves that carries information to and from your brain and the rest of your body. Your spinal cord runs from your brain down your back to your hips through the holes in your vertebrae.

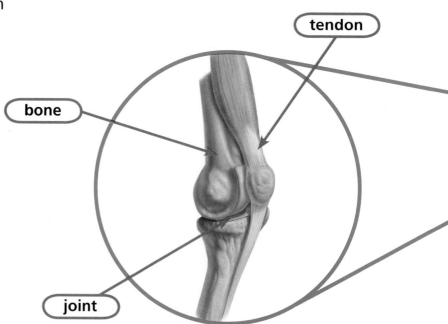

tendon

bone

joint

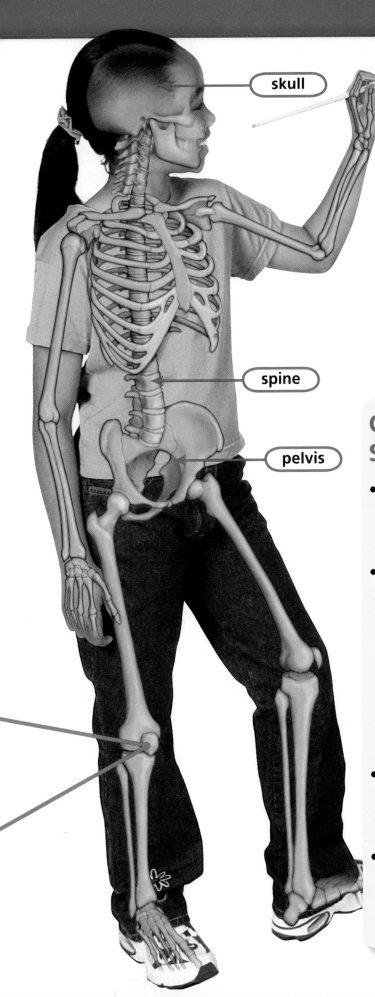

skull

spine

pelvis

Caring for Your Skeletal System

- Always wear a helmet and proper safety gear when you play sports, skate, or ride a bike or a scooter.

- Your bones are made mostly of calcium and other minerals. To keep your skeletal system strong and to help it grow, you should eat foods that are rich in calcium, such as milk, cheese, and yogurt. Dark green, leafy vegetables such as broccoli, spinach, and collard greens are also good sources of calcium.

- Exercise to help your bones stay strong and healthy. Get plenty of rest to help your bones grow.

- Stand and sit with good posture. Sitting slumped over puts strain on your muscles and on your bones.

Your Muscular System

A muscle is a body part that produces movement by contracting and relaxing. All of the muscles in your body make up the muscular system.

Voluntary and Involuntary Muscles

Voluntary Muscles are the muscles you use to move your arms and legs, your face, head, and fingers. You can make these muscles contract or relax to control the way your body moves.

Involuntary Muscles are responsible for movements you usually don't see or control. These muscles make up your heart, your stomach and other organs of your digestive system, and your diaphragm. Your heart beats and your diaphragm controls your breathing without your thinking about them. You cannot stop the actions of these muscles.

How Muscles Help You Move

All muscles pull when they contract. Moving your body in more than one direction takes more than one muscle. To reach out with your arm or to pull it back, you use a pair of muscles. As one muscle contracts to stretch out your arm, the other muscle relaxes. As you pull your arm back, the muscles reverse their functions.

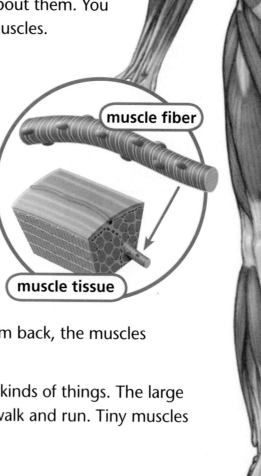

muscle fiber

muscle tissue

Your muscles let you do many kinds of things. The large muscles in your legs allow you to walk and run. Tiny muscles in your face allow you to smile.

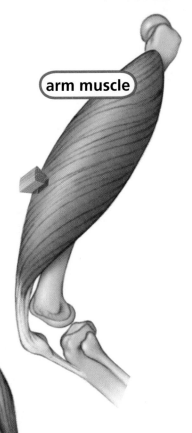

arm muscle

Your Muscles and Your Bones

The muscles that allow you to move your body work with your skeletal system. Muscles in your legs that allow you to kick a ball or ride a bicycle pull on the bones and joints of your legs and lower body. Your muscles are connected to your skeletal system by strong, cordlike tissues called tendons.

Your Achilles tendon just above your heel connects your calf muscles to your heel bone. When you contract those muscles, the tendon pulls on the heel bone and allows you to stand on your toes, jump, or push hard on your bicycle's pedals.

Caring for Your Muscular System

- Always stretch and warm your muscles up before exercising or playing sports. Do this by jogging or walking for at least ten minutes. This brings fresh blood and oxygen into your muscles and helps prevent injury or pain.

- Eat a balanced diet of foods to be sure your muscles have the nutrients they need to grow and remain strong.

- Drink plenty of water when you exercise or play sports. This helps your blood remove wastes from your muscles and helps you build endurance.

- Always cool down after you exercise. Walk or jog slowly for five or ten minutes to let your heartbeat slow and your breathing return to normal. This helps you avoid pain and stiffness after your muscles work hard.

- Stop exercising if you feel pain in your muscles.

- Get plenty of rest before and after you work your muscles hard. They need time to repair themselves and to recover from working hard.

Your Eyes and Vision

Your eyes allow you to see light reflected by the things around you. This diagram shows how an eye works. Light enters through the clear outer surface called the cornea. It passes through the pupil. The lens bends the incoming light to focus it on the retina. The retina sends nerve signals along the optic nerve. Your brain uses the signals to form an image. This is what you "see."

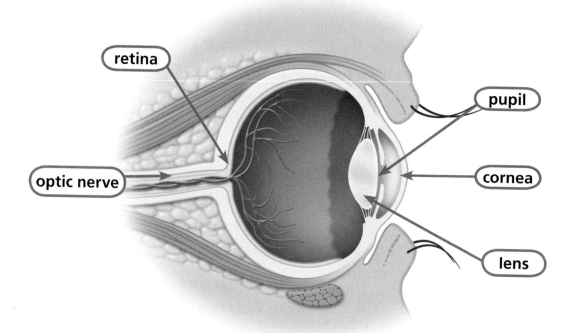

Caring for Your Eyes

- You should have a doctor check your eyesight every year. Tell your parents or your doctor if your vision becomes blurry or if you are having headaches or pain in your eyes.

- Never touch or rub your eyes.

- Protect your eyes by wearing safety goggles when you use tools or play sports.

- Wear swim goggles to protect your eyes from chlorine and other substances in the water.

- Wear sunglasses to protect your eyes from the sun's ultraviolet rays. Looking directly at the sun can damage your eyes permanently.

Your Ears and Hearing

Sounds travel through the air in waves. When those waves enter your ear, you hear a sound. This diagram shows the inside of your ear.

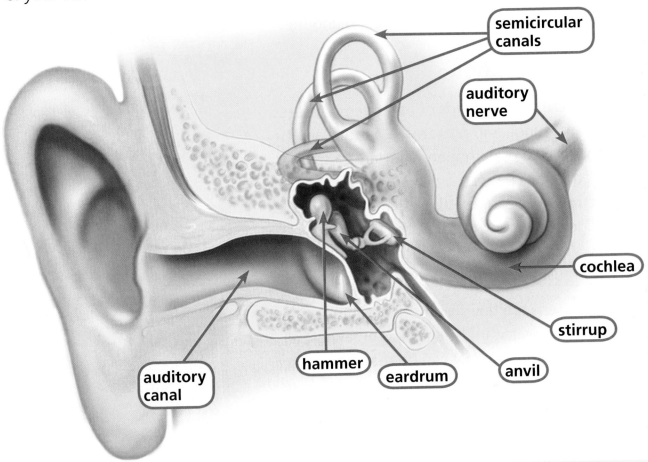

semicircular canals

auditory nerve

cochlea

stirrup

anvil

eardrum

hammer

auditory canal

Caring for Your Ears

- Never put anything in your ears.

- Wear a helmet that covers your ears when you play sports.

- Keep your ears warm in winter.

- Avoid loud sounds and listening to loud music.

- Have your ears checked by a doctor if they hurt or leak fluid or if you begin to have trouble hearing.

- Wear earplugs when you swim. Water in your ears can lead to infection.

Your Immune System

Pathogens and Illness

You may know someone who had a cold or the flu this year. These illnesses are caused by germs called pathogens. Illnesses spread when pathogens move from one person to another.

Types of Pathogens

There are four kinds of pathogens—viruses, bacteria, fungi, and protozoans. Viruses are the smallest kind of pathogen. They are so small that they can be seen only with very powerful electron microscopes. Viruses cause many types of illnesses, including colds, the flu, and chicken pox. Viruses cannot reproduce by themselves. They must use living cells to reproduce.

Bacteria are tiny single-cell organisms that live in water, in the soil, and on almost all surfaces. Most bacteria can be seen only with a microscope. Not all bacteria cause illness. Your body needs some types of bacteria to work well.

The most common type of fungus infection is athlete's foot. This is a burning, itchy infection of the skin between the toes. Ringworm is another skin infection caused by a fungus. It causes itchy round patches to develop on the skin.

Protozoans are the fourth type of pathogen. They are single-cell organisms that are slightly larger than bacteria. They can cause disease when they grow in food or in drinking water.

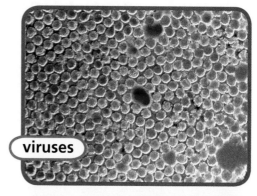

viruses

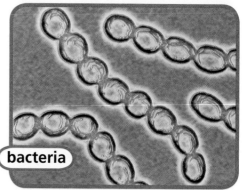

bacteria

fungi

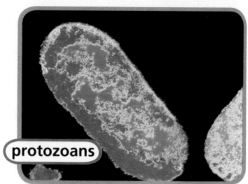

protozoans

Fighting Illness

Pathogens that can make you ill are everywhere. Following good health habits will prevent the spread of pathogens and protect you and others from the illnesses they can cause.

The best way to avoid spreading pathogens is to wash your hands with soap and warm water. This will remove germs from your skin. You should wash your hands often. Always wash them before and after eating, after handling animals, and after using the bathroom. Avoid touching your mouth, eyes, and nose. Never share cups or drinking straws. If you get a cut or scrape, pathogens can enter your body. It is important to wash cuts and scrapes carefully with soap and water. Then cover the injury with a sterile bandage to keep out germs.

When you are ill, you should avoid spreading pathogens to others. Cover your nose and mouth when you sneeze or cough. Don't share anything that has touched your mouth

or nose. Stay home from school until an adult family member tells you that you are well enough to go back.

Even though pathogens are all around, most people become ill only once in a while. This is because the body has systems that protect it from pathogens. These defenses keep pathogens from entering your body.

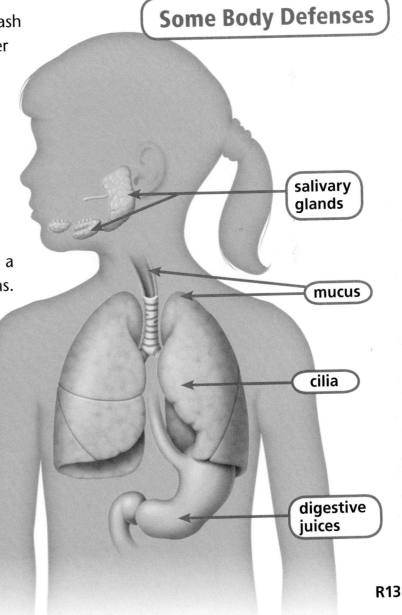

Some Body Defenses

salivary glands

mucus

cilia

digestive juices

Eat a Balanced Diet

Eating the foods your body needs to grow and fight illness is the most important thing you can do to stay healthy. A balanced diet of healthful foods gives your body energy. Your body's systems need nutrients to function properly and to work together.

Choosing unhealthful foods can cause you to gain excess weight and to lack energy. Inactivity and poor food choices can lead to your becoming ill more frequently. Unhealthful foods can also cause you to develop noncommunicable diseases. Unlike communicable diseases, which are caused by germs, these illnesses occur because your body systems are not working properly.

Exercise Regularly

Exercise keeps your body healthy. Regular exercise helps your heart, lungs, and muscles stay strong. It helps your body digest food. It also helps your body fight disease. Exercising to keep your body strong also helps prevent injury when you play sports.

Exercise allows your body to rest more effectively. Getting enough sleep prepares your body for the next day. It allows your muscles and bones to grow and to recover from exercise. Getting the rest you need also helps keep your mind alert so you can learn well.

Identify the Main Idea and Details

Focus Skill

Many of the lessons in this science book are written so that you can understand main ideas and the details that support them. You can use a graphic organizer like this one to show a main idea and details.

Main Idea: The most important idea of a selection

Detail: Information that tells more about the main idea	**Detail:** Information that tells more about the main idea	**Detail:** Information that tells more about the main idea

Tips for Identifying the Main Idea and Details

- To find the main idea, ask *What is this mostly about?*

- Remember that the main idea is not always stated in the first sentence of a passage.

- Look for details that answer questions such as *who, what, where, when, why,* and *how.* Use pictures as clues to help you.

Here is an example.

Main Idea

An environment that meets the needs of a living thing is called its habitat. Some habitats are as big as a whole forest. This is often true for birds that fly from place to place. Some habitats are very small. For example, fungi might grow only in certain places on a forest floor.

Detail

Here is what you could record in the graphic organizer.

Main Idea: An environment that meets the needs of a living thing is called its habitat.

Detail: Some habitats are as big as a whole forest.	**Detail:** A bird's habitat might be a whole forest.	**Detail:** Fungi might grow only in certain places on a forest floor.

More About Main Idea and Details

Sometimes the main idea is not stated at the beginning of a passage. If the main idea is not stated, it can be understood from the details. Look at the details in this graphic organizer. What do you think the main idea of the passage is?

Main Idea:

Detail:
Green plants are the producers in a food chain. They make their own food.

Detail:
Consumers make up the next level of a food chain. They eat plants and other living things for energy.

Detail:
Decomposers are another level. They feed on the wastes of consumers or on their remains.

A paragraph's main idea may be supported by details of different types. In the following paragraph, identify whether the details give reasons, examples, facts, steps, or descriptions.

A group of the same species living in the same place at the same time is called a population. A forest may have populations of several different kinds of trees. Trout may be one of several populations of fish in a stream. Deer may be one population among many in a meadow.

Skill Practice

Read the following paragraph. Use the Tips for Identifying the Main Idea and Details to answer the questions.

Animals do not get their energy directly from the sun. Many eat plants, which have used sunlight to make food. Animals that don't eat plants still depend on the energy of sunlight. They eat animals that have eaten plants. The sun is the main source of energy for all living things.

1. What is the main idea of the paragraph?

2. What supporting details give more information about the main idea?

3. What details answer any of the questions *who, what, where, when, why,* and *how?*

Compare and Contrast

Some lessons are written to help you see how things are alike or different. You can use a graphic organizer like this one to compare and contrast.

Topic: Name the two things you are comparing and contrasting.

Alike
List ways the things are alike.

Different
List ways the things are different.

Tips for Comparing and Contrasting

- To compare, ask *How are the people, places, objects, ideas, or events alike?*

- To contrast, ask *How are the people, places, objects, ideas, or events different?*

- When you compare, look for signal words and phrases such as *similar, alike, both, the same as, too,* and *also.*

- When you contrast, look for signal words and phrases such as *unlike, different, however, yet, while,* and *but.*

Here is an example.

Compare

Mars and Venus are the two planets closest to Earth. They are known as inner planets. Venus and Earth are about the same size, but Mars is a little smaller. Venus does not have any moons. However, Mars has two moons.

Contrast

Here is what you could record in the graphic organizer.

Topic: Mars and Venus

Alike
Both are inner planets.
Both are close to Earth.

Different
Mars is smaller than Venus.
Mars has two moons.

More About Compare and Contrast

You can better understand new information about things when you know how they are alike and how they are different. Use the graphic organizer from page R18 to sort the following items of information about Mars and Venus.

Mars	Venus
Mars is the fourth planet from the sun.	Venus is the second planet from the sun.
A year on Mars is 687 Earth days.	A year on Venus is 225 Earth days.
Mars has a diameter of 6794 kilometers.	Venus has a diameter of 12,104 kilometers.
The soil on Mars is a dark reddish-brown.	Venus is dry and has a thick atmosphere.

Sometimes a paragraph compares and contrasts more than one topic. In the following paragraph, one topic being compared and contrasted is underlined. Find the second topic being compared and contrasted.

Radio telescopes and optical telescopes are two types of telescopes that are used to observe objects in space. A radio telescope collects radio waves with a large, bowl-shaped antenna. An optical telescope collects light. There are two types of optical telescopes. A refracting telescope uses lenses to magnify an object. A reflecting telescope uses a curved mirror to magnify an object.

Skill Practice

Read the following paragraph. Use the Tips for Comparing and Contrasting to answer the questions.

Radio telescopes and optical telescopes work in the same way. However, optical telescopes collect and focus light, while radio telescopes collect and focus invisible radio waves. Radio waves are not affected by clouds and poor weather. Computers can make pictures from data collected by radio telescopes.

1. How are radio and optical telescopes alike and different?

2. What signal words can you find in the paragraph?

Cause and Effect

Some of the lessons in this science book are written to help you understand why things happen. You can use a graphic organizer like this one to show cause and effect.

Cause		Effect
Cause A cause is an action or event that makes something happen.	→	**Effect** An effect is what happens as a result of an action or event.

Tips for Identifying Cause and Effect

- To find an effect, ask *What happened?*

- To find a cause, ask *Why did this happen?*

- Remember that actions and events can have more than one cause or effect.

- Look for signal words and phrases such as *because* and *as a result* to help you identify causes and effects.

Here is an example.

Cause

Effect

A pulley is a simple machine. It helps us do work. It is made up of a rope or chain and a wheel around which the rope fits. When you pull down on one end of the rope, the wheel turns and the other end of the rope moves up.

Here is what you could record in the graphic organizer.

Cause One end of the rope in a pulley is pulled down.	→	**Effect** The pulley wheel turns, and the other end of the rope moves up.

More About Cause and Effect

Actions and events can have more than one cause or effect. For example, suppose the paragraph on page R20 included a sentence that said *The pulley can be used to raise an object.* You could then identify two effects of operating a pulley, as shown in this graphic organizer.

Cause
One end of the rope in a pulley is pulled down.

Effect
The pulley wheel turns, and the other end of the rope moves up.

Effect
An object is raised.

Some paragraphs contain more than one cause and effect. In the following paragraph, one cause and its effect are underlined. Find a second cause and its effect.

A fixed pulley and a movable pulley can be put together to make a compound machine. The movable pulley increases your force. As more movable pulleys are added to a system, the force is increased. The fixed pulley changes the direction of your force.

Skill Practice

Read the following paragraph. Use the Tips for Identifying Cause and Effect to help you answer the questions.

A lever can be used to open a paint can. The outer rim of the can is used as the fulcrum. Your hand supplies the effort force. The force put out by the end of the lever that is under the lid is greater than the effort force. As a result, the lid is popped up.

1. What causes the paint can's lid to pop up?

2. What is the effect when an effort force is applied?

3. What signal phrase helped you identify the cause and effect in this paragraph?

Sequence

Some lessons in this science book are written to help you understand the order in which things happen. You can use a graphic organizer like this one to show a sequence.

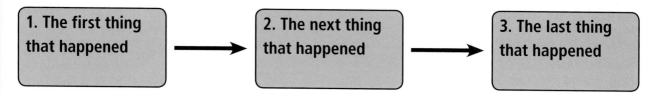

| 1. The first thing that happened | → | 2. The next thing that happened | → | 3. The last thing that happened |

Tips for Understanding a Sequence

- Pay attention to the order in which events happen.

- Recall dates and times to help you understand the sequence.

- Look for signal words such as *first, next, then, last,* and *finally.*

- Sometimes it is helpful to add your own time-order words to help you understand a sequence.

Here is an example.

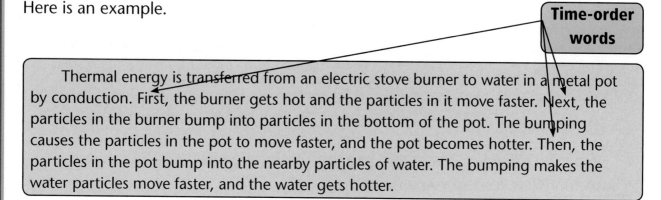

Time-order words

Thermal energy is transferred from an electric stove burner to water in a metal pot by conduction. First, the burner gets hot and the particles in it move faster. Next, the particles in the burner bump into particles in the bottom of the pot. The bumping causes the particles in the pot to move faster, and the pot becomes hotter. Then, the particles in the pot bump into the nearby particles of water. The bumping makes the water particles move faster, and the water gets hotter.

Here is what you could record in the graphic organizer.

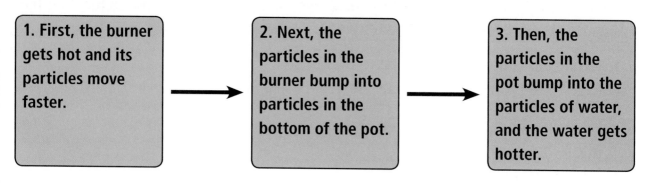

| 1. First, the burner gets hot and its particles move faster. | → | 2. Next, the particles in the burner bump into particles in the bottom of the pot. | → | 3. Then, the particles in the pot bump into the particles of water, and the water gets hotter. |

More About Sequence

Sometimes information is sequenced by time. For example, in an experiment to measure temperature change over time, a graphic organizer could sequence the steps of the procedure.

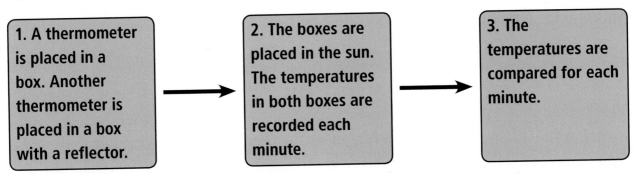

When time-order words are not given, add your own words to help you understand the sequence. In the paragraph below, one time-order word has been included and underlined. What time-order words can you add to understand the paragraph's sequence?

Convection is the transfer of thermal energy in a fluid—a liquid or a gas. As the fluid near a hot object gets hot, it expands. The hot fluid is forced up by the cooler, denser fluid around it. Then, as the hot fluid is forced up, it warms the fluid around it. It slowly cools as it sinks.

Skill Practice

Read the following paragraph. Use the Tips for Understanding a Sequence to answer the questions.

Solar energy can be used to heat water in a home. First, solar panels are placed on the roof of a house. Next, the panels absorb infrared radiation from the sun. Then, the radiation heats the water as it flows through the panels.

1. What is the first thing that happens in the sequence?

2. How many steps are involved in the process?

3. What three signal words helped you identify the sequence in this paragraph?

Summarize

At the end of every lesson in this science book, you are asked to summarize. When you summarize, you use your own words to tell what something is about. In the lesson, you will find ideas for writing your summary. You can also use a graphic organizer like this one to summarize.

| Main Idea: Tell about the most important information you have read. | + | Details: Add details that answer important questions such as *who, what, where, when, why,* and *how.* | = | Summary: Retell what you have just read, including only the most important details. |

Tips for Summarizing

- To write a summary, first ask *What is the most important idea of the paragraph?*

- To add details, ask *who, what, when, where, why,* and *how.*

- Remember to use fewer words than the original.

- Tell the information in your own words.

Here and on the next page is an example.

Main Idea

Details

The water cycle is the constant recycling of water. As the sun warms the ocean, water particles leave the water and enter the air as water vapor. This is evaporation, the process of a liquid changing to a gas. Clouds form when water vapor condenses high in the atmosphere. Condensation occurs when the water vapor rises, cools, and changes from a gas to a liquid. When the drops are too large to stay up in the air, precipitation occurs as the water falls back to Earth.

Here is what you could record in the graphic organizer.

Main Idea:
The water cycle is the constant recycling of water.

+

Details:
Evaporation is the change from a liquid to a gas. Condensation is the change from a gas to a liquid. Precipitation is water that falls to Earth.

=

Summary:
The constant recycling of water is the water cycle. It includes evaporation, condensation, and precipitation.

More About Summarizing

Sometimes a paragraph has details that are not important enough to be included in a summary. The graphic organizer remains the same because those details are not important to understanding the paragraph's main idea.

Skill Practice

Read the following paragraph. Use the Tips for Summarizing to answer the questions.

Tides are the changes in the ocean's water level each day. At high tide, much of the beach is covered with water. At low tide, waves break farther away from the shore and less of the beach is underwater. Every day most shorelines have two high tides and two low tides. High tides and low tides occur at regular times and are usually a little more than six hours apart.

1. If a friend asked you what this paragraph was about, what information would you include? What would you leave out?

2. What is the main idea of the paragraph?

3. Which two details would you include in a summary of the paragraph?

Draw Conclusions

At the end of each lesson in this science book, you are asked to draw conclusions. To draw conclusions, use the information that you have read and what you already know. Drawing conclusions can help you understand what you read. You can use a graphic organizer like this.

| **What I Read** Use facts from the text to help you understand. | + | **What I Know** Use your own experience to help you understand. | = | **Conclusion:** Combine facts and details in the text with personal knowledge or experience. |

Tips for Drawing Conclusions

- To draw conclusions, first ask *What information from the text do I need to think about?*

- Then ask *What do I know from my own experience that could help me draw a conclusion?*

- Ask yourself whether the conclusion you have drawn is valid, or makes sense.

Here is an example.

Plants need air, nutrients, water, and light to live. A plant makes its own food by a process called photosynthesis. Photosynthesis takes place in the plant's leaves. In an experiment, a plant is placed in a dark room without any light. It is watered every day.

Text information

Here is what you could record in the graphic organizer.

| **What I Read** A plant needs air, nutrients, water, and light to live. | + | **What I Know** Plants use light to make the food they need to live and grow. | = | **Conclusion:** The plant will die since it is not getting any light. |

More About Drawing Conclusions

Sensible conclusions based on your experience and the facts you read are valid. For example, suppose the paragraph on page R26 included a sentence that said *After a day, the plant is removed from the dark room and placed in the sunlight.* You could then draw a different conclusion about the life of the plant.

What I Read A plant needs air, nutrients, water, and light to live.	+	**What I Know** Plants use light to make the food they need to live and grow.	=	**Conclusion:** The plant will live.

Sometimes a paragraph might not contain enough information to draw a valid conclusion. Read the following paragraph. Think of one valid conclusion you could draw. Then think of one conclusion that would be invalid or wouldn't make sense.

Cacti are plants that are found in the desert. Sometimes it does not rain in the desert for months or even years. Cacti have thick stems. The roots of cactus plants grow just below the surface of the ground.

Skill Practice

Read the following paragraph. Use the Tips for Drawing Conclusions to answer the questions.

Animals behave in ways that help them meet their needs. Some animal behaviors are instincts, and some are learned. Tiger cubs learn to hunt by watching their mothers hunt and by playing with other tiger cubs. They are not born knowing exactly how to hunt.

1. What conclusion can you draw about a tiger cub that is separated from its mother and from other tigers?

2. What information from your own experience helped you draw the conclusion?

3. What text information did you use to draw the conclusion?

Using Tables, Charts, and Graphs

As you do investigations in science, you collect, organize, display, and interpret data. Tables, charts, and graphs are good ways to organize and display data so that others can understand and interpret your data.

The tables, charts, and graphs in this Handbook will help you read and understand data. The Handbook will also help you choose the best ways to display data so that you can draw conclusions and make predictions.

Reading a Table

A scientist is studying the rainfall in Bangladesh. She wants to know which months are part of the monsoon season, or the time when the area receives the greatest amount of rainfall. The table shows the data she has collected.

Monthly Rainfall in Chittagong, Bangladesh	
Month	Rainfall (inches)
January	1
February	2
March	3
April	6
May	10
June	21
July	23
August	10
September	13
October	7
November	2
December	1

Title ← (points to title)
Headings ← (points to headings)
Data ← (points to data)

How to Read a Table

1. **Look** at the title to learn what the table is about.

2. **Read** the headings to find out what information is given.

3. **Analyze** the data. Look for patterns.

4. **Draw conclusions.** When data is displayed in a graph, you are able to see patterns easily.

By studying the table, you can see how much rain fell during each month. If the scientist wanted to look for patterns, she might display the data in a graph.

Reading a Bar Graph

The data in this bar graph is the same as that in the table. A bar graph can be used to compare data about different events or groups.

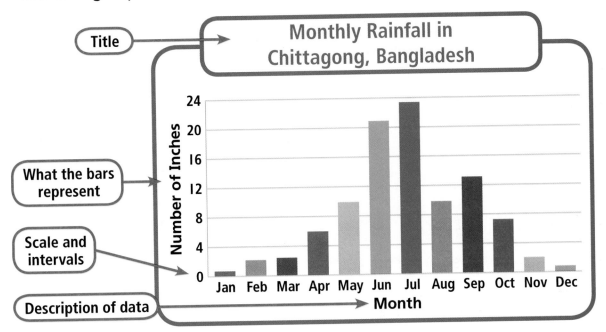

Title

Monthly Rainfall in Chittagong, Bangladesh

What the bars represent

Scale and intervals

Description of data

How to Read a Bar Graph

1. **Look** at the title to learn what kind of information is shown.

2. **Read** the graph. Use the numbers and labels to guide you.

3. **Analyze** the data. Study the bars to compare the measurements. Look for patterns.

4. **Draw conclusions.** Ask yourself questions like the ones under Skills Practice.

Skills Practice

1. In which two months does Chittagong receive the most rainfall?

2. Which months have the same amounts of rainfall?

3. **Predict** During which months are the roads likely to be flooded?

4. How does the bar graph help you identify the monsoon season and the rainfall amounts?

5. Was the bar graph a good choice for displaying this data? Explain.

Reading a Line Graph

A scientist collected this data about temperatures in Pittsburgh, Pennsylvania.

Average Temperatures in Pittsburgh	
Month	Temperature (degrees Fahrenheit)
January	28
February	29
March	39
April	50
May	60
June	68
July	74
August	72
September	63
October	52
November	43
December	32

How to Read a Line Graph

1. **Look** at the title to learn what kind of information is shown.

2. **Read** the graph. Use the numbers and labels to guide you.

3. **Analyze** the data. Study the points along the lines. Look for patterns.

4. **Draw conclusions.** Ask yourself questions like the ones under Skills Practice.

Here is the same data displayed in a line graph. A line graph is used to show changes over time.

Title

What the points represent

Scale and intervals

Description of data

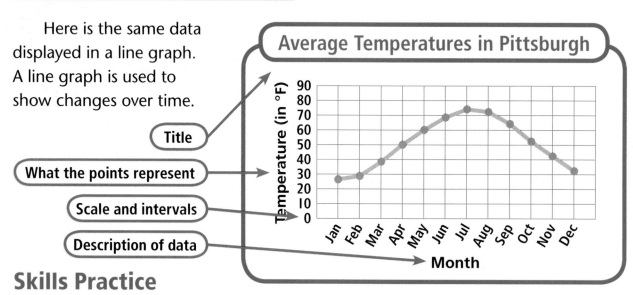
Average Temperatures in Pittsburgh

Skills Practice

1. In which three months are the temperatures the warmest in Pittsburgh?

2. **Predict** During which months are ponds in Pittsburgh likely to freeze?

3. Was the line graph a good choice for displaying this data? Explain.

Reading a Circle Graph

Some scientists counted 100 animals at a park. The scientists wanted to know which animal group had the most animals. They classified the animals by making a table. Here is their data.

Animal Groups at the Park	
Animal Group	**Number Observed**
Mammals	7
Insects	63
Birds	22
Reptiles	5
Amphibians	3

The circle graph shows the same data as the table. A circle graph can be used to show data as a whole made up of parts.

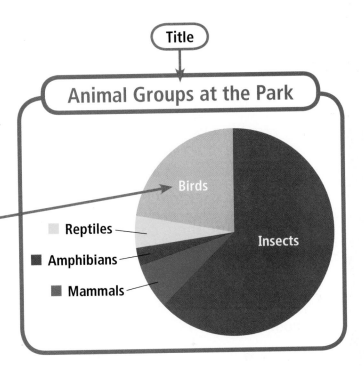

Title

Animal Groups at the Park

Label for a section

Birds

Reptiles

Amphibians

Mammals

Insects

How to Read a Circle Graph

1. **Look** at the title to learn what kind of information is shown.

2. **Read** the graph. Look at the label of each section to find out what information is shown.

3. **Analyze** the data. Compare the sizes of the sections to determine how they are related.

4. **Draw conclusions.** Ask yourself questions like the ones under Skills Practice.

Skills Practice

1. Which animal group had the most members? Which one had the fewest?

2. **Predict** If you visited a nearby park, would you expect to see more reptiles or more insects?

3. Was the circle graph a good choice for displaying this data? Explain.

Measurements

When you measure, you compare an object to a standard unit of measure. Scientists almost always use the units of the metric system.

Measuring Length and Capacity in Metric Units

When you measure length, you find the distance between two points. The table shows the metric units of **length** and how they are related.

Equivalent Measures
1 centimeter (cm) = 10 millimeters (mm)
1 decimeter (dm) = 10 centimeters (cm)
1 meter (m) = 1000 millimeters
1 meter = 10 decimeters
1 kilometer (km) = 1000 meters

You can use these comparisons to help you learn the size of each metric unit of length:

A **millimeter (mm)** is about the thickness of a dime.

A **centimeter (cm)** is about the width of your index finger.

A **decimeter (dm)** is about the width of an adult's hand.

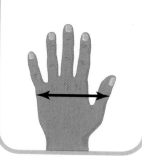

A **meter (m)** is about the width of a door.

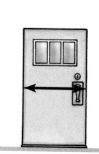

The following diagram shows how to multiply and divide to change to larger and smaller units.

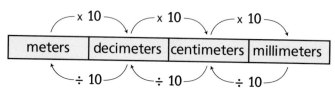

When you measure capacity, you find the amount a container can hold when it is filled. The images show the metric units of **capacity** and how they are related.

A **milliliter (mL)** is the amount of liquid that can fill one section of a dropper.

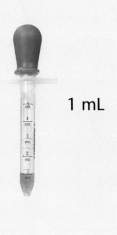

1 mL

A **liter (L)** is the amount of liquid that can fill a plastic water bottle.

1 L = 1000 mL

You can use multiplication to change liters to milliliters.

You can use division to change milliliters to liters.

2 L = _____ mL	4000 mL = _____ L
Think: There are 1000 mL in 1 L.	Think: There are 1000 mL in 1 L.
2 L = 2 x 1000 = 2000 mL	4000 ÷ 1000 = 4
So, 2 L = 2000 mL.	So, 4000 mL = 4 L.

Skills Practice

Complete. Tell whether you multiply or divide.

1. 3 L = _____ mL

2. 5000 mL = _____ L

3. 7000 mL = _____ L

4. 6 L = _____ mL

5. 500 dm = _____ cm

6. 4 m = _____ mm

7. 8 _____ = 80 cm

8. _____ m = 1400 cm

Measuring Mass

Matter is what everything is made of. **Mass** is the amount of matter that is in something. The metric units of mass are the gram (g) and the kilogram (kg). You can use these comparisons to help you understand the masses of some everyday objects:

A paper clip is about **1 gram (g)**. 	A slice of wheat bread is about **20 grams**. 	A box of 12 crayons is about **100 grams**. 	A large wedge of cheese is about **1 kilogram (kg)**. 

You can use multiplication to change kilograms to grams.

You can use division to change grams to kilograms.

2 kg = _____ g Think: There are 1000 g in 1 kg. 2 kg = 2 x 1000 = 2000 g So, 2 kg = 2000 g.	4000 g = _____ kg Think: There are 1000 g in 1 kg. 4000 ÷ 1000 = 4 So, 4000 g = 4 kg.

Skills Practice

Complete. Tell whether you multiply or divide by 1000.

1. 5000 g = _____ kg

2. 3000 g = _____ kg

3. 4 kg = _____ g

4. 7 kg = _____ g

Measurement Systems

SI Measures (Metric)

Temperature
Ice melts at 0 degrees Celsius (°C).
Water freezes at 0°C.
Water boils at 100°C.

Length and Distance
1000 meters (m) = 1 kilometer (km)
100 centimeters (cm) = 1 m
10 millimeters (mm) = 1 cm

Force
1 newton (N) = 1 kilogram x 1 meter/second/second (kg-m/s²)

Volume
1 cubic meter (m³) = 1 m x 1 m x 1 m
1 cubic centimeter (cm³) = 1 cm x 1 cm x 1 cm
1 liter (L) = 1000 milliliters (mL)
1 cm³ = 1 mL

Area
1 square kilometer (km²) = 1 km x 1 km
1 hectare = 10,000 m²

Mass
1000 grams (g) = 1 kilogram (kg)
1000 milligrams (mg) = 1 g
1000 kilograms = 1 metric ton

Rates
km/hr = kilometers per hour
m/sec = meters per second

Customary Measures

Temperature
Ice melts at 32 degrees Fahrenheit (°F).
Water freezes at 32°F.
Water boils at 212°F.

Length and Distance
12 inches (in.) = 1 foot (ft)
3 ft = 1 yard (yd)
5280 ft = 1 mile (mi)

Force
16 ounces (oz) = 1 pound (lb)
2000 pounds = 1 ton (T)

Volume of Fluids
2 cups (c) = 1 pint (pt)
2 pt = 1 quart (qt)
4 qt = 1 gallon (gal)

Area
1 square mile (mi²) = 1 mi x 1 mi
1 acre = 4840 sq ft

Rates
mph = miles per hour
ft/sec = feet per second

Safety in Science

Doing investigations in science can be fun, but you need to be sure you do them safely. Here are some rules to follow.

1. **Think ahead.** Study the steps of the investigation so you know what to expect. If you have any questions, ask your teacher. Be sure that you understand all caution statements and safety reminders.

2. **Be neat.** Keep your work area clean. If you have long hair, pull it back so it doesn't get in the way. Roll or push up long sleeves to keep them away from your activity.

3. **Oops!** If you should spill or break something, or you get cut, tell your teacher right away.

4. **Watch your eyes.** Wear safety goggles anytime you are directed to do so. If you get anything in your eyes, tell your teacher right away.

5. **Yuck!** Never eat or drink anything during a science activity.

6. **Don't get shocked.** Be especially careful if an electric appliance is used. Be sure that electrical cords are in a safe place where you can't trip over them. Don't ever pull a plug out of an outlet by pulling on the cord.

7. **Keep it clean.** Always clean up when you have finished. Put everything away, and wipe your work area. Wash your hands.

Visit the Multimedia Science Glossary to see illustrations of these words and to hear them pronounced.
www.hspscience.com

Every entry in the glossary begins with a term and a *phonetic respelling*. A phonetic respelling writes the word the way it sounds, which can help you pronounce new or unfamiliar words. The definition of the term follows the respelling. An example of how to use the term in a sentence follows the definition.

The page number in ( ) at the end of the entry tells you where to find the term in your textbook. All of these terms are highlighted in yellow in the chapter in your textbook. Each entry has an illustration to help you understand the term. The Pronunciation Key below will help you understand the respellings. Syllables are separated by a bullet (•). Small, uppercase letters show stressed syllables.

Pronunciation Key

Sound	As in	Phonetic Respelling	Sound	As in	Phonetic Respelling
a	bat	(BAT)	oh	over	(OH•ver)
ah	lock	(LAHK)	oo	pool	(POOL)
air	rare	(RAIR)	ow	out	(OWT)
ar	argue	(AR•gyoo)	oy	foil	(FOYL)
aw	law	(LAW)	s	cell	(SEL)
ay	face	(FAYS)		sit	(SIT)
ch	chapel	(CHAP•uhl)	sh	sheep	(SHEEP)
e	test	(TEST)	th	that	(THAT)
	metric	(MEH•trik)		thin	(THIN)
ee	eat	(EET)	u	pull	(PUL)
	feet	(FEET)	uh	medal	(MED•uhl)
	ski	(SKEE)		talent	(TAL•uhnt)
er	paper	(PAY•per)		pencil	(PEN•suhl)
	fern	(FERN)		onion	(UHN•yuhn)
eye	idea	(eye•DEE•uh)		playful	(PLAY•fuhl)
i	bit	(BIT)		dull	(DUHL)
ing	going	(GOH•ing)	y	yes	(YES)
k	card	(KARD)		ripe	(RYP)
	kite	(KYT)	z	bags	(BAGZ)
ngk	bank	(BANGK)	zh	treasure	(TREZH•er)

Multimedia Science Glossary: www.hspscience.com

A

abiotic [ay•by•AHT•ik] Describes a nonliving part of an ecosystem: Water and rocks are *abiotic* parts of an ecosystem. (342)

acceleration [ak•sel•er•AY•shuhn] Any change in the speed or direction of an object's motion: This racing car is capable of great *acceleration*. (221)

adaptation [ad•uhp•TAY•shuhn] A body part or behavior that helps an organism survive: This insect's stick-like body is an *adaptation* that makes it look like part of a tree. (362)

air mass [AIR MAS] A large body of air that has similar temperature and humidity throughout: The blue arrows represent cool *air masses*. (134)

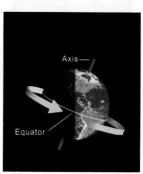

anemometer [an•uh•MAHM•uht•er] An instrument for measuring wind speed: Wind makes an *anemometer* spin. (132)

axis [AK•sis] An imaginary line that runs through the center of Earth from the North Pole to the South Pole: Earth's tilted *axis* is responsible for seasonal changes in climate. (60)

Axis

Equator

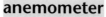

B

barometer
[buh•RAHM•uht•er]
An instrument for measuring air pressure: A falling *barometer* usually means a greater chance of rain. (132)

basic needs [BAY•sik NEEDZ] **Food, water, air, and shelter that an organism needs to survive:** These living things have the same *basic needs.* (360)

biotic [by•AHT•ik] **Describes a living part of an ecosystem:** Plants and animals are *biotic* parts of an ecosystem. (340)

C

camouflage
[KAM•uh•flahzh] **A color or shape that helps an animal hide:** Because of this insect's *camouflage,* it is hard to detect among the leaves. (362)

carnivore
[KAR•nih•vawr]
An animal that eats only other animals: *Carnivores* have sharp teeth to help them eat meat. (316)

climate [KLY•muht] **The pattern of weather an area experiences over a long period of time:** The living things in this desert are adapted to a dry *climate.* (138)

comet [KAHM•it] A ball of ice, rock, and frozen gases that orbits the sun: The fiery tail of a *comet* may be seen from Earth. (77)

community [kuh•MYOO•nuh•tee] All the populations of organisms living in an environment: A *community* has many kinds of interdependent organisms. (304)

concave lens [kahn•KAYV LENZ] A lens that is thicker at the edges than it is at the center: Light waves are spread apart as they pass through this *concave lens*. (194)

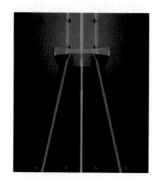

condensation [kahn•duhn•SAY•shuhn] The process by which a gas changes into a liquid: *Condensation* caused droplets to form on the outside of the glass as water in the air lost heat energy and cooled off. (111)

constellation [kahn•stuh•LAY•shuhn] A pattern of stars that form an imaginary picture or design in the sky: Ursa Major is a *constellation* that looks like a bear to many people. (88)

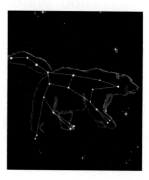

consumer [kuhn•SOOM•er] A living thing that can't make its own food and must eat other living things: Animals are *consumers*. (314)

convex lens

[kahn•VEKS LENZ] **A lens that is thicker at the center than it is at the edges:** Light waves are brought together by a *convex lens.* (194)

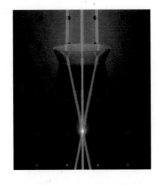

current [KUR•uhnt] **A stream of water that flows like a river through the ocean:** Ocean *currents* flow in only one direction. (118)

 D

decomposer

[dee•kuhm•POHZ•er] **A living thing that feeds on the wastes and remains of plants and animals:** Mushrooms are one kind of *decomposer.* (318)

 E

ecosystem

[EE•koh•sis•tuhm] **A community of living things and the community's physical environment:** This *ecosystem* includes water, fish, grass, flowers, and air. (300)

energy pyramid

[EN•er•jee PIR•uh•mid] **A diagram showing how much energy is passed from one organism to the next in a food chain:** *Energy pyramids* have producers at the bottom and higher-level consumers at the top. (333)

environment

[en•VY•ruhn•muhnt] **All of the living and nonliving things surrounding an organism:** Clean water is essential to the health of this wetland *environment.* (300)

estimate

[ES•tuh•mit] **A careful guess about the amount of something:** If you can't measure an object, you might make *estimates* of its length and width. (22)

evaporation

[ee•vap•uh•RAY•shuhn] **The process by which a liquid changes into a gas:** *Evaporation* of water by the sun causes these footprints to dry up. (110)

experiment

[ek•SPER•uh•muhnt] **A controlled test of a hypothesis:** In order to compare the results of different *experiments,* they must be carried out under similar conditions. (23)

extinction

[ek•STINGK•shuhn] **The death of all the members of a certain group of organisms:** The *extinction* of dinosaurs took place about 65 million years ago. (376)

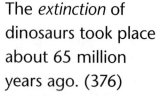

food chain [FOOD CHAYN] **A series of organisms that depend on one another for food:** A *food chain* begins with a producer. (328)

food web [FOOD WEB] **A group of food chains that overlap:** A *food web* shows the interdependence of organisms in an ecosystem. (330)

force [FAWRS] **A pull or push that causes an object to move, stop, or change direction:** Each of these animals applies a *force* to the other. (222)

frequency [FREE•kwuhn•see] **The number of vibrations per unit of time:** In this diagram, the *frequency* of the wave decreases from left to right. (162)

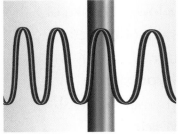

friction [FRIK•shuhn] **A force that resists motion between objects that are touching:** When you rub your hands together, *friction* changes the motion into heat. (237)

front [FRUHNT] **The border where two air masses meet:** Sometimes you can locate a *front* by watching the clouds. (135)

fulcrum [FUL•kruhm] **The fixed balance point on a lever:** As the girl sweeps, the broom pivots about its *fulcrum*. (254)

fulcrum

lever

G

galaxy [GAL•uhk•see] **A grouping of gas, dust, and many stars, plus any objects that orbit those stars:** Our solar system is located on the edge of the Milky Way *Galaxy*. (88)

gravitation [grav•ih•TAY•shuhn] **The pull of all objects in the universe on one another:** *Gravitation* holds Earth in its orbit around the sun. (235)

gravity [GRAV•ih•tee]
The force of attraction between Earth and other objects: On a roller coaster, you experience the effects of *gravity*. (235)

 H

habitat [HAB•ih•tat]
An environment that meets the needs of an organism: A gopher tortoise's *habitat* includes its burrow. (326)

herbivore [HER•buh•vawr] **An animal that eats only plants or other producers:** Cows are *herbivores*. (316)

hibernation [hy•ber•NAY•shuhn] **A dormant, inactive state in which normal body activities slow:** During *hibernation*, animals live off stored fat. (373)

humidity [hyoo•MID•uh•tee]
A measurement of the amount of water vapor in the air: When *humidity* is high, your sweat evaporates slowly. (122)

hygrometer [hy•GRAHM•uht•er]
An instrument for measuring humidity: A decreasing *hygrometer* reading usually indicates a lower chance of rain. (132)

hypothesis [hy•PAHTH•uh•sis]
A scientific explanation that can be tested: A scientist carries out an experiment in order to test a *hypothesis*. (23)

inclined plane
[IN•klynd PLAYN] **A simple machine that is a slanted surface:** Pushing an object up an *inclined plane* is easier than lifting it. (274)

inertia [in•ER•shuh] **The property of matter that keeps an object at rest or moving in a straight line:** You must overcome an object's *inertia* in order to change its motion. (224)

inference
[IN•fuhr•uhns] **An untested interpretation of observations:** An *inference* can be restated in the form of a hypothesis that you can test. (18)

instinct [IN•stingkt] **A behavior that an animal begins life with and that helps it meet its needs:** These ospreys' *instincts* include building nests and hunting for fish. (372)

interpret
[in•TER•pruht] **To evaluate evidence or data in order to draw a conclusion:** Scientists *interpret* their results to explain what happened in their experiments. (32)

L

lever [LEV•er] **A simple machine made of a bar that pivots on a fixed point:** The girl is using a broom, which is a kind of *lever.* (254)

fulcrum

lever

R45

M

meteorology [mee·tee·uh·RAHL·uh·jee] **The study of weather:** Students use weather stations to help them learn about *meteorology.* (132)

microscope [MY·kruh·skohp] **A science tool that makes tiny things look bigger:** You can use a *microscope* to see things that you can't see with your eyes alone. (8)

migration [my·GRAY·shuhn] **The movement of animals from one region to another and back:** Canada geese fly south during their fall *migration.* (374)

moon [MOON] **A natural body that revolves around a planet:** It takes about a month for the *moon* to revolve around Earth. (64)

motion [MOH·shuhn] **A change in position of an object:** This boy and his bike are in *motion.* (208)

N

niche [NICH] **The role a living thing plays in its habitat:** Every living thing has a *niche.* (327)

O

observation [ahb·zuhr·VAY·shuhn] **Information that you gather with your senses:** You can make an *observation* with your eyes or ears. (18)

omnivore [AHM•nih•vawr] **An animal that eats both plants and other animals:** Bears, raccoons, and people are *omnivores.* (316)

opaque [oh•PAYK] **Not allowing light to pass through:** You cannot see through *opaque* objects. (183)

orbit [AWR•bit] **The path of one object in space around another object:** Earth's *orbit* is almost a perfect circle. (62)

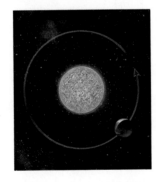

 P

phase [FAYZ] **One of the shapes the moon seems to have as it orbits Earth:** The moon waxes and wanes through its cycle of *phases.* (64)

pitch [PICH] **How high or low a sound is:** The girl produces sounds of different *pitch* by striking the different-sized metal bars on this instrument. (162)

planet [PLAN•it] **A large body that revolves around a star:** Saturn is one of eight *planets* that revolve around the sun. (72)

population [pahp•yuh•LAY•shuhn] **All the individuals of one kind living in the same ecosystem:** *Populations* compete for resources in an ecosystem. (302)

position [puh•ZISH•uhn] **The location of an object:** The runners' *positions* do not change as they wait for the race to begin. (208)

precipitation
[pree•sip•uh•TAY•shuhn] **Water that falls from clouds to Earth's surface:** *Precipitation* can be solid, like snow, or liquid, like rain. (122)

predator
[PRED•uh•ter] **A consumer that eats prey:** A wolf hunts living animals, so it is a *predator.* (328)

prediction
[pree•DIK•shuhn] **A statement of what will happen, based on observations and knowledge of cause-and-effect relationships:** To make a *prediction,* you combine what you already know with things you have observed. (19)

prey [PRAY]
Consumers that are eaten by predators: *Prey* have adaptations that allow them to escape or hide from predators. (328)

producer
[proh•DOOS•er] **A living thing, such as a plant, that can make its own food:** Grasses are *producers.* (314)

pulley [PUHL•ee] **A simple machine that consists of a wheel with a line around it:** This single fixed *pulley* changes the direction, but not the amount, of the applied force. (264)

T

translucent

[tranz•LOO•suhnt]
Allowing only some light to pass through: You can see light through *translucent* objects, but you cannot see clearly through them. (182)

transparent

[tranz•PAIR•uhnt]
Allowing light to pass through: You can see clearly through *transparent* objects. (182)

U

universe

[YOO•nuh•ve
Everythin nat exists in ace: Many axies make up th niverse. (88)

V

velocity

[vuh•LAHS•uh•tee] **The measure of the speed and direction of motion of an object:** The *velocity* of this hammer includes both its speed and the direction in which it is moving. (220)

vibration

[vy•BRAY•shuhn] **A quick back-and-forth movement of matter:** *Vibrations* of the strings of this guitar cause sounds. (160)

volume [VAHL•yoom]

The loudness of a sound: Over time, listening to sounds of high *volume* can damage your hearing. (161)

W

water cycle [WAW•ter SY•kuhl] **The constant movement of water from the surface of Earth to the air and back again:** The sun's energy drives the *water cycle.* (108)

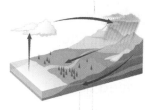

water vapor [WAW•ter VAY•per] **The gas form of water:** *Water vapor* forms when water boils or evaporates. (108)

weather [WETH•er] **The condition of the atmosphere at a certain place and time:** *Weather* can affect people's activities, especially if it is severe. (122)

wedge [WEJ] **A simple machine made of two inclined planes placed back to back:** When a downward force is applied to the *wedge,* it pushes the wood apart. (278)

weight [WAYT] **A measure of the gravitational force acting on an object:** The boy is using a spring scale to find the *weight* of the stapler. (236)

wheel-and-axle [weel•and•AK•suhl] **A simple machine made of a wheel and an axle that turn together:** This fishing reel is an example of a *wheel-and-axle* because the crank (wheel) and axle turn together. (266)

axle

wheel

work [WERK] **The use of a force to move an object over a distance:** The girl does *work* by pushing a chair across the room. (252)

Index

KEY: (*t*) top, (*b*) bottom, (*l*) left, (*r*) right, (*c*) center, (*bg*) background, (*fg*) foreground

INTRODUCTION
1 RonSherman.com; **2** (*r*) NASA/JPL/LMSS; **9** (*cl*) Sinclair Stammers/Science Photo Library; **11** (*tr*) Paul Horsted/Stock Connection; **13** (*tl*) Blend Images/PictureQuest, (*cl*) Cordleia Molloy/Photo Researchers; **14** (*c*) © RonSherman.com - All Rights Reserved; **16** (*bl*) Ron Niebrugge/Alamy; **26** (*bl*) Getty Images; **27** (*cl*) Courtesy of the National Institute of Standards and Technology. Not Copyrightable in the USA, (*bl*) Liquidlibrary/PictureQuest; **28** (inset) AFP/Getty Images; **30** (*r*) Vince Streano/Corbis; **32** (*b*) © Doug Pensinger/Getty Images; **34** (*b*) © Taxi/Getty Images; **33** (*b*) Craig Lovell/Eagle Visions Photography/Alamy; **34** (*b*) © Taxi/Getty Images; **35** (*br*) David R. Frazier Photolibrary, Inc./Alamy; **37** (*bl*) © CORBIS; **38** (*r*) Roger Ressmeyer/Corbis; **40** (*bl*) Model by Konstantinos Papadimitrakopoulos; **42** (*bl*) Mark Gibson/Index Stock Imagery, (*b*) Robert Llewellyn/Corbis. **52** (*c*) Julian Baum/Photo Researchers, Inc.

UNIT A
55 (*tc*) © RonSherman.com- All Rights Reserved; **56** (*c*) © James Leynse/CORBIS; **58** (*bl*) © Betsy Strasser/Visuals Unlimited; **60** International Stock Photography/Getty Images; **61** (*tr*) © Harris Hatcher Photography; **66** (*bl*) Gianni Dagli Orti/CORBIS; **67** (*tl*) © Erik S. Lesser/Getty Images; **68** (*c*) NASA; **72** (*bg*) StockTrek/Getty Images; (*bcr*) USGS /Photo Researchers; **73** (*tr*) US Geological Survey/Photo Researchers; (*bcr*) Getty Images; **74** (*bg*) Getty Images; (*br* & *cl*) NASA; **75** (*tr*) NASA; (*c*) Getty Images; (*bl*) STScl/NASA/Photo Researchers; **76** (*b*) © IAU/Martin Kommesser/Handout/epa/Corbis; **77** (*bl*) Reuters/CORBIS; (*c*) Jerry Lodriguss/Photo Researchers; **82** Reuters/CORBIS; **79** (*tl*) NASA; **82** (*c*) © RonSherman.com–All Rights Reserved; **86** (*bl*) GoodShoot/SuperStock; **88** (*bl*) John Chumack/Photo Researchers; **89** (*bg*) Celestial Image Co./Photo Researchers; (*bl*) NASA; **90** (*bl*) © Bettmann/CORBIS; **90** (*br*) ©JOHN SANFORD/PHOTO RESEARCHERS, INC.; **94** (*tl*) Courtesy of Georgia State University; **94** (*br*) Courtesy of Georgia State University; **94** (*b*) Courtesy of Georgia State University; **95** (*b*) NASA/JPL/Caltech/The Image Works, (*tr*) Courtesy of Adriana C. Ocampo; (*br*) NASA/JPL/Malin Space Science Systems; **101** (*tc*) © Macduff Everton/CORBIS; **102** (*c*) © James Randklev/CORBIS; **103** (*c*) Creatas/PictureQuest; **104** (*bl*) © Royalty-Free/Corbis; **106** (*bl*) Getty Images; **110** (tr & tl) Keate/Masterfile; **111** (*tl*) Japack Company/Corbis; **112** (*bl*) Gerd Ludwig/VISUM/The Image Works; **113** (*tl*) © Stone/Getty Images; **113** (*bl*) © William A. Bake/CORBIS; **114** (*c*) © Joanne Wells/DanitaDelimont.com; **115** (*cr*) J.A. Kraulis/Masterfile, (*br*) Peter Cade/Getty Images; **123** (*t*) Jonathan Nourok/Photo Edit, (*b*) Prints & Photographs Division, Edward S. Curtis Collection, [reproduction number, LC-USZ62-118588]/Library of Congress; **114** (*c*) Gary Randall/Getty Images; **115** (*cr*) J.A. Kraulis/Masterfile, (*br*) Peter Cade/Getty Images; **116** (*bl*) David Young-Wolff/Photo Edit; **287** (*t*) T. Gerson/L.A. Daily News/Corbis SYGMA; **122** (*bg*) K.H. Hanel/Panoramic Images/National Geographic Image Collection, (*bc*) Paul Nicklen/National Geographic Image Collection, (*br*) John Eastcott and Yva Momatiuk/National Geographic Image Collection; **125** (*t*) A. Ramey/Photo Edit, (*c*) John Foster/Masterfile, (*b*) Corbis; **126** (*c*) © Graeme Teague Photography; **126** (*bc*) NASA; **128** (*c*) © RonSherman.com - All Rights Reserved.; **129** (*c*) J.Emilio Flores/Corbis; **130** (*bl*) Frank S. Balthis; **132** (*tcl*) ANA/The Image Works, (*bl*) Mark Antman/The Image Works, (*cl*) David Young-Wolff/Photo Edit, (*tc*) Tony Freeman/Photo Edit; **133** (*t*) Hartmut Schwarzbach/Peter Arnold Inc.; **137** (*tl*) © Reuters/CORBIS;**143** (*bl*) NASA; **144** (*bl*) Faidley/Agliolo/Imagestate, (*br*) John Foster/Masterfile; **147** (*cr*) K.H. Hanel/Panoramic Images/National Geographic Image Collection; **155** (*tc*) © Getty Images Sport/Getty Images; **156** (*c*) © Fernando Bengoechea/Beateworks/Corbis; **160** Robert Holmes/CORBIS; **161** (*l*) Brooks Kraft/CORBIS; (*r*) Gary Braasch/Getty Images; **164** Erik Butler/Getty Images; **165** Macduff Everton/CORBIS; (*l*) Stephen Dalton/Animals Animals; (*cr*) Color-Pic/Animals Animals; (*br*) Fabio Colombini Medeiros/Animals Animals; **166** (*bl*) Stephen Dalton/Animals Animals; (*br*)Fabio Colombini Medeiros/Animals Animals; (*cr*) Color-Pic/Animals Animals; **167** (*t*) © Arthur Morris/Corbis; **167** (inset) P. Granli/ElephantVoices; **169** (*bl*) © George Hall/CORBIS; **169** (*cl*) Photodisc Green/Getty Images RF; **170** AP/Wide World Photos; **171** Reuters/Newscom; **172** (*c*) © Bob Krist/CORBIS; **174** (*bl*) Samuel R. Maglione/Photo Researchers, Inc.; **176** (*bl*) Royalty-Free/CORBIS; (*bc*) PictureQuest; (*br*) E.R. Degginger/Color-Pic; **177** (*tr*) Science Photo Library; (*br*) Simon Wilkinson/Getty Images; **179** (*cr*) Rosenfeld Images Ltd./Photo Researchers; (*b*) Juan Carlos Munoz/AGE fotostock; **180** (inset) Richard Megna/Fundamental Photographs; **180** (*r*) Sergio Piumatti/Sergio Piumatti, Inc.; **181** (*tr*) R. Ian Lloyd/Masterfile; (*tl*) David Parker/Photo Researchers, Inc.

UNIT B
185 (*bl*) © Taxi/Getty Images; **186** (*br*) Ann Hamilton, Atlanta VA Medical Center, Decatur, GA; **186** (*tl*) Peter R. B. Grattan, Atlanta VA Medical Center, Decatur, GA; **187** (*br*) Photo-Disc, (*bg*) Bob Winsett/Corbis; **188** (*c*) © RonSherman.com- All Rights Reserved.; **190** (*bl*) Danita Delimont/Alamy; **192** (*b*) © Matthias Kulka/zefa/Corbis; **192** (inset) © William Whitehurst/CORBIS; **194** (*c*) © Nicholas Eveleigh /SuperStock; **196** (*bl*) Blend Images/Getty Images RF; **197** (*bl*) © Bettmann/CORBIS; **201** (*tr*) SSPL/The Image Works; **203** (*tc*) AP Wide World Images; **204** (*c*) © Taxi/Getty Images; **208** (*b*) Jim Cummins/CORBIS; **210** (*bc*) C Squared Studios/Getty Images; (*b*) David Young-Wolff/PhotoEdit; **211** (*tl*) Leslie O'Shaushnessy/Visuals Unlimited; (*tr*) Spencer Grant/PhotoEdit; **212** (br & bcl) Dennis MacDonald/PhotoEdit; **215** (*tl*) AP Images/Mary Ann Chastain; **215** (*bl*) AP Images/Richard Vogel; **216** (*c*) © Pascal Rondeau /Allsport/Getty Images; **220** (*b*) Jim Craigmyle/CORBIS; (*br*) CORBIS; **221** (*tr*) Bill Bachmann/PhotoEdit; (*tcl*) Jonathan Nourok/PhotoEdit; **222** (*tcl*) Wally McNamee/CORBIS; **223** (*tr*) Chris Trotman/Duomo/CORBIS; **189** (tc & tcl) Lon C. Diehl/PhotoEdit; **227** (*bl*) © Bettmann/CORBIS; **227** (*tl*) © Royalty-Free/Corbis; **227** (*cl*) AP Images/Porsche; **228** (*cr*) © Marc Serota/Reuters/Corbis; **228** (*br*) Grant Halverson/Getty Images; **229** (*tr*) © Marc Serota/Reuters/Corbis; **229** (*b*) Doug Pensinger/Getty Images **230** Tom Sanders/CORBIS; **235** (*b*) Bill Bachmann/PhotoEdit; **236** (*tr*) Roy Morsch/Bruce Coleman; (*b*) Jose Luis Pelaez, Inc./CORBIS; **240** Matthew Stockman/Getty Images; **241** Robert LaBerge/Getty Images; **247** (*tc*) © RonSherman.com–All Rights Reserved.; **248** (*c*) © RonSherman.com- All Rights Reserved.; **253** (*t*) Grant Heilman Photography; **254** (*r*) William Sallaz/Duomo/CORBIS; **255** (*tl*) Cindy Charles/Photo Edit; **258** (*cr*) © PhotoEdit; **258** (*tl*) © Rick Friedman/Corbis; **258** (*br*) © Rick Friedman/Corbis; **259** (*c*) European Space Agency/DLR/FU Berlin /G. Neukum /Photo Researchers, Inc.; **259** (*tr*) Michael Grecco/Icon International; **259** (*br*) NASA; **260** (*c*) © RonSherman.com–All Rights Reserved; **264** (*b*) Farley Lewis/Photo Researchers; **265** (*br*) Philip Gould/CORBIS; (*tr*) Ted Spiegel/CORBIS; **269** (*bl*) © Julian Worker/Visuals Unlimited; **269** (*tl*) AP Images/Cheboygan Daily Tribune, Mike Fornes; **270** Will Funk/Alpine Aperture; **274** (*b*) Richard Cummins/CORBIS; **275** (*tr*) Tony Freeman/Photo Edit; (*bcl*) David Young-Wolff/Photo Edit; (*br*) Lori Adamski Peek/Getty Images; **277** (*cl*) Tom Schierlitz/Getty Images; tr) Image Farm/PictureQuest; **278** (*bl*) Marshall Gordon/Cole Group/Getty Images; **281** (*tl*) © David Young-Wolff/Photo Edit Inc.; **281** (*bl*) © The Bridgeman Art Library/Getty Images; **282** (*c*) © Graeme Teague Photography; **283** (*tr*) © Graeme Teague Photography; **283** (*br*) Georgia Department of Economic Development; **286** (*br*) Sky Bonillo/PhotoEdit; **287** K.Hackenberg/Masterfile.

UNIT C
295 (*tc*) © Graeme Teague Photography; **296** (*c*) © Science Faction/Getty Images; **300** (*cr*) Bob & Clara Calhoun/Bruce Coleman; (*br*) Beth Davidow/Visuals Unlimited; **300** (*b*) Cathy Melloan/PhotoEdit; **301** (*t*) E. R. Degginger/Bruce Coleman, Inc.; (*cl*) George Sanker/Bruce Coleman, Inc.; **302** (*t*) Dennis MacDonald/PhotoEdit; (*tl*) Dennis MacDonald/PhotoEdit; **303** (*bl*) Steve Maslowski/Visuals Unlimited; (*b*) Kenneth Fink/Bruce Coleman, Inc.; **304** (*br*) © David Muench/CORBIS; **304** (*bl*) © Graeme Teague Photography; **305** (*b*) © James Randklev/CORBIS; **308** (*tl*) Jargal Jamsranjav, (*bg*) Adrian Arbib/Corbis; **309** (*br*) Courtesy of Hargrett Rare Book and Manuscript Library/University of Georgia Libraries; **309** (*tr*) University of Georgia; **310** (*c*) © Bill Beatty/Visuals Unlimited; **309** (*br*) Courtesy of Hargrett Rare Book and Manuscript Library/University of Georgia Libraries; **309** (*tr*) University of Georgia; **310** (*c*) © Bill Beatty/Visuals Unlimited; **315** (*cr*) © Jeff Vanuga/CORBIS; **315** (*tl*) © RonSherman.com–All Rights Reserved; **317** (*bl*) Michael Fogden/Animals Animals; (*cr*) Bob Barber/Barber Nature Photography; (*tc*) Lynn Stone/Animals Animals; (*cl*) Kevin Schafer/CORBIS; **318** (*cr*) Wolfgang Kaehler/CORBIS; (*b*) Jim Brandenburg/Minden Picures; (*cl*) Ken Lucas/Visuals Unlimited; **320** (*br*) D.Hurst/Alamy Images; **322** CDC/PHIL/CORBIS; **326** (*tr*) ZSSD/MINDEN PICTURES; **327** (*br*) Dale Sanders/Masterfile; (*tl*) CORBIS; (*c*) Andrew J. Martinez/Photo Researchers; (*tr*) Dale Sanders/Masterfile; **328** (*bl*) © Joseph Sohm; ChromoSohm Inc./CORBIS; **328** (*br*) © Lynda Richardson/CORBIS; **328** (*b*) © Science Faction/Getty Images; **329** (*bl*) © Michael Redmer/Visuals Unlimited; **329** (*br*) © RonSherman.com- All Rights Reserved; **336** (*c*) © Graeme Teague Photography; **340** (*c*) Jerome Wexler/Visuals Unlimited; (*bl*) Adam Jones/Visuals Unlimited; (*br*) Rob Simpson/Visuals Unlimited; **341** David L. Shirk/Animals Animals; **345** (*tr*) Greg Neise/Visuals Unlimited; (*cl*) Adam Jones/Visuals Unlimited; (*tl*) Julie Eggers/Bruce Coleman, Inc.; (*br*) Eastcott-Momatiuk/The Image Works; (*bl*) Patrick Endres/Visuals Unlimited; (*cr*) Richard Thom/Visuals Unlimited; **347** (*tl*) Charles T. Bryson, USDA Agricultural Research Service, www.forestryimages.org; **347** (*bl*) © Riser/Getty Images; **348** (*c*) © Jerry Cooke/Animals Animals- Earth Scenes; **348** (*bl*) Courtesy of Georgia Mountain Research and Education Center; **348** (*cl*) Wisconsin Department of Natural Resources; **349** (*tl*) Wisconsin Department of Natural Resources; **349** (*bl*) Wisconsin Department of Natural Resources **355** (*tc*) Stephen J. Krasemann/Photo Researchers, Inc.; **356** (*c*) © National Geographic/Getty images; **360** Peter Arnold/Peter Arnold, Inc.; **361** (*br*) Gil Lopez Espina/Visuals Unlimited; (*cr*) E & P Bauer/Bruce Coleman, Inc.; **361** (*cl*) Masa Ushioda/Bruce Coleman, Inc.; **362** (*bl*) Michael & Patricia Fogden/Minden Pictures; (*br*) David Moore/Alamy Images; (*cl*) Jean Paul Ferrero/Ardea London; (*cr*) Lynn Stone/Animals Animals; **363** (*cl*) © Charles Philip Cangialosi/CORBIS; **363** (*tr*) © Michael & Patricia Fogden/CORBIS; **363** (*cr*) © Naturfoto Honal/CORBIS; **363** (*tl*) © Photodisc Green/Getty Images RF; **366** (*bl*) Animals Animals; **367** (*t*) Wildlife Conservation Society; (*b*) Animals Animals; **368** (*c*) © SeaPics.com; **370** (*bl*) © Joe & Mary Ann McDonald/Visuals Unlimited; **372** (*bl*) Bernard Castelein/Nature Picture Library; (*bcr*) Hanne & Jens Eriksen/Nature Picture Library; **373** (*tr*) Patti Murray/Animals Animals; (*tcr*) Georgette Douwma/Nature Picture Library; (*cr*) Dietmar Nill/Nature Picture Library; (*bl*) Jennifer Loomis/Animals Animals; (*br*) Doug Wechsler/Animals Animals; **374** (*tr*) Nigel Bean/Nature Picture Library; (*br*) Bob Cranston/Animals Animals; **375** (*tr*) Staffan Widstrand/Nature Picture Library; (*bcr*) Arthur Morris/CORBIS; **376** (*cr*) © John Dick/VIREO; **377** (*tl*) © Carol Nourse; **377** (*tr*) © Richard Thom/Visuals Unlimited; **379** (*tl*) © Rob Lewine/CORBIS; **380** (*cr*) Barry Mansell/npl/Minden Pictures; **380** (*bc*) Kevin McIntyre, Joseph W. Jones Ecological Research Center at Ichauway; **381** (*r*) Jeffrey Lepore/Photo Researchers, Inc.; **381** (*tr*) Jonathan Stober, Joseph W. Jones Ecological Research Center at Ichauway; **385** (*tl*) Hal Brindley/VWPICS/Alamy Images.

Glossary
R44 (*bl*) Leonard Lee Rue III/Photo Researchers, Inc.; **R46** (*bl*) © Chase Swift/CORBIS; **R51** (*br*) STEVE ALLEN/Photo Researchers, Inc.

Health Handbook
R5 Dennis Kunkel/Phototake; **R12** (*t*) CNRI/Science Photo Library/Photo Researchers; **R12** (*tc*) A. Pasieka/Photo Researchers; **R12** (*bc*) CNRI/Science Photo Library/Photo Researchers; **R12** (*b*) Custom Medical Stock Photo; **R15** (inset) David Young-Wolff/PhotoEdit; **R15** (*b*) Bill O'Connor/Peter Arnold, Inc.

All other photos © Harcourt School Publishers. Harcourt Photos provided by the Harcourt Index, Harcourt IPR, and Harcourt photographers; Weronica Ankarorn, Eric Camden, Doug Dukane, Ken Kinzie, April Riehm, and Steve Williams.

BEHAVIOR Most black bears feed in the cool of the evening or early morning. During the heat of the day, they often seek shade in dense underbrush.

COMMUNICATION Bears communicate using sounds that include moans, bellows, and grunts.

BEHAVIOR Bear cubs are taught to climb trees to escape danger. Black bears are excellent climbers.

CHARACTERISTICS Adult black bears are 5 to 6 feet tall.

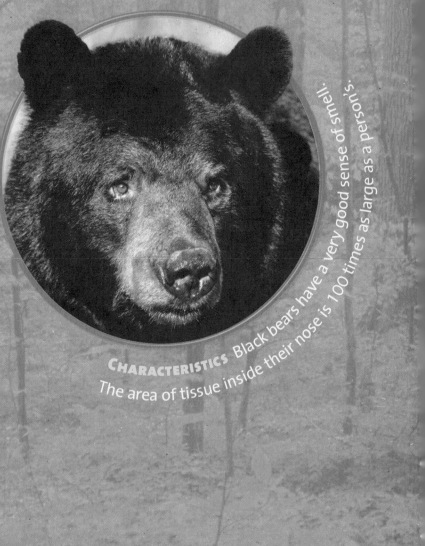

CHARACTERISTICS Black bears have a very good sense of smell. The area of tissue inside their nose is 100 times as large as a person's.